Basic
COMMODORE
64™
BASIC

Basic COMMODORE 64™ BASIC

JAMES S. COAN

HAYDEN BOOK COMPANY, INC.
Hasbrouck Heights, New Jersey

Equipment Needed

To use the programs in this book you will need:

- a Commodore 64 microcomputer
- a black and white or color television set (color is required for certain programs)
- one disk drive (a Commodore Datassette can be used to save programs)

Production Editor: TERRY DONOVAN
Production Service: EDITING, DESIGN & PRODUCTION, INC.
Art Director: JIM BERNARD
Printed and bound by: COMMAND WEB OFFSET INC.

1	2	3	4	5	6	7	8	9	PRINTING
84	85	86	87	88	89	90	91	92	YEAR

Preface

Regrettably, computer programming has acquired a mystique it doesn't deserve. Of course, professional programmers are highly skilled people. Race car drivers are also highly skilled people. That doesn't seem to prevent the average person from learning to drive a car. And learning to drive a car doesn't suggest that we aspire to be a race car driver. Anybody who can manage a checking account can write a computer program. Many important and useful programs are written without any more mathematics than addition, subtraction, multiplication, and division. If your problem can be solved on the computer and you understand it enough to solve it by using pencil and paper, then you can probably write a computer program to solve it, too. While much of programming is mathematically oriented, an effort has been made in preparing this book to include topics and develop programming ideas that do not require advanced mathematics.

This book is suitable for use as a textbook in schools and colleges. It is equally appropriate for use by individuals wishing to learn programming in BASIC on a Commodore 64 computer.

The approach in this book is to begin with short complete programs and then carefully and gently build them into larger programs that solve larger problems. Each capability or organization of capabilities is introduced to create a desired effect in a program. Generally, details are introduced in the context of their effect on a program. Even though some of the topic headings appear to be oriented toward the BASIC language, each feature is brought in at a point where it helps to solve a problem. The topic headings can be used as a reference after the reader has learned to program.

Programming has developed tremendously since its early days. This book takes advantage of many of the good programming practices we have learned in that time. We always divide the program into small manageable segments. Most segments will fit on a single screen. Longer programs include a control routine at the beginning that handles all program management by using subroutines.

Chapter 1 gets us started on the Commodore 64: entering data and obtaining results from the computer. Chapter 2 introduces some ideas for planning a program. Commodore character graphics are presented in Chapter 3, which also covers subroutines and presents more on program design and organization. Chapter 4 contains a potpourri of BASIC features and programming techniques, including functions and logical operators. Chapter 5 presents strings and string functions, while Chapter 6 covers numeric and string arrays. Chapter 7 is a collection of miscellaneous applications. Sequential files are presented in Chapter 8. Some bit-map high-resolution (Hi-Res) graphics features of the Commodore 64 are presented in Chapter 9 with examples. Chapter 10 tells how to use Sprite graphics, including a simple Sprite editor and an introduction to animation. Music and sound are developed in Chapter 11.

Each chapter is followed by special sections, or Programmer's Corners, that highlight special features or advanced programming ideas. Programmer's Corner 1 discusses the Commodore 64 screen editor. Immediate Mode Execution is covered in Programmer's Corner 2. Programmer's Corner 4 explains how to control the keyboard buffer to avoid accidental keystrokes while entering a program. Programmer's Corner 5 reveals a way to place the color PRINT codes in a string for easy 0 to 15 access in programs, while Programmer's Corner 6 presents integer variables. The bitwise nature of operations with AND, OR, and NOT is discussed in Programmer's Corner 7. Programmer's Corner 9 presents useful information about using memory for graphics and graphics programs. Miscellaneous Sprite graphics information is offered in 10. Programmer's Corner 11 covers complex sounds and effects.

Appendix A is a chart of certain special print characters on the Commodore 64 as they appear in quote mode. Charts for the screen codes make up Appendix B. Appendix C contains the CHR$ and ASC codes. Appendix D describes the features of the VIC 1541 single disk drive needed for saving and loading programs. Appendix E is an index of the programs in this book. Solution programs for the even-numbered problems appear in Appendix F.

Commodore markets at least two software products that will be of interest to the serious programmer. The VSP cartridge adds numerous high-resolution (Hi-Res) graphics commands to Commodore 64 BASIC. Simons BASIC adds 114 commands to Commodore 64 BASIC in 12 categories. Graphics plotting is included, with commands for lines, circles, and arcs. Sprite animation commands are also included. There are commands to control such music parameters as wave, envelope, and volume. Programming aids, such as TRACE, AUTO, UNNEW, and renumbering, are included. All this does require a sacrifice of about 8K of memory.

I thank Barbara Garris, Neil Harris, Jim Gracely, and Andy Finkel who all supplied important information for the preparation of this book.

New Hope, PA   JAMES S. COAN

To the Reader

Learning to program a computer can be a very exhilarating experience. The thrill of seeing your first apparently complicated idea implemented in a simple program is wonderful. You will be well advised to look upon the computer as a machine to be mastered and not as some impersonal monster that is out to do you in. Everything that the computer does is explainable and predictable. You should take care to evaluate the results that the computer produces: do not blindly accept computer results as faultless. That is not to say that the computer is going to make many mistakes. In fact, under normal conditions, the computer will execute your instructions exactly. Mistakes in the results of a program execution are usually caused by errors in the instructions written by the programmer. Once in a great (and I mean great) while, the problem may be with the machine itself. Don't count on it, because it is most unlikely. Machine error is absolutely the remotest possible cause of faulty program behavior: it almost never happens. Strongly resist the temptation to blame anything other than your programming for incorrect or unexpected results.

Learning to program a computer is not so complicated. You will probably find that an iterative process works best. Read some of this book, and try a few things on the computer. Then read more of the book and test out more of what you have learned on the computer. There are certain aspects of programming that you cannot possibly know without being told, and others that will just make sense based on what you know so far. You will find that reading the text will help with writing the next program; writing and executing a program will help with reading the text.

I hope that you are soon stimulated by your work in programming to bring to the computer new and exciting problems. Above all, to be successful, you will have to be an active participant. Actually write programs. Execute them. Then try to see how what you have learned fits into the picture of the BASIC language and programming in general.

Experiment. Write programs to solve problems of interest to you. Try anything—you can't do any physical damage to the computer by typing the wrong thing at the keyboard. Don't be afraid to try new and different things.

GOOD LUCK!

Contents

Chapter 1

Introduction to Commodore 64 BASIC 1

PROGRAMMER'S CORNER 1

Chapter 2

Writing a Program 22

PROGRAMMER'S CORNER 2

Chapter 3

Commodore Character Graphics and Much More 39

Chapter 4

Miscellaneous Features and Techniques 57

PROGRAMMER'S CORNER 4

Chapter 5

Character Strings and String Functions 73

PROGRAMMER'S CORNER 5

Chapter 6

Arrays 88

PROGRAMMER'S CORNER 6

Chapter 7

Miscellaneous Applications 107

PROGRAMMER'S CORNER 7

Chapter 8

Sequential Files 126

Chapter 9

Bit-Map Graphics: Hi-Res 139

PROGRAMMER'S CORNER 9

Chapter 10

Sprite Graphics 160

PROGRAMMER'S CORNER 10

Chapter 11

by Scott Banks

Programming Sound and Music 177

PROGRAMMER'S CORNER 11

Appendix A

Special Print Characters 197

Appendix B

Commodore 64 Screen Codes 199

Appendix C

PRINT Codes on the Commodore 64 203

Appendix D

The Disk 209

Appendix E

Appendix F

Basic
COMMODORE 64™
BASIC

Chapter 1

Introduction to Commodore 64 BASIC

A *program* consists of a set of instructions that causes a computer to perform in a predictable way. The process of writing such instructions is called *programming*. We can write programs to do an amazing variety of things. The Commodore 64 can perform a wide range of arithmetic operations. Using the built-in electronic music synthesizer, it can be programmed to play music on the speaker of a TV or other sound system. We can make it draw graphs and pictures of all kinds—in color no less. Paddles or joysticks can be used to provide a continuous range of responses by moving a lever or rotating a dial. We can even write programs to respond to a light pen drawing on a TV screen. The Sprite graphics are particularly suited to games. There are many ways in which this computer can be used to help students learn subject matter unrelated to computers. This same computer can be used to keep track of all kinds of data necessary in the operation of a small business.

Every instruction used in a program has its own precise definition. The total collection of these instructions is called a *programming language*; BASIC is one such language. Each instruction in the language also has a form associated with it. This form is called the *instruction syntax*. The syntax of each instruction that we enter into the computer must be one of those the computer "recognizes." For example, the computer will reject the instruction QUIT, while it will find END perfectly acceptable and, on encountering the END instruction, it will indeed end. Even though QUIT and END have similar meanings in English, they don't to the computer. Words that make up a computer language are called *keywords*. END is a BASIC keyword.

Commodore 64 BASIC is the BASIC that is built right into the Commodore 64. It resembles the BASIC that was developed at Dartmouth College by John G.

Kemeny and Thomas E. Kurtz, with numerous enhancements. BASIC is designed so that anyone from a rank amateur to an exotic engineer can quickly and easily write programs pertinent to their own interests.

Using Commodore 64 BASIC, we can easily calculate numeric results to nine decimal digits. Or we might want to use the special feature that allows us to limit calculations to integers in the range -32768 to 32767. It is just as easy to work with the written word.

1-1...Getting Started

There are a number of things that we need to know, all at once, to get going. After this initial burst of information, we can introduce things in smaller doses. So, here we go!!

The computer is turned on, the word "READY." appears on the screen, and a little light blue block is blinking at us. That little block is the cursor. It is there to show us where the next thing we type will appear. This makes it easy to follow along with our eyes. We type

```
NEW
```

and then press the RETURN key. NEW erases any BASIC program in memory. Never type NEW unless you really mean it: the old program is not recoverable. Appendix D deals with the subject of saving programs for future use. Any time you make a typing error you may simply press the RETURN key and begin the line again. Commodore 64 BASIC includes a nice screen editor that you will want to use shortly after you begin to do some actual typing. The editor is fully discussed with examples in Programmer's Corner 1, immediately following this chapter.

The Commodore 64 responds by displaying

```
READY.
```

This means just what it says. The computer is ready for our next step, and we are ready to type in our first program. It all looks like Program 1-1:

```
NEW
READY.

100 PRINT "HERE IS AN EXAMPLE"
110 PRINT "OF A PROGRAM IN"
120 PRINT "COMMODORE 64 BASIC."
```

Program 1-1. Our first Commodore 64 BASIC program.

There you have it. Each line we type must be followed by pressing the RETURN key. Every time we hit the RETURN key the 64 responded by moving to the next line.

Our program consists of three statements, each labeled with a line number. Line numbers may be any integer from 0 to 63999. After the READY message, we typed:

```
100 PRINT "HERE IS AN EXAMPLE"
```

and then pressed the RETURN key. We then typed the next two lines in the same manner. Get into the habit of striking the RETURN key after everything. If nothing happens, it is probably because you pressed RESTORE instead. That's okay; just press RETURN and proceed.

Each of these three statements is an example of a PRINT statement. When the program is run, each PRINT statement is an instruction to the computer that something is to be printed out to the screen of the TV monitor.

```
RUN
HERE IS AN EXAMPLE
OF A PROGRAM IN
COMMODORE 64 BASIC.

READY.
```

Figure 1-1. Execution of Program 1-1.

After entering the three PRINT statements, we typed RUN and then pressed the RETURN key. In this case, as with the NEW instruction, we did not assign a line number to the instruction. The presence of a line number implies that the line is to be stored for later use by the computer. The absence of a line number implies that the computer should immediately process whatever is on the line as an instruction. The RUN instruction causes the computer to process the instructions of the program stored in the computer's memory. That is what is meant by *running a program*. The RUN instruction may also be followed by a line number that names a line in the program where the run should begin. For example, to use our little program to display "COMMODORE 64 BASIC.", simply enter RUN 120.

The result of running our first program is that the three PRINT statements cause whatever is enclosed within quotes to be printed on the monitor.

When the computer runs out of instructions in the stored program, it simply displays the READY message and politely waits for us to tell it what to do next. If we now type RUN again, the 64 will again display the same three-line message on the monitor.

Note the difference between the letter oh and the digit zero. The Commodore 64 uses an oval with a slash through it for the digit zero and an open oval for the letter oh. You might just type O's, zeroes, and eights so that you can study them on the monitor. You will find the zero key between 9 and + in the top row of keys, while the oh is in the second row from the top between I and P.

Here is a way to change the displayed message:

```
READY.
110 PRINT "OF A PROGRAM"
115 PRINT "WRITTEN IN"
```

Figure 1-2. Changing Program 1-1.

We have changed line 110 by retyping it, and we have inserted a new line numbered 115. Instructions are always processed in numerical order, so by choosing a line number that falls between two existing ones, we have told the computer that we want line 115 to be processed after line 110 and before line 120. It is a good idea to leave intervals in your line numbering. The computer will always arrange the lines of the program in increasing order. Now, if we tell the computer to follow the instructions of the new program, we get:

```
RUN
HERE IS AN EXAMPLE
OF A PROGRAM
WRITTEN IN
COMMODORE 64 BASIC.

READY.
```

Figure 1-3. Execution of the modified version of Program 1-1.

The process of carrying out the instructions of program statements is termed *execution*. Thus, when we type RUN, we are telling the computer to *execute* the program.

At this point, we have a program that we have created in two distinct steps. We first entered three lines and then some time later we entered two lines. One of those two lines replaced a line of the earlier program, and the other added a new instruction. The resulting program contains four lines.

It is now desirable to look at the program in its entirety by using the LIST instruction.

```
LIST

100 PRINT "HERE IS AN EXAMPLE"
110 PRINT "OF A PROGRAM"
115 PRINT "WRITTEN IN"
120 PRINT "COMMODORE 64 BASIC. "

READY.
```

Figure 1-4. Demonstration of LIST.

The instructions NEW, RUN, and LIST are commonly called *commands* because they are used to command the computer to manipulate the program as an entity rather than perform a program instruction.

What happens when we make typing errors? That depends upon the error. If we type LOST instead of LIST, we get the following message:

```
?SYNTAX  ERROR
READY.
```

No harm has been done; merely correct the request and proceed. If we type

```
100 PRIMT A
```

instead of

```
100 PRINT A
```

nothing will happen until the statement is executed. At that time, execution will cease and Commodore 64 BASIC will display the following message:

```
?SYNTAX   ERROR IN 100
READY.
```

Whenever READY is displayed, you know that the computer is waiting for you to do something. We will begin to leave it out of our printed listings.

We can look at the statement where the computer has identified an error by using an extension of the LIST command.

```
LIST 100
```

will display only line 100 of our program, if it exists. LIST 100–200 will display all of the lines in our program from 100 to 200, inclusive. LIST 100– will display from line 100 to the end of the program. LIST –400 will display from the beginning of the program to line 400. Now type the line correctly and execute the new program. A detailed discussion of the special editing features of the Commodore 64 appears in Programmer's Corner 1.

If we type

```
100 PRINT B
```

instead of

```
100 PRINT A
```

we have a different kind of error that the computer will never find for us. The value of B will be displayed where we expected to see the value of A. It is important to evaluate our results for correctness.

...SUMMARY

A computer language is a defined set of instructions that have a specific meaning to the computer. In BASIC each instruction of a program begins with a line number. The PRINT statement is used to display a message on the computer monitor.

The NEW command prepares BASIC for a new program, the RUN command causes the computer to carry out the instructions of the program stored in its memory, and the LIST command displays the stored program on the monitor. LIST 100 displays the line numbered 100, while LIST 100–200 displays all lines in the interval from 100 to 200, including 100 and 200. LIST –200 displays from the beginning of the program to line 200. LIST 200– displays from line 200 to the end of the program.

1-2...Printing Messages

In the last section, there were no long program statements. The Commodore 64 monitor screen is 40 characters wide. (There is a way to make it 38.) The screen width can be something of a limitation. However, we will very quickly get used to it. When typing program statements that are longer than 40 characters, just keep on typing. The computer will take care of everything. It looks like this:

```
100 PRINT "HERE IS AN EXAMPLE OF A LONG
PROGRAM LINE"

RUN
HERE IS AN EXAMPLE OF A LONG PROGRAM LIN
E

LIST
100 PRINT "HERE IS AN EXAMPLE OF A LONG
PROGRAM LINE"
```

Figure 1-5. Demonstration of the 40-column display screen.

Notice that the Commodore 64 listed our program just as we typed it. Indeed, the computer will take care that no characters are lost. In the interest of making the results of printing readable, we should plan ahead so that the screen doesn't break the line in an awkward place during program execution. To print the little message of the above program, we might prefer the following:

```
100 PRINT "  THIS IS AN EXAMPLE OF A LON
G PROGRAM"
110 PRINT "LINE."

RUN
  THIS IS AN EXAMPLE OF A LONG PROGRAM
LINE.
```

Figure 1-6. Planning messages on the Commodore 64 screen.

Now we can easily read the message. With a little practice, printing messages will become second nature to us.

Some people appreciate anything that reduces typing. PRINT can be indicated by typing a question mark. So, we might enter the above program as Program 1-2:

```
100 ? "  THIS IS AN EXAMPLE OF A LONG PROGRAM"
```

Program 1-2. Using question mark as PRINT.

We have saved a little typing, but the Commodore will replace the question mark with PRINT when we LIST the program. Most other BASIC keywords can be abbreviated by typing the first character and then holding down the shift for the second character. For example we can LIST a program by pressing L and SHIFT I. When we type SHIFT I the right graphics character appears on the screen. So, we will see the L followed by the rounded corner that appears to the right on the I key, but the program is listed just the same.

We may make messages as long or as short as we like. A program could consist of hundreds of PRINT statements. All programs should have at least one PRINT statement. How would we know what the program does if it displays no message?

...**Upper-case, lower-case**

The Commodore defaults to upper-case mode. That is, left to itself, BASIC will type all capital letters. Often it is nice to have messages displayed in upper- and lower-case. You can access the lower-case characters by pressing the Commodore key (**C**) and the SHIFT key at the same time. When you do this, you will see all upper-case characters on the screen suddenly displayed in lower-case. Press them again and the display reverts to upper-case. This is known as a *toggle action*. The mode is changed every time those two keys are pressed simultaneously. We might like to display a message using both upper- and lower-case. First, check that the computer is in lower-case mode. Then type a program normally. For upper-case characters, simply press the SHIFT key and the desired letter, just as you would do on a typewriter. (See Program 1-3.)

```
100 print "This is a demonstration of up
per and lower case"
```

Program 1-3. Demonstration of lower-case mode.

It's that simple. Don't make the mistake of trying to type PRINT by holding down the SHIFT key or using SHIFT LOCK. That will result in ?SYNTAX ERROR. Now, if we press the Commodore key and the SHIFT key, the upper-case T displays as its corresponding graphics symbol, a vertical bar near the left of the character space. We should be consistent for any one program, entering it in either upper-case mode or lower-case mode. Do not change within a single program.

For more information about the keyboard, see Programmer's Corner 1.

1-3...**Calculations**

Now that we know how to display messages, we might like to have something for the messages to talk about. The Commodore 64's ability to perform calculations is readily available to us.

The --> shown in the following program and in other programs throughout this book, is included to point out program lines that are specifically discussed in the text and is *not* to be considered part of the program.

```
    100 PRINT "THE NUMBERS ARE:"
    105 PRINT "234.56 AND 43901"
    110 PRINT "THE SUM IS"
-->120 PRINT 234.56 + 43901
    130 PRINT "THE DIFFERENCE IS"
-->140 PRINT 234.56 - 43901
    150 PRINT "MULTIPLY THEM"
-->160 PRINT 234.56 * 43901
    170 PRINT "NOW DIVIDE"
-->180 PRINT 234.56 / 43901
```

Program 1-4. Calculations.

Here we have a program that adds, subtracts, multiplies, and divides two numbers. As you can see in lines 120, 140, 160, and 180, the Commodore 64 uses +, −, *, and / as the symbols for these arithmetic operations. Let's look at an execution of this program:

```
RUN
THE NUMBERS ARE:
234.56 AND 43901
THE SUM IS
 44135.56
THE DIFFERENCE IS
-43666.44
MULTIPLY THEM
 10297418.6
NOW DIVIDE
 5.34293069E-03
```

Figure 1-7. Execution of Program 1-4.

Notice that the product displays nine digits. This is the maximum precision available in Commodore 64 BASIC. That is not to say that all answers are accurate to nine digits; the computer has to round things off from time to time. So, it is up to you to verify the accuracy of computed results. In addition to evaluating the accuracy of the computations that the computer carries out, you will need to know the accuracy of the numbers that you give the computer to work with.

For the division problem in our program, something else interesting happens. We get 5.34293069E-03 as the answer. This is another way of writing 0.00534293069, which takes 11 digits to express. Commodore 64 BASIC uses scientific notation for displaying very small and very large numbers. Ten-to-the-minus-third (10^{-3}) is written "E-03" to get it on one line of display. This is often called *E-format*; any value less than 0.01 or greater than 999999999.1 will be displayed in this manner.

Commodore 64 BASIC limits numbers to a range of from −1E38 to +1E38. That should be entirely adequate for our needs for some time to come.

So far, we have been printing each item on a separate line. Often we would like to display several items on the same line. This is easy to do by entering a semicolon or a comma between the items that belong together. A semicolon calls for close spacing, while a comma is used to divide the screen into four fields that are 10 characters wide. Symbols used to separate items in a list are called *delimiters*. So, we now know about the comma and semicolon delimiters in a PRINT statement. Program 1-5 demonstrates this nicely.

```
100 PRINT 1/4; 2/4; 3/4; 4/4
110 PRINT 1/4, 2/4, 3/4, 4/4
```

Program 1-5. Demonstration of using comma and semicolon for spacing.

We have used semicolons in line 100 and commas in line 110. If we want to skip a 10-character field, we can use an extra comma.

```
.25  .5  .75  1
.25         .5        .75         1
```

Figure 1-8. Execution of Program 1-5.

Commodore 64 BASIC includes a space before and after every numeric display in a PRINT statement. If the value is negative, then the space before the value is replaced by a minus sign.

Program 1-6 demonstrates printing a few values using scientific notation.

```
   100 PRINT "EXAMPLES OF SCIENTIFIC NOTATI
   ON"
-->120 PRINT ".0001",, "=";  .0001
-->125 PRINT ".00058293",, "=";  .00058293
   130 PRINT ".00123456789", "=";  .00123456
   789
   140 PRINT "1234567890", "=";  1234567890
   150 PRINT "3939382827347456", "=";  39393
   82827347456
```

Program 1-6. Demonstration of scientific notation.

Here we are using commas and semicolons to produce a readable display. Lines 120 and 125 use a double comma to skip a 10-column field. This way, all the results are nicely lined up on the display screen.

Now let's look at the display produced by Program 1-6.

```
RUN
EXAMPLES OF SCIENTIFIC NOTATION
.0001                   = 1E-04
.00058293               = 5.8293E-04
.00123456789            = 1.23456789E-03
1234567890              = 1.23456789E+09
3939382827347456        = 3.93938283E+15
```

Figure 1-9. Execution of Program 1-6.

We will indeed get used to the 40-character screen on the Commodore 64. However, we are not limited to 40 characters on the printed page. Therefore, we will present most of our program listings in a wider format. If you type exactly what is displayed in the programs of this book, BASIC will take care of the rest. We present here Program 1-6 reformatted without any line breaks.

```
100 PRINT "EXAMPLES OF SCIENTIFIC NOTATION"
120 PRINT ".0001",, "=";  .0001
125 PRINT ".00058293",, "=";  .00058293
130 PRINT ".00123456789", "=";  .00123456789
140 PRINT "1234567890", "=";  1234567890
150 PRINT "3939382827347456", "=";  3939382827347456
```

Program 1-6a. Demonstrate program listings without line breaks.

1-4...Numeric Variables

We can do some interesting things with what we know at this point, but some of the real power of the computer begins to emerge when we can save the results of calculations.

A *variable* may be thought of as a pigeonhole or a mailbox in which we may save the value of any result as a computer program goes about solving our problem for us. We establish an hourly wage and save it in W1. Then we determine the number of hours worked and save the value in N. Next, we might find the net pay by multiplying W1 by N and then saving it in N9. Or we might want to take the average of some numbers. Program 1-7 uses numeric variables to do just that.

```
100   LET S1 = 34 + 45 + 65 + 89 + 91 + 56
110   LET N1 = 6
120   LET AV = S1 / N1
130   PRINT "AVERAGE ="; AV
140   END
```

Program 1-7. Calculating a simple average.

If we want to calculate an average for a different set of values, we need only retype lines 100 and 110 of this simple program.

We have used three variables in this program. They are S1, N1, and AV. We are free to choose a wide variety of names for variables. Commodore 64 BASIC variables may begin with any letter, followed by digits or letters. However, only the first two characters of the variable name are used to distinguish between two variables. Thus, OLDNUMBER and OLDSCORE will be the same variable. You should avoid names like this. One method of avoiding trouble is to limit variable names to a single letter, two letters, or a letter followed by a digit. While variable names like WAGES, NETPAY, PAYCHECK, PAYRATE, and NETTAXES are descriptive, we run the risk of ambiguity. Besides, very long variable names will tend to push program statements over to the second line, which makes the program harder to read. Program statements are limited to 80 characters in length. If we attempt to type a longer one, we are greeted with

```
?SYNTAX  ERROR
```

BASIC keywords are reserved for use by BASIC itself. Errors caused by incorrectly using reserved words for variable names can be tough to find. NEW, LIST, RUN, and PRINT are reserved words. So is END. A statement such as

```
100 LEFTEND = 5
```

will produce the message

```
?SYNTAX  ERROR IN 100
```

That is easy to see, because we know about the END statement. But, what about

```
100 TOP = 7
```

We get the same message. We will find out about the keyword TO in Chapter 2.

...The Assignment Statement (LET)

Each of the statements 100, 110, and 120 in Program 1-7 is an example of an *assignment statement*. The effect of statement 100 is that the computer will calculate the sum of the six numbers shown there and store it in the slot labeled S1. Line 110 causes the value 6 to be stored in a pigeonhole labeled N1. And line 120 causes the computer to divide the value found in the slot labeled S1 by the value found in the slot labeled N1 and place the result in a slot labeled AV.

```
RUN
AVERAGE = 63.3333333
```

Figure 1-10. Execution of Program 1-7.

The assignment statement in BASIC may take one of two forms.

```
100  LET X = 15              and              100 X = 15
```

are functionally equivalent. In practice, most programmers drop the use of LET. However, many beginners find it helpful to include the LET keyword while learning BASIC.

1-5...The INPUT Statement

The INPUT statement is used to provide data for a BASIC program to work on. When BASIC encounters an INPUT statement, it causes the computer to wait for data to be typed at the keyboard.

When the statement

```
200 INPUT X
```

executes, it will display a question mark as the signal to us that we are to type in a single number.

```
200 INPUT X,Y,Z
```

will also display a question mark. However, we have provided for three values to be entered and the computer will insist on getting three.

Suppose we enter only one. Commodore 64 BASIC will gently prod us by displaying two question marks repeatedly until we have entered the proper amount of data.

Suppose we enter too much data. Commodore 64 BASIC will quietly display the following message:

```
?EXTRA IGNORED
```

and proceed with the rest of the program.

Suppose we just hit the RETURN key. Then Commodore 64 BASIC will use whatever value the variable had before the INPUT statement. If we want RETURN to mean zero, then we'll have to set that value before the INPUT statement.

11

```
205 X = 0
210 INPUT X
```

will take care of it. But, suppose we type a letter or other symbol instead.

```
? I
?REDO FROM START
? 1,2,3
```

A decimal point alone is taken as a zero.

Suppose we have the following record of gasoline purchases for a brand new car:

Gallons	Odometer
19.3	230.3
12.7	456.7
17.7	709.4
11.1	895.5
13.8	1131.6

We want a program that will calculate the gas mileage for each tankful of gasoline. We have been careful to fill the tank each time. Since we do not know whether the tank was full when we got the car, we should discard the figure for the first purchase. What we do know is that 12.7 gallons took us 226.4 miles, 17.7 gallons took us 252.7 miles, etc. Program 1-8 asks the right questions and does the miles-per-gallon calculation for us.

```
-->100 PRINT "FIRST READING";
-->110 INPUT M1
   195 PRINT
-->200 PRINT "GALS,READING";
-->210 INPUT GA, M2
   220 LET MI = M2 - M1
   230 LET MG = MI / GA
   240 PRINT MG; "MPG"
   250 LET M1 = M2
   260 GOTO 195
```

Program 1-8. Calculating gasoline mileage.

Note the use of the semicolon at the end of lines 100 and 200. This enables us to compose a single line of display on the screen from several lines in a program. Thus the question mark displayed by the INPUT statement at line 110 will appear immediately following FIRST READING from line 100, and the question mark displayed by the INPUT statement at line 210 will appear immediately following GALS, READING from line 200.

It is always a good idea to display a label for an INPUT request. We may know right now what that question mark means, but nobody else will and next week we probably won't either.

Since we want the miles traveled, the program must subtract the previous reading from the current one. This is done in line 220. MI is the miles traveled, GA is the number of gallons used, and MG is the number of miles per gallon. Once the computer has calculated the number of miles traveled, the current reading becomes the previous reading for the next data to be entered. This is the purpose of line 250. Line 195 is referred to as *blank PRINT*. A blank PRINT will display as a blank line. We use this to provide nice spacing on the screen.

...GOTO

We must introduce the GOTO statement at this point. The GOTO 195 you see at line 260 is an instruction to the computer to execute the statement numbered 195 next in sequence. In this way, we are able to control the order in which BASIC executes the statements of a program.

```
RUN
FIRST READING? 230.3

GALS,READING? 12.7,456.7
17.8267717 MPG

GALS,READING? 17.7,709.4
14.2768362 MPG

GALS,READING? 11.1,895.5
16.7657658 MPG

GALS,READING? 13.8,1131.6
17.1086956 MPG

GALS,READING? [enter STOP RESTORE here]

READY.
```

Figure 1-11. Execution of Program 1-8.

Clearly the value 17.8267717 shown in Figure 1-11 is more precise than 12.7, 456.7, or 230.3, but it is not more accurate. We may safely say that we got about 17.8 miles per gallon for the first calculation. The results of a calculation can never be more accurate than the data. Soon we will learn how to round off results to any desired precision.

This program would go on forever if we didn't have a special procedure to get out of an INPUT statement. We pressed the STOP and RESTORE keys at the same time. Not only did this get us out of the program execution, but it also cleared the screen. This is okay for programmers, but soon we will learn better ways to exit from our programs. We should not require others who will be using our programs to use STOP-RESTORE in this way.

1-6...READ...DATA

There are numerous ways to provide programs with data. We have entered numbers into our programs by including them in PRINT statements, by assigning values to variables with the assignment statement using LET, and by programming with the INPUT statement. Now we add READ and DATA to the list.

The READ statement assigns values to variables by using a DATA statement as the source. READ and DATA are always coordinated to solve the problem at hand; it is not workable to have one without the other. Let's simply convert the INPUT-based program on gasoline mileage to an equivalent program using READ and DATA. In this case the data will not be entered from the keyboard during execution, so we display the gallons and miles traveled along with the miles-per-gallon figure. The logic here is identical to the logic of our Program 1-8.

```
90 PRINT "GAL", "MILES", "MPG"
100 READ M1
200 READ GA, M2
210 LET MI = M2 - M1
220 LET MG = MI / GA
230 PRINT GA, MI, MG
240 LET M1 = M2
250 GOTO 200
900 DATA 230.3
902 DATA 12.7,  456.7
904 DATA 17.7,  709.4
906 DATA 11.1,  895.5
908 DATA 13.8,  1131.6
```

Program 1-9. Program 1-8 with READ...DATA.

Note that we have arranged the data so that the numbers are grouped to look like the table of values first presented. The computer doesn't care how many or how few lines we use for data. The important point is that the values in DATA statements must be in the correct order, matching the variables in the READ statements. We may arrange the data so that it is well organized for humans to read. Since the computer will never be confused, we should take care to make things better for us.

```
RUN
GAL        MILES      MPG
  12.7       226.4      17.8267717
  17.7       252.7      14.2768362
  11.1       186.1      16.7657658
  13.8       236.1      17.1086956

?OUT OF DATA  ERROR IN 200
```

Figure 1-12. Execution of Program 1-9.

We do indeed obtain the expected calculation results. However, we also triggered an error message. The cause is clear enough: the program has read all of the data; there is no more. Soon, we will learn a more orderly way to handle the end-of-data condition in our programs.

Occasionally we come upon a situation in a program where we want to read data over again. This is made possible with the RESTORE statement. After RESTORE the data will be read from the very first item in the first DATA statement of the program. Do not confuse this with the RESTORE key on the keyboard; we are talking now about a statement in a program.

...SUMMARY

We have covered a lot of ground in this first chapter. Very soon, nearly everything presented here will be second nature to you. You can make your job easier by remembering the right things. Don't bother remembering exact error messages; your job will be simply to recognize them. You need to remember NEW, LIST, RUN, PRINT, LET, END, line numbers, GOTO, INPUT, variables, quotes, and READ...DATA. Remember also that Commodore 64 BASIC allows numbers in the range of $-1E38$ to $+1E38$.

The PRINT statement in BASIC is used to display labels in quotes, numeric values expressed literally, and values stored in variables individually or in combination. Items may be separated with semicolon or comma delimiters.

Variables are used in programs to retain numeric values during program execution. Variable names must begin with a letter and may consist of letters and digits intermixed after the first character. Commodore 64 BASIC accepts very long variable names, but distinguishes only the first two characters. Keywords that are part of the programming language, such as LET, PRINT, and END, may not be used as variable names; they are reserved for use by BASIC only.

Values may be assigned to variables by using the BASIC assignment statement. The use of the keyword LET in such statements is optional. Values may also be assigned through the keyboard by using INPUT statements. When we have run out of data, we can halt a program waiting for input by entering STOP and RESTORE simultaneously.

Commodore 64 BASIC provides the companion statements READ and DATA for storing data within the program itself.

Execution of an END statement halts the run of a program.

We have learned three commands for program manipulation thus far. RUN calls for our program to be executed. RUN 100 calls for our program to be executed beginning at line 100. LIST displays our program or a segment of our program on the screen. NEW clears the BASIC work area for a new project.

Problems for Chapter 1 . . . .

You should not feel that you must limit yourself to the problems offered here. As you get some programming under your belt, you should find lots of interesting problems to try on the computer. Learning to program is unique in that the computer itself will provide you with a measure of your success: you do not need an answer book or a teacher to know how you are doing. The real joy of learning anything comes when you begin to formulate the problems, solve them, and verify that your solutions are correct all on your own. (It helps to have a computer.)

At this point you can write programs for printing messages of all kinds, request data from the keyboard, and perform a variety of arithmetic operations.

1. Write a program to display the sum of 123.45, 654, 1920, 114423, and 0.01.
2. Write a program to display the sum of five numbers to be supplied during execution.
3. Write a program to print a decimal value of 2/3.
4. Assign 1/3 to the variable X. Display the value of X, 3*X, and X + X + X.
5. Write a program to display decimal values for 1/7, 2/7, through 6/7.
6. Write a program to find a value for the following expression:

$$\frac{1/2 + 1/3}{1/3 - 1/4}$$

7. Write a program to find the sum of the first ten counting numbers. (integers).
8. Write a program to find the product of the first ten counting numbers.
9. Have the computer request the numerator and denominator for two fractions to be multiplied. Print the numerator and denominator of the product. (This problem does not call for the computer to perform division.)
10. Have the computer request the numerator and denominator for two fractions to be added. Print the numerator and denominator of the sum. (This problem does not call for the computer to perform division.)

PROGRAMMER'S CORNER 1

Screen Editing . . . .

There is a wide range of typing skills among people who wish to learn about computer programming. The Commodore 64 is designed to accommodate us all. For the expert typist, the keyboard is laid out nicely, and there are only a few special keys to learn about. For the novice, several keys are included to make it easy to fix typing errors. Even without these special editing keys, we can always press the RETURN key and begin again.

...The DEL Key

It often happens that we notice our typing errors almost immediately after we make them. These are the easiest to fix. Suppose we have just begun a line as follows:

```
100  PRINT "THIS IS A TRIIL K==
```

and the cursor is right there after the L. We have not finished the line yet. It is easy to press the INST/DEL key in the upper-right corner of the keyboard twice. (Be sure not to press the SHIFT key here; that does something else.) This is the way to delete the L and then the I. After this it is a simple matter to type AL and the rest of the line, as originally intended.

At any time we may use DEL to erase characters to the left. If the key is held down, it will repeat automatically, so it is easy to delete several characters quickly. If that is what we want, it is very nice. If we only want to delete a single character, then we simply press the key and release it right away. The beginner should experiment with this to learn the feel of it. With a little practice this key will help us produce accurate program lines quickly and easily.

At first we made changes in program lines by simply retyping the entire line. If the line we wish to change is a long one and we merely want to change a character or two, we may just end up making another typing error. Commodore 64 Basic includes a set of commands that allow us to move the cursor around the screen to change what is displayed there.

Whatever appears on the screen is stored in memory. In fact, program lines that appear on the screen are stored in two places. One place is invisible to us, the location in memory where BASIC keeps the entire program. When we type a line of a program and press RETURN, BASIC incorporates it into any existing program already stored in that invisible part of memory. The visible line on the screen is stored in the visible part of memory used for text display and for some graphics.

The best possible way to learn about these screen editing features for your machine is to sit down with the computer and experiment. Try everything described here. Soon you will be doing all of this automatically.

...CRSR Left and Right Key

The two keys at the very right of the bottom row of keys are marked with arrows. They can be used to save us a lot of typing effort. One of those keys moves the cursor up and down, depending on whether or not it is shifted. The other key moves the cursor right or left, again depending on whether or not it is shifted. Both of these keys have a built-in repeat feature: the cursor will move repeatedly until we release the key. Thus, if we have begun typing a line as follows:

```
100 LRT K = 76342.91
```

and we spot that we have mistyped LET we may immediately press the cursor left key enough times to place the cursor over the R. To move the cursor left, we hold down the SHIFT key while pressing the key with the right and left arrows. Sometimes when we use the repeat feature, the cursor moves too far. That is no problem: just move it back to the correct spot with the cursor right key. That is the same key, only unshifted. Practice this a little until it becomes comfortable for you to move the cursor back and forth without looking at the keyboard. When the cursor is finally blinking over the R, we simply type an E and then press RETURN. It is not necessary to retrace the line with the cursor. Whenever we press RETURN, the whole line is read into the program. This is a great convenience. Thus it may often make sense to finish typing a line even though we see a typing error at the beginning. Then we can use the cursor left key to go back and make the correction.

Or, it may make sense to use the CRSR left key to back up, make a change, and then use the CRSR right key to retrace to the end of the line and finish typing as planned.

...The INST Key

The INST key may be used to provide space to insert characters on any line. Suppose we type

```
300   LET X = 3245982
```

and before pressing RETURN we realize that the number should have been 32459.82. That is easy to correct, too. Just use the CRSR left key to place the cursor over the 8 and press INST. We access INST by holding down SHIFT and pressing the INST/DEL key. This opens up a space on the line between the 9 and the 8. That is exactly where we want the decimal point. Press the dot key and press RETURN. The line now reads

```
300   LET X = 32459.82
```

The various editing keys may be used in combination to achieve the desired results. We may move the cursor right or left and then insert or delete characters as needed to make one change and then do it again to make another change on the same line. Even if the program line extends to a second line on the screen, the editing will move back and forth between the two just fine.

...CRSR Up and Down Key

It often happens that we want to change a line in a program after we have gone on to other things. This may come up because we spot a typing error, or because we want to change what the program does. Either way the editing works the same. As an example, let's work with the following program segment:

```
LIST

100   PRINT "THIS IS A EDIT EXAMPLE"
120   PRINT "IF WE FOLLLOW ALONE WITH THE
COMPUTER,"
130   PRINT "THEN WE WILL BECOM EDITTING E
XPRTS"
```

Program 1-10. An editing example.

Each statement of Program 1-10 needs attention. With the program listed as shown, we can move the cursor to line 100 by holding down the SHIFT key and pressing the CRSR up key. Use this to place the cursor over the 1 in 100. Next, hold down the CRSR right key until the cursor is over the space between the A and EDIT, as shown in Figure 1-13.

```
100   PRINT "THIS IS A█EDIT EXAMPLE"
```

Figure 1-13. Editing a program line.

Now hold down the SHIFT key and press the INST/DEL key once. This

18

introduces the space we need for the letter N. Press N and the RETURN key. Now the cursor is in place to work on line 120.

To fix line 120 we need to eliminate the triple L in FOLLLOW.

```
120  PRINT "IF WE FOLLLOW ALONE WITH THE
COMPUTER,"
```

Using the CRSR right key we place the cursor over either the second or the third L and press DEL. Watch as the C on the second line moves up to the first line. Next we fix ALONE by using the CRSR right key until the cursor is over the E and typing G. Pressing RETURN now takes care of that line. The cursor moves to line 130.

There are three things to fix on line 130

```
130  PRINT "THEN WE WILL BECOM EDITTING E
XPRTS"
```

Use CRSR right to place the cursor to the right of the M. Press SHIFT INST once and the letter E. Next, move the cursor to the second T in EDITTING. Press DEL once. Now move the cursor to the R in EXPRTS. Press SHIFT INST once and the letter E. Finally, press RETURN and the job is done.

At this point the cursor is flashing over the R in READY. We need to use the CRSR down key to get a clear spot on the screen so that we can type RUN to test our program. If we just type RUN at this point, the computer will try to process the command

```
RUNDY.
```

That will produce the display

```
?UNDEF'D STATEMENT  ERROR
```

On the other hand, if we simply press the RETURN key to move the cursor down into a clear area of the screen, the computer will process "READY." as our instruction. Since the first four letters, READ, are part of READ...DATA, we get the following message:

```
?OUT OF DATA  ERROR
```

If it happens that the program in memory has a DATA statement in it, then something else happens. The value of Y becomes whatever numeric value occurs in the DATA statement. This is because the computer reads "READY." as READY. We still get the ?SYNTAX ERROR message, because BASIC doesn't recognize the dot as anything.

...Quote Mode

Whenever a quotation mark is typed, something happens to the CRSR keys and the CLR/HOME key. Typing any one of these keys after typing a quote transmits that character to the program. In this way we may enter some of the editing functions right in PRINT statements. The editing occurs when the program is run rather than at the keyboard. Typing a second quote cancels Quote Mode and returns these keys to their normal immediate editing functions. Each of these keys displays a reversed graphics character when entered in Quote Mode, as shown in Table 1-1.

Keystroke	Character
HOME	▤
CLR (SHIFT)	▢
CRSR down	▣
CRSR up (SHIFT)	▢
CRSR right	▮
CRSR left (SHIFT)	▮▮

Table 1-1. Cursor controls in Quote Mode.

Note that DEL still works as before here. However, INST displays as an inverse graphic character with a vertical bar near the left edge. This is the same graphics we get with the inverse shifted T.

We may use Quote Mode to create interesting effects. For example, try Program 1-11.

```
100  PRINT "▯▯▯▯▯▯▯▯C▯O▯M▯M▯O▯D▯O▯R▯E▯▯
▯▯▯▯▯"
```

Program 1-11. Demonstration of CLR and CRSR keys in a PRINT statement.

Note the "special" characters in line 100. The ▢ is obtained by pressing the SHIFT and CLR/HOME keys, the ▣ s are obtained by pressing the CRSR down key each time, and the ▢ s are obtained by pressing SHIFT and CRSR down each time. These characters and others used in this book are all shown in Appendix A. Later we will learn about the numeric codes associated with the editing keys and about ways to use them in programs. Figure 1-14 shows the result.

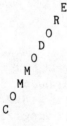

```
            E
           R
          O
         D
        O
       M
      M
     O
     C
```

READY.

Figure 1-14. Execution of Program 1-11.

Note that it is the typing of the quote that produces all these effects. We may still use the editing keys normally to change an existing program statement having quotes in it. But, suppose we want to enter cursor controls in an existing statement. In this situation, INST puts BASIC in Quote Mode. So we can place the cursor where we want it and then make room in the statement with INST. Now any cursor keys will behave as they do in Quote Mode. That is, they will be entered as controls for when the program is run rather than moving the cursor immediately. Also, in INST mode the DEL key now displays as an inverse T and causes the deletion when the program is run, not immediately. So, be careful. The best way to see all this is to experiment on the computer.

Anytime we use DEL to fill characters inserted with INST we get an inverse T. When the program is run or listed the inverse T's do not appear. Instead, the deletions are made.

It is worth noting that we can change line numbers with the screen editor in the same way that we change any other characters on the screen. It may be necessary to delete the old line when this is done. Be careful not to replace the wrong lines with this technique.

Chapter 2

Writing a Program

2-1...Planning Your Program

Computer programs are linear. That is, they define a single step at a time. Many problems brought to the computer for solution, however, are nonlinear in nature. For example, we would like to do many things in at least two dimensions. Many computerized processes are outlined by using large charts in which each item in the chart represents a complete subsystem consisting of a whole collection of very long computer programs. We need to develop some ideas that will help us begin with the big ideas and systematically arrive at a completed project whose smallest elements are computer program statements.

Good programming requires a plan. The planning should be completed before any program statements are written down. You should write out the entire program on paper before you sit down to type it into the computer. Major changes in program organization are easy to deal with before the program has been typed into the computer, as there is less inertia to overcome. Once a program has been typed into the computer, part of the problem becomes how to make the desired change while preserving as much as possible of what exists. While the program is still written out longhand, such changes are much easier. Sure, we can easily write a program to add two numbers without much fuss. The plan can be in our head and we can "write down" the program statements directly at the computer keyboard. But try writing a system to launch a satellite or a payroll system, or even a program to find all prime integers from 1000 to 2000. Good planning requires a complete understanding of the problem. What is known? What is the question? What will be the form of the solution? How do I get from the known information to the solution?

...Counting on the Computer

Let's start with something simple—developing a plan for instructing the computer to count. This is a good first problem, since it is something we are all familiar with. A thorough understanding of the problem at hand is essential for writing computer programs. It is highly unlikely that we can write a program to solve a problem we do not understand.

We can describe counting as a process of starting with the number 1 and repeatedly adding 1 to obtain the next counting number in sequence. That is easy! There are only two ingredients here: beginning and adding 1 repeatedly.

We can begin with a statement such as

```
110 C1 = 1
```

But, how do we add 1? Here's a way:

```
120 C2 = C1 + 1
125 C1 = C2
```

In mathematics, the equal sign (=) usually asserts that two expressions have the same value. However, assignment statements in BASIC use the equal sign for a special purpose—to assign the result of a calculation on the right to a variable named on the left. This allows us to combine statements 120 and 125 above into the single statement

```
120 C1 = C1 + 1
```

The variable C1 contains one value before execution of this statement and another value after execution of this statement. The prior value is replaced by the new value. A variable cannot store two values simultaneously. Even though pigeonholes and mail boxes may hold more than one item, variables cannot.

Now we need to tell the computer to repeat the work of line 120 over and over again. We resist any possible urge to include a statement $130\ C1 = C1 + 1$, and so on. To count to 100 this way would require more than 100 statements. Computers are supposed to save work, not make things harder. The way to repeat the action of line 120 over and over again is to include the following line:

```
130 GOTO 120
```

This will put the computer into a loop. Now we have three lines that would indeed cause the Commodore 64 to count, beginning with 1:

```
110 C1 = 1
120 C1 = C1 + 1
130 GOTO 120
```

Program 2-1. First counting program.

However, we have overlooked an important ingredient. We will never know which number the computer is up to at any particular time, except when it gets to something above 1E38. What we need here is to display each number as the computer gets to it. Therefore, we will insert a PRINT statement between lines 110 and 120. In order for this statement to be executed every time the computer adds 1, the GOTO statement at line 130 must be changed. The loop must include the PRINT statement, as shown in Program 2-2.

```
    110 C1 = 1
-->115 PRINT C1
    120 C1 = C1 + 1
-->130 GOTO 115
```

Program 2-2. Counting with display.

Several comments and one warning are in order here. Program 2-2 has no natural termination. If you execute this program, it will run for a very long time. You will have to press the RUN/STOP key, pull the plug, or wait for BASIC to overflow. In order to make this a useful counting program, we need to replace the unconditional statement 130 GOTO 115 with one that can make a decision. This brings us to the IF...THEN statement.

...IF...THEN

Our counting program would be more useful if we had a way for it to terminate when some predetermined number was reached. BASIC has the ability to alter the order in which statements are executed, depending on the outcome of a decision. This is called a *conditional transfer*. Suppose we want the computer to count to seven and quit. In this case, we want to GOTO 115 on the condition that C1 is less than or equal to seven. That is easy in BASIC:

```
    130 IF C1 <= 7 THEN GOTO 115
```

Line 130 will do the job for us. Here "less than or equal to" is symbolized by $<=$. The $<$ symbol represents "less than" and the $=$ symbol represents "equals."

...REM: What's It All About?

While all of our programs are clear to us at the time that we write them, it is difficult to come back to an old program and recall all of the clear thoughts that we had way back when. BASIC offers the REM statement so that we may include REMarks as part of the program. The computer will ignore all REM statements during program execution, but it will list them along with the others in response to the LIST command. Not only will those REM statements remind us about our own old programs, but they will be invaluable to others reading our programs. No program should be considered complete without REM statements. Some programmers consider REM statements so vital to the program development process that they write them first. Not a bad idea!

REM statements should describe the action of a program or segment of a program. Remarks like LOAD Y WITH 17 actually detract from the readability of a program, while INITIALIZE LOW TEMPERATURE CUTOFF describes the function of part of a program. And now we have a program to type into the Commodore 64 and run.

```
100 REM ** COUNTING FROM 1 TO 7
110 C1 = 1
115 PRINT C1
120 C1 = C1 + 1
130 IF C1 <= 7 THEN GOTO 115
999 END
```

Program 2-3. Counting from 1 to 7.

```
RUN
1
2
3
4
5
6
7
```

Figure 2-1. Execution of Program 2-3.

When using IF...THEN, there are six options available:

$<$	less than
$<=$	less than or equal to
$=$	equal to
$<>$	not equal to
$>$	greater than
$>=$	greater than or equal to

These symbols are called *relational operators.* Any BASIC expression may appear on either side of a relational operator.

Counting is a process that pervades computer programming. We do it all the time. How many players? How many problems? Count the number of specimens so that we may compute the average for this lab test. The examples go on endlessly. We might be interested in only the odd numbers. How would we change our counting program to do that? That is easy—just change line 120 to read:

```
120 C1 = C1 + 2
```

Now don't forget to change the REM statement to correctly reflect the new function of the program.

```
100 REM ** ODD INTEGERS FROM 1 TO 7
```

Misleading REM statements are terrible. The extra time spent to make sure they are right will pay off in the end. Suppose we have a problem that requires even integers. In this case, line 110 should set the value of C1 to start at 2 or whatever we require as the first even integer. Again, note that the REM statement should reflect the function of the program.

Our little program has four important components.

1. We initialize, or set the initial value of, the counting variable.
2. Some action is programmed. In our example, we display the current value of the counter.

3. The counter is incremented.

4. We test the value of the counter to determine whether or not to loop back and repeat the programmed action.

Most counting routines are used for some higher purpose than merely displaying the current value of the counter. Suppose we have a relative who has promised to give us five times our age in dollars on each of our first 21 birthdays. We might like to know the total number of dollars we will have received upon reaching 21. This problem can be solved with the logic of our counting program. Here the programmed action consists of adding five times C1 for each year. We will use the variable D1 for this. We initialize D1 to zero. We test for 21 rather than 7. When the IF test fails, the program should print the value of D1 with an appropriate label. Program 2-4 does all this.

```
      50 REM ** TOTAL $5 EACH YEAR ON EACH BIR
      THDAY
-->100 D1 = 0
      110 C1 = 1
-->120 D1 = D1 + 5 * C1
      140 C1 = C1 + 1
      150 IF C1 <= 21 THEN GOTO 120
      160 PRINT "$"; D1; "AFTER 21 YEARS"
      999 END
```

Program 2-4. Birthday dollars.

Look at line 100. It turns out that BASIC automatically sets the values of all variables to zero when we type the RUN command. So, for our little problem, D1 would be initialized to zero for us. However, it is good programming practice to include an assignment statement anyway. Having that statement in the program makes the meaning of line 120 less mysterious—not to the computer, but to anyone reading our program.

```
RUN
$ 1155 AFTER 21 YEARS
```

Figure 2-2. Execution of Program 2-4.

Now, imagine you are the inspector in a packaging plant. Quality Control requires that for any lot to be accepted, the average weight of five packages selected at random must be at least 180 grams. You want to write a program that asks the right questions and accepts or rejects the lot. Here we have the four components listed above. In this case, the programmed action is a little more complex. We print a label for the INPUT request, request INPUT, and add the entered weight to a variable designated for keeping track of the total weight of the five packages. This last can be done with the statement

```
235 T1 = T1 + WT
```

where T1 is the running total weight and WT is the weight of each package in turn. Before we have entered any package weights, the value of T1 must be zero. When the value of the counter has passed 5, we will calculate the average in AV. If the value of AV is less than the required 180 grams then we want a reject message. Otherwise, we want an accept message.

```
    100 REM ** CHECK AVERAGE PACKAGE WEIGHT
        FOR 180 GRAM MINIMUM
-->200 T1 = 0
    210 C1 = 1
    220 PRINT "WT"; C1;
    230 INPUT WT
    235 T1 = T1 + WT
    240 C1 = C1 + 1
    250 IF C1 <= 5 THEN GOTO 220
    260 AV = T1 / 5
-->270 IF AV < 180 THEN GOTO 290
    275 PRINT "ACCEPT THIS LOT"
-->280 GOTO 295
    290 PRINT "REJECT THIS LOT"
    295 END
```

Program 2-5. Package weight monitor.

We have included a REM statement describing the purpose of the program. Look at line 200. Note again that we have initialized a variable to zero even though we could let BASIC do it for us. Later, if we want to include this routine as part of a more complex program, the value of T1 will be reset to zero every time this program segment is executed. Failure to include such a statement would cause the value of T1 to grow ever larger as more and more lots are sampled. Thus the program would erroneously accept every sample after the first. (Doubtless, the computer would be blamed for this obvious programmer error.) Note that we have selected C1 for counting, T1 for totaling, WT for the package weight, and AV for the average. Selecting variable names carefully will make the meaning of each program statement clearer. Don't use A9 for weight or TF for counting. While TO might have been nice for the total, that two-letter word is reserved. If we had used TO as a variable in line 200, the Commodore 64 would have reported ?SYNTAX ERROR. Soon, we will discover what TO is reserved for. Line 270 determines which message will be displayed according to the average weight. Line 280 assures that we get exactly one message. Now let's run the program.

```
RUN
WT 1 ? 182
WT 2 ? 190
WT 3 ? 180
WT 4 ? 179
WT 5 ? 177
ACCEPT THIS LOT
```

Figure 2-3. Execution of Program 2-5.

To check another lot, simply run the program again.

If this were all that the program did, it might be more practical to use a hand-held calculator. In practice, there are many more factors to consider in the above problem. While it may be illegal to be underweight, it is unprofitable to sell overweight packages. So, in addition to checking for minimum average, our program ought to check for any package over a certain weight, say 185. Furthermore, there may be a legal minimum weight, say 178.

The program can also easily be modified to process several batches of data. Simply change

```
280 GOTO 295
```

to

```
280 GOTO 200
```

and replace

```
295 END
```

with

```
295 GOTO 200
```

Now, how do we terminate execution of the program? We may enter a value of zero to indicate that there are no more batches to process. Then the statement

```
232 IF WT = 0 THEN GOTO 999
```

may be used to divert program execution to statement 999 for a weight of zero. We had better include the statement

```
999 END
```

to avoid the following error message:

```
?UNDEF'D STATEMENT  ERROR IN 232
```

Special data values used as signals to control the action of a program are sometimes called dummy data. These changes are left as exercises.

While we could use STOP-RESTORE in response to an INPUT request, it is not desirable to depend on this method to terminate the program. That is more for programmers to use during program development. Our programs should provide for more orderly control. We often want further computing after the last INPUT item. STOP-RESTORE not only terminates the program, it clears the screen as well, while the use of a special data value allows us to direct the program to continue processing.

...SUMMARY

Know your problem well before coding your solution program. Have a plan. It is easier to make major changes on paper than it is to make major changes in a program that has already been typed into the computer.

The IF...THEN statement may be used to determine the next statement to be executed while the program is running.

Use remarks freely, but properly. Don't state the obvious. State the purpose of a statement or group of statements. It is vital that REM statements be accurate. Make sure that your program documentation keeps up with any changes in your program at all times. It is very frustrating to sort through a program code that does not agree with the documentation; this can be worse than no documentation at all. However, don't use that comment as an excuse to omit REM statements.

Artificial values, called dummy data, may be used as data to control what statements will be executed next.

Problems for Section 2-1 . . . .

At this point, we know enough about BASIC to program solutions to a wide variety of problems. We could find the sum of the counting numbers from 1 to 100 (or from A to B) as long as we don't exceed 1E38. We could find sums of even integers or odd integers or those divisible by five, etc. We could do something as simple as having the computer display "I LIKE BASIC" some specified number of times. Use your imagination—you needn't limit yourself to the problems listed here. If you have a Commodore 64 to yourself, then you can answer all of those "I wonder what would happen if . . ." questions with, "I'll try it." The computer never raises its voice or remembers our "dumb" questions; it just quietly tells us when we have made a mistake.

1. In the birthday problem (Program 2-4), have the computer print the amount received for this birthday and the total so far for each birthday.

2. In the package inspection problem (Program 2-5), make the changes necessary to repeat processing for many batches of data in a single execution. Insert at least one blank PRINT statement so that the batches are separated on the screen.

3. Rewrite the package inspection program (Program 2-5) to test for a minimum package weight of 178 grams and a maximum of 183. Have the program report the reason for rejecting a lot and repeat for another batch.

4. Four test scores were 100, 86, 71, and 92. Write a program to determine the average.

5. Write a program to count the number of odd integers from 5 to 1191 inclusive.

6. Write a program to find the number and sum of all integers greater than 1000 and less than 2213 that are evenly divisible by 11. (Start with 1001.)

7. Three pairs of numbers follow in which the first is the base and the second is the altitude of a triangle. 10,21; 12.5,8; 289,114. Write a program to print the area of each triangle. Use dummy data to end the program.

8. A person is paid $0.01 the first day of a job, $0.02 the second day, $0.04 the third day, and so on, with the pay doubling each day on the job for 30 days. Write a program to calculate the wages for the 30th day and the total for the 30 days.

9. Write a program to print the integers from 1 to 15, paired with their reciprocals.

10. A customer put in an order for four books that retail at $10.95 and carry a 25% discount, three records at $7.98 with a 15% discount, and one record player for $59.95 on which there is no discount. In addition, there is a 2% discount allowed on the total order for prompt payment. Write a program to compute the amount of the order.

11. In the song "The Twelve Days of Christmas," gifts are bestowed upon the singer in the following pattern: the first day she received a partridge in a pear tree; the second day two turtle doves and a partridge in a pear tree; the third day three French hens, two turtle doves, and a partridge in a pear tree. This continues for 12 days. On the 12th day she received $12 + 11 + \ldots + 2 + 1$ gifts. Write a program to determine how many gifts she received altogether. Another way to ask this question is to ask: If she had to return one gift each day after the first, on what day would she return the last gift?

12. For problem 11, have the computer print the number of gifts on each of the 12 days and the total up to that day.

13. George took tests in two courses. For the first course the scores were 83, 91, 97, 100, 89. For the second course the scores were 65, 72, 81, and 92. Write a program that will compute test averages for both courses. You will need two dummy data values—one to signal the end of each set of scores and the other to signal the end of each execution of the program.

2-2 . . . Random Events

How do programmers instruct a computer to flip coins, deal cards, or roll dice? These actions are really very easy to simulate. All we need is the ability to generate numbers at random. BASIC includes exactly what we need for this—RND(X), an instruction that produces a random number. RND is a little "black box" in BASIC that brings forth a number at random each time it is invoked, producing decimal numbers in the range 0 to 0.999999999. The number enclosed in the parentheses and symbolized above by X is called the *argument* and is very important.

Here are the rules:

RND(I)   I > 0   Yields a different random value for each successive access.
RND(I)   I = 0   Produces the last random number used.
RND(I)   I < 0   Produces the same value each time the same value of I is used.

If we want the same sequence every time a program is run, then we must use the same negative value for I for the first access and a positive number for all succeeding accesses. Then, to change the random sequence, simply use a different negative number or any positive number for the first access. The ability to repeat a random sequence is useful for program testing.

Program 2-6 prints 10 random numbers.

```
100 REM ** GENERATE A FEW RANDOM NUMBERS
200 I = 1
230 PRINT RND(1)
240 I = I + 1
250 IF I <= 10 THEN GOTO 230
999 END
```

Program 2-6. Generating 10 random numbers.

We have built a counting routine that enables us to print RND(1) 10 times. Here is a sample run of our program.

```
RUN
.936928502
.620447973
.98411756
.228080195
.0444301156
.929139704
.228214184
.954965809
.641032259
.946861798
```

Figure 2-4. Execution of Program 2-6.

Now we will adapt this new ability to simulate flipping a coin. Let's flip it 39 times, to just fill one line of the screen without moving to the next line. There are three parts to this problem. We need to count to 39, generate a random flip, and print an H or a T depending on whether the toss comes up heads or tails. We know all about counting. We can decide whether to print an H or a T if we know how to tell which came up. All that remains is to distinguish heads from tails. We want half of each. So if we designate all of the random numbers from 0 to 0.499999999 as heads and all of the numbers from 0.5 to 0.999999999 as tails, the problem is solved. We merely test RND(1) in an IF...THEN statement. If the value is less than 0.5, then branch to a statement that displays an H; otherwise "drop through" to a statement that displays a T. Following the PRINT "T"; statement, we must be sure to put in a GOTO statement to divert execution around the PRINT "H"; statement. Here is a program to do just that.

```
198 REM ** FLIP A COIN 39 TIMES
200 FL = 1
230 IF RND (1) < .5 THEN GOTO 270
250 PRINT "T";
260 GOTO 280
270 PRINT "H";
280 FL = FL + 1
290 IF FL <= 39 THEN GOTO 230
999 END
```

Program 2-7. Flip a coin 39 times.

```
RUN
HHTHTHTHHHHTTHTHTTTHHHTTHHTHTTHTHTTTTHTH
```

Figure 2-5. Execution of Program 2-7.

There you have it.

We have accomplished what we set out to do. However, we really want to know as much about BASIC as possible. So, let's probe further.

...A RaNDom Exploration

The random number generator may be bent to our needs in many ways. We have chosen to select two equal halves by forming a boundary at 0.5. This works fine for flipping a coin, but suppose we want to roll a die. Now, to deal with six numbers by using the method of Program 2-7 there would be five boundaries, with values like 0.166666667 and 0.833333333. There is a much better way.

If we multiply all numbers in the range from 0 to 1 (including 0 and excluding 1) by 6 then we get results in the range from 0 to 6 (including 0 and excluding 6). Then we could successively test to see if the result is less than 1, then 2, and so on through 6, to obtain a value for the face of a die. This will certainly work, but we can do even better. Once again BASIC comes to the rescue. This time it is INT(N) that makes life simple.

...INT(N)

INT(N) is a special mechanism for developing an integer value that is the greatest integer less than or equal to the argument. Thus, INT (3.9876919) = 3, INT(4) = 4, and INT(− 9.8) = − 10. So, if we simply generate random numbers in the range from 0 to 5.99999999, we can apply INT(N) to obtain integers in the range from 0 to 5. We merely add 1 to the values 0 to 5 to get values in the range 1 to 6. This is, of course, exactly what we want for rolling dice. Bingo, another problem solved. Let's look at Program 2-8 to roll a die ten times.

```
    198 REM ** ROLL A DIE TEN TIMES
    200 I = 1
    210 V1 = RND(1) * 6 + 1
    220 PRINT V1, INT(V1)
    230 I = I + 1
-->240 IF I <= 10 THEN GOTO 210
```

Program 2-8. Rolling a die ten times.

```
RUN
    4.89597147         4
    3.61340997         3
    6.85094379         6
    6.8514799          6
    3.62058533         3
    2.96008383         2
    4.86195681         4
    4.10220501         4
    3.16562905         3
    2.9053821          2
```

Figure 2-6. Execution of Program 2-8.

...IF...THEN Revisited

IF...THEN is used so frequently in BASIC to transfer program control that an abbreviated form exists.

```
240 IF I <= 10 THEN 210
```

may be used in place of line 240 in our die rolling program above. Using this new form of the IF...THEN statement, our coin flipping of Program 2-7 may be rewritten as follows:

```
     198 REM ** FLIP A COIN 39 TIMES
     200 FL = 1
-->230 IF RND(1) < .5 THEN 270
     250 PRINT "T";
     260 GOTO 280
     270 PRINT "H";
     280 FL = FL + 1
-->290 IF FL <= 39 THEN 230
     999 END
```

Program 2-9. Program 2-7 showing shortened IF...THEN statement.

Lines 230 and 290 in Program 2-9 use the shortened form of IF...THEN.

...SUMMARY

RND(X) provides a source of random numbers. We get numbers in the range from 0 to 0.999999999. The argument of RND(X) affects the result. A positive value simply produces a value at random. Any negative number gives us the same result every time it is used. Zero recalls the last value produced by RND(X).

INT(X) returns the greatest integer not greater than X.

IF...THEN has an abbreviated form that we may use for conditional transfer. 100 IF $X < 5$ THEN 230 will transfer control to line 230 if $X < 5$ is true.

Problems for Section 2-2 ....

1. Modify the coin-flipping program (Program 2-9) to repeat the 39 flips five times.
2. Modify the coin-flipping program (Program 2-9) to count the number of times tails comes up in 39 flips.
3. Write a program to flip a coin 1000 times. Count the number of tails. You might choose not to display H's and T's.
4. Write a program to roll two dice ten times.
5. Write a program to provide math drill problems in addition. Request limits and the number of problems by using INPUT. Display the number of correct answers at the end.

2-3...A Better Way to Count (FOR and NEXT)

Having written numerous counting loops, we imagine that there is some more compact method for doing this. After all, just about everything we do seems to involve counting of some sort.

...BASIC Loops

FOR and NEXT in BASIC automate the control functions of a program loop. Thus our earlier program to count from one to seven becomes Program 2-10:

```
    100 REM ** COUNTING WITH FOR...NEXT
-->110 FOR C1 = 1 TO 7
    115 PRINT C1
-->130 NEXT C1
    999 END
```

Program 2-10. Program 2-3 using FOR...NEXT.

Statement 110 automatically establishes the limits on C1 as 1 and 7. Statement 130 automatically adds 1 to the value of C1 and tests to determine if C1 is less than or equal to 7. The value of C1 will be 8 when execution reaches line 999 of this program. Look again at line 110. Now we know why TO is a BASIC keyword and therefore must not be used in a variable name. If you want to save the last value used of the loop variable, then you need a statement such as 120 C2 = C1 in this program. It is important to note that the statements between FOR and NEXT will always be executed at least once. If we program the statement FOR X = 4 TO 1, then the loop will be executed for X = 4. The NEXT statement will add 1 to 4, getting 5, and then find that X is greater than 1. Execution will "drop through," behaving in exactly the same way as our hand-built loops. To count from A to B by twos, simply code FOR C1 = A TO B STEP 2. The value of STEP may be − 3 or even N. Decimals are allowed.

The FOR...NEXT statements provide several important benefits. FOR... NEXT loops execute dramatically faster than hand-built ones. Their use reduces the number of ideas that we have to keep in mind as we write our programs. Those simple BASIC keywords embody the more complex controls actually used to construct the loop itself, without requiring us to think about the details each time that we use them, thus freeing our mental processes for the specific problem at hand. The ability to make a small number of program statements represent complex solutions greatly simplifies the writing of correct computer programs.

Now we can think about some of the counting loops we have looked at before. Consider the birthday dollars program (Program 2-4). In the original program, we had a line 110 C1 = 1. That line happened to be the opening statement of a counting loop. But, that statement could have set the value of C1 at 1 for any number of reasons. On the other hand, the statement

```
110 FOR C1 = 1 TO 21
```

is crystal clear. It can mean only one thing—we are going to do something 21 times.

In exactly the same manner, NEXT C1 conveys much more information to the person reading the program than

```
150 IF C1 <= 21 THEN GOTO 120.
```

FOR and NEXT are designed to go together. Don't try to initialize a loop with

```
100 C1 = 1
```

and later close it with

```
200 NEXT C1
```

Luckily, if you do this you will receive the following message from the Commodore 64:

```
?NEXT WITHOUT FOR   ERROR IN 200
```

Occasionally, you will be sure you have a loop that will repeat something several times. But, alas, it only happens once and the computer sends no error messages. While the computer requires that a NEXT statement be preceded by a FOR statement, it does not necessarily report that a FOR statement was not followed by a NEXT statement. Now you know.

...SUMMARY

FOR and NEXT are paired up to control program loops in BASIC. FOR A = B TO C STEP D opens a loop by assigning the value of B to A. Each iteration of the loop is accomplished by adding the value of D to the value of A. When the value of A goes past the value of C, the loop is finished. NEXT A causes the next iteration of the loop that was opened with a FOR A statement. If STEP is omitted, the step value is assumed to be 1.

Problems for Section 2-3 . . . .

For each of the problems here, use FOR and NEXT where appropriate.

1. Modify the package inspection program (2-5) to use FOR...NEXT.
2. Write a program to count the number of odd integers from 5 to 1191 inclusive.
3. Write a program to find the number of and the sum of all integers greater than 1000 and less than 2213 that are divisible by 11. (Start with 1001.)
4. A person is paid $0.01 the first day of a job, $0.02 the second day, $0.04 the third day, and so on, with the pay doubling each day on the job for 30 days. Write a program to calculate the wages for the 30th day and the total for the 30 days.
5. Write a program to print the integers from 1 to 15, paired with their reciprocals.
6. Solve the "Twelve Days of Christmas" problem from Section 2.1 by using FOR...NEXT.

7. For problem 6, have the computer print the number of gifts on each of the 12 days and the total up to that day.

8. Modify the coin-flipping program (Program 2-7) to repeat the 39 flips five times.

9. Modify Program 2-7 to count the number of times tails comes up in 39 flips.

10. Write a program to flip a coin 1000 times. Count the number of tails. You might choose to not display H's and T's.

11. Write a program to roll two dice ten times.

12. Write a program to provide math drill problems in addition. Request limits and the number of problems by using INPUT. Display the number of correct answers at the end.

13. Examine the following program:

```
100 FOR I = 1 TO 1.3 STEP .1
110 PRINT I
120 NEXT I
```

What values do you think it will display? Run it. Do you get what you expect? Write a program to display the four values you expected.

PROGRAMMER'S CORNER 2

Immediate Execution . . . .

We have performed a variety of calculations using LET and PRINT statements in programs. This method of calculation is called *deferred execution*, and it is used for most computing. Programs prepared for deferred execution may be saved and used over and over again.

The features of our BASIC programs may be used in a second important way, known as *immediate execution*. We can simply type BASIC instructions whenever a BASIC prompt is displayed. Suppose we want to know the number of hours in a year. We are not required to enter a program line number to obtain such a simple result. Simply type

```
PRINT 365*24
```

Press the RETURN key and instantly BASIC will execute our instruction to produce the desired value.

```
8760
```

```
READY.
```

We can even type a series of BASIC instructions without creating a stored program. We could find the number of hours in a year as follows:

```
D=365

READY.
H=24

READY.
PRINT D*H
8760

READY.
```

With this technique, each statement is executed immediately. The keyword PRINT may be replaced with a question mark (?). This means that we may command the computer to display a result with a single keystroke instead of the five keystrokes required for PRINT.

Immediate mode execution may be used for several purposes. BASIC can be used as a sophisticated calculator. Detailed and complex calculations can be performed quickly and easily. Whatever we enter remains on the screen for us to examine (up to 23 lines with spaces). Generally, calculators retain only a single visible number on the display. The large screen provides the opportunity to check our work. We can be more secure than with most calculators.

...Stepping through a Program

We can press the STOP key at any time to halt execution of a program. If the program is waiting for a response to INPUT, then we must press STOP and RESTORE at the same time. We can select strategic locations in our program to insert END statements. When the program stops, we can switch to immediate mode. The value of any variable can be displayed with a PRINT statement. If the values are all okay, then we can proceed by typing the keyword

```
CONT
```

to continue the program. Or we can pick up execution with a GOTO statement. If 355 is the next line in the program, then we would key in

```
GOTO 355
```

If we find a strange value with one of our PRINT statements, we need to determine what it is in our program that produced it. We can still test the rest of the program, however, by setting the expected value and going on with execution, using CONT or GOTO statements as above.

We cannot enter a new line in the program or change an existing one in immediate mode, however. This will set the values of all variables at zero. You will have to run the program after this.

...STOP

In addition, the STOP statement may be used to cause a program to stop at selected points.

```
945 STOP
```

will cause execution to cease at line 945. When BASIC encounters a STOP statement, a message will be printed as follows:

```
BREAK IN 945
```

If we are inserting temporary STOP statements, it is very nice to know which one the program just encountered. When we have fixed everything, we can remove all unwanted STOP statements.

Of course, certain BASIC statements make no sense entered directly from the keyboard without line numbers. Keywords like READ, DATA, and INPUT are clearly intended for use in executing programs. Entering INPUT A without a line number evokes

```
?ILLEGAL DIRECT   ERROR
```

However, INPUT #1, A produces

```
?FILE NOT OPEN   ERROR
```

We'll get to files.

On the other hand, certain commands are intended for the keyboard. LIST does work in a program, but execution stops after the program is listed.

...Deleting Program Lines

We may delete any program line by typing the line number. But, suppose we want to delete lines 100 through 190. If we have left intervals of 10, that's 10 lines. We could type 100, then 110, then 120, and so on, but that is a little tedious. Type this line instead:

```
FOR I = 100 TO 190 STEP 10 : PRINT I : NEXT I
```

The numbers of the lines we want to delete are now on the screen. Place the cursor at the beginning of the 100 and press RETURN 10 times. Like magic the program lines are deleted. The screen editor has saved us much typing. We have also avoided potential errors from typing incorrect line numbers by hand.

Chapter 3

Commodore Character Graphics and Much More

3-1...Using the Commodore Graphics Keys

We can easily use the Commodore graphics characters directly from the keyboard. If we want an arrow pointing left, we simply press the leftmost key in the upper row of keys. If we want to display this character in a program, we simply enclose it in quotes in a PRINT statement. Normally, the Commodore displays the character that appears on the top of the key. Where there are two characters on the top of the key, we get the upper one by pressing the SHIFT key while also pressing the desired character key. Thus, we have accessed the quote mark for our PRINT statements by pressing SHIFT and 2. Many of the keys are labeled on the front with two graphics characters. To display the right character, simply press SHIFT and the desired character. To display the left character, simply press the Commodore sign (Ⓒ) and the desired character. All of these characters can be displayed within a program by enclosing them in quotes in PRINT statements.

We can control the appearance of the characters provided in two important ways. It is easy to display characters in reverse mode. To do this, we press the CTRL key and 9. The 9 key is labeled ReVerSe ON. Now, instead of a light blue character on a dark blue background, we get a dark blue character on a light blue background. RVS ON is in effect until the RETURN key is struck or the program issues a RETURN at the end of a PRINT statement. When we include RVS ON in a PRINT statement, it appears as an "R" in reverse. The reverse feature takes effect only when the program is run. In addition, we can control the color of each character. This we do by using the 1 through 8 keys and either the CTRL key or the

Commodore key (⬚). Using the CTRL key causes subsequent characters to be displayed in the color labeled on the front of the corresponding key. Besides these eight colors another eight are available by holding the (⬚) key and any of the keys 1 through 8 (see Table 3-1).

KEY	CTRL KEY	(⬚) KEY
1	Black	Orange
2	White	Brown
3	Red	Light Red
4	Cyan	Gray 1
5	Purple	Gray 2
6	Green	Light Green
7	Blue	Light Blue
8	Yellow	Gray 3

Table 3-1. Colors from the keyboard.

You can use this to adjust the colors on your television or your color monitor. Simply turn reverse on by pressing CTRL and 9, then display each of the colors in turn by pressing the space bar a few times for each color. Notice that without RVS ON, pressing the space bar simply leaves spaces in the screen color. At any time we may restore the screen to its original condition by pressing STOP-RESTORE. This also stops execution of any program in progress.

If we want to clear the screen for more work in the latest color while maintaining RVS ON, SHIFT/CLR is the key to press. SHIFT/CLR may also be used in a PRINT statement. It will appear as a reversed heart, but upon execution the screen will be cleared. Further, we may simply begin again at the top of the screen without clearing by pressing HOME. In a PRINT statement, this shows up as a reversed letter S.

It is a good idea to experiment with these capabilities. Notice that some of the graphics characters are grouped sensibly. The four corners of a circle appear at the corners of a box on keys U, I, K, and J. The four open square half corners appear on A, S, X, and Z, while the four filled square half corners appear on D, F, V, and C. All we need is a little imagination and some patience to display interesting figures.

...The Character Graphics Screen

The character graphics screen on the Commodore 64 is the same screen that we use for regular text display. Normally, we have 25 lines of 40 characters each. We may mix graphics characters and text on the screen at any time, because the letters are simply included among the graphics characters.

For some graphics applications, we will just PRINT what we want on the screen. For others it will be important to lay out a screen gridwork. Each position on the screen may be identified by its line and column. The position in the upper left corner is labeled 0, 0. The position in the lower right corner is labeled 39, 24. We may think of the lines as being numbered from 0 to 24 and the positions on each line as being numbered from 0 to 39. This permits us to think of the screen as a 40-by-25 grid. We have 1000 positions on the screen. We may easily place any character in any of them with PRINT statements. (There is one exception: we cannot print a

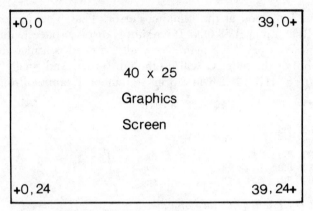

Figure 3-1. The graphics screen layout.

character in the lower right corner without having it scroll the screen up one line.) Columns are numbered from 0 to 39 from left to right and rows are numbered from 0 to 24 from top to bottom. This is not the same as the conventional rectangular coordinate system widely used in mathematics, but this difference presents no great obstacle. The screen is not exactly square, so we call the plotted points blocks rather than squares. No special graphics keywords are required here; we just design a figure and print it on the screen.

...A Graphic Example

In Chapter 2, we learned how to display values for "rolling" dice at random by using RND( ). Now we can use the Commodore 64 graphics features to display dice on the screen. This will be surprisingly easy to do. Let's concentrate on the nature of a picture of one face of a die.

Think of drawing the six possible faces of a die on ordinary graph paper. This can be done nicely, if we use a rectangle seven blocks wide and five blocks high. We come up with the following sketch:

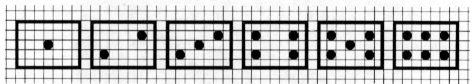

Figure 3-2. The six dice.

Now the computer problem separates into two parts. First, we need the die background. And second, we need six different configurations for the dots in some contrasting color. Let's see what solutions the Commodore 64 provides for these two problems.

...Drawing a Die

How are we going to display the die background? A search of the keyboard fails to reveal any completely solid blocks. The closest we can get is the left-graphics character on the plus sign key. That character is a lot like the checkered flag in a

41

stock car race. But, look at the blinking cursor. That would make a good die background. Remember RVS ON? If we simply display spaces with RVS ON, we will have the background we need. Now all we need is a nice dot. The right-graphics symbol of the letter Q will do the job for us. And finally, let's clear the screen by putting SHIFT CLR in a print statement. Examine Program 3-1.

```
98 REM ** THE "1" FACE OF A DIE
100 PRINT "♡";
110 PRINT "▩        "
120 PRINT "▩        "
130 PRINT "▩    ●   "
140 PRINT "▩        "
150 PRINT "▩        "
```

Program 3-1. Draw the one face of a die.

The reversed heart in line 100 is the CLR character. The reversed R in each statement from 110 to 150 assure that we have RVS ON for each line. Once we have typed in line 110, the rest are very easy to obtain by using the screen editor described in Programmer's Corner 1. Simply place the cursor over the second 1 in 110 and press 2 RETURN to get line 120. Three more times and we have the blank die. LIST the program and place the SHIFT-q in line 130.

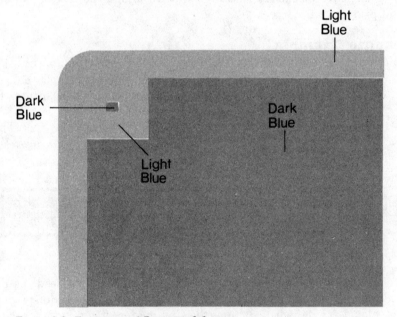

Figure 3-3. Execution of Program 3-1.

That is pretty nice. But, with the colors the way they are, we can't distinguish the die from the border. We can do two things. We can change the color, or we can place the die away from the edge of the screen. We can easily experiment with colors right at the keyboard. Press CTRL 2 and run the program. This gives a nice white die with a blue dot.

We can move the die away from the border by inserting 105 PRINT and by inserting a leading space in lines 110 through 150. Alternatively, we can move the die down the screen one line by removing the semicolon in line 100. This is left as an exercise. How do we get a three face? Simply use the screen editor to change lines 120 and 140 to produce Program 3-2.

```
98 REM ** THE "3" FACE OF A DIE
100 PRINT "▢";
110 PRINT "▨          "
120 PRINT "▨       ●  "
130 PRINT "▨     ●    "
140 PRINT "▨ ●        "
150 PRINT "▨          "
```

Program 3-2. Draw the three face of a die.

After we have had a chance to study the graphics screen, we may press STOP RESTORE to return the screen to normal. We may easily edit this program to display any of the six faces of a die.

...SUMMARY

We have examined numerous graphics features of the keyboard. The 40-by-25 text screen is also used for the graphics characters supplied with the Commodore 64. We can display characters in any of 16 colors. We can display them in reverse or normal mode. We can easily clear the screen.

Problems for Section 3-1 . . . .

1. Write a program to display a die showing the six face in the lower left corner of the screen.
2. Write a program to display a pair of dice, one showing a one and the other showing a three.
3. Write a program to request a number from one to six and display the appropriate die (try using colors if you have a color monitor).
4. Modify Program 3-1 to move the die away from the corner of the screen.
5. Write a program to draw a bar graph picturing the following temperatures for a seven-day period:

Day	Temp
1	30
2	27
3	26
4	31
5	26
6	30
7	38

Make the bars horizontal and label each one with the day number and the temperature. Experiment with different colors.

6. Write a program to display the three of hearts. Form the corners of the card with right graphics characters on the O, P, @, and L keys. Form the boundaries with the left graphics characters on the H, P, N, and Y keys. For now we will settle for a figure with all symbols facing the same way. The advanced programmer could create an inverted heart and an inverted 3 to make the card even more realistic.

3-2...Divide and Conquer (Subroutines)

Once we have written the code to display a die of a particular color having a particular face value in a particular place, it is hard to be inspired to write new code to display that same die in another location or another color. And it is even less exciting to consider displaying five dice in this way. When we find ourselves writing routine after routine, each of which is only a slight variation of the one just finished, programming becomes tedious. The more experience we gain in programming, the more opportunity we will have to use what we have already coded. Often a current problem is only a slight variation of an old, already solved one.

If we want to display a black die and then a white die in the same location, the only thing that changes is the color. Clearly, it is a nuisance to duplicate the code that does the actual graphing. We can easily isolate that code and direct the computer to execute it at will by using GOSUB and RETURN.

...GOSUB and RETURN

GOSUB 1000 causes the computer to execute line 1000 next regardless of where you are in a program. However, GOSUB 1000 differs from GOTO 1000 in that GOSUB remembers its place in the program. When a RETURN statement is encountered, execution resumes following the most recent GOSUB. The program statements that begin with the line number after the keyword GOSUB and end with a RETURN statement are grouped together and referred to as a *subroutine*. Thus GOSUB means "GO do the SUBroutine."

For our black-die-followed-by-a-white-die problem we need to have the program pause between the two displays. Otherwise, things will happen so quickly that we will not see the first die. This pause can be accomplished with a time-waster FOR...NEXT loop that does nothing else. The problem is solved in six easy steps:

1. Set green color.
2. Display the die.
3. Waste some time.
4. Set pink color.
5. Display the die.
6. End.

Putting off for the moment writing the actual die-display subroutine, let's look at a program to display our black and white dice. See Program 3-3a.

```
     98 REM ** CONTROL DIE DISPLAY
    110 PRINT "CLR■LK"
-->120 GOSUB 1000
-->130 FOR X = 1 TO 1500
-->135 NEXT X
    140 PRINT "CLR=⊏T"
    150 GOSUB 1000
    190 END
```

Program 3-3a. The control segment of a die-drawing program.

We have been able to embody a group of statements in the single statement

```
    120 GOSUB 1000
```

As with FOR loops, we have a method for organizing our thoughts more easily by concentrating many computing steps in a single statement. We can think of

```
    GOSUB 1000
```

as "display a die" without having to think about the actual BASIC statements required to do the display. Look at 130 and 135. Those two lines make up a delay loop. For a longer delay, use a value larger than 1500. Without a delay, we would not even see the first die, because it would be replaced so quickly with the second.

Finally, the display routine is very easy. We may simply select those statements from our earlier die-drawing program and use appropriate line numbers. We may concentrate on the display without having to think about other parts of the program. We know that the first line should be numbered 1000 and the last statement should be RETURN. See Program 3-3b.

```
    998 REM ** THE "1" FACE OF A DIE
   1000 PRINT "⊡"
   1010 PRINT " ℝ        "
   1020 PRINT " ℝ        "
   1030 PRINT " ℝ    ●   "
   1040 PRINT " ℝ        "
   1050 PRINT " ℝ        "
   1090 RETURN
```

Program 3-3b. Subroutine to display a one face of a die.

Programs 3-3a and 3-3b together make up a complete program to display the one face of a die in two different colors, with a brief delay in between.

It is important to realize the impact of the END statement at 190 in Program 3-3a on the subroutine beginning at line 1000. It is improper to execute a RETURN statement without a matching GOSUB. If we fail to obey this rule, the Commodore 64 will deliver the following message:

```
?RETURN WITHOUT GOSUB  ERROR IN 1090
```

190 END assures that the routine beginning at line 1000 is not executed an extra time.

...Make It Handle the General Case

Wouldn't it be nice to be able to display a die anywhere on the screen? With the idea of subroutines well in hand, this new twist is easy. All we need is to "send" values to our subroutine that specify where a corner of the die is to be. Let's use X and Y as the horizontal and vertical position on the screen where we want the upper left corner of our die to be placed (refer to Figure 3-1). The value of Y will tell the subroutine how many blank lines to display before showing the die on the screen. We could use the value of X to display the appropriate number of blank spaces in a FOR loop. But we would have to do that for each line in the graphics display. It will be much easier to use a special feature in BASIC to do this.

...TAB( )

TAB(X) in a PRINT statement causes the computer to tab to column X, much like a tab key on a typewriter. It is important to remember that the first column on each line is numbered zero and the first line at the top of the screen is numbered zero.

Let's use this idea to display a message exactly in the center of the screen. We need a FOR loop to print 12 blank lines and we need to calculate a TAB value to center our display on the screen. Examine Program 3-4.

```
90 PRINT "⬜RT";
98 REM ** CENTER A MESSAGE
100 FOR L = 0 TO 11
110 PRINT
120 NEXT L
150 PRINT TAB(14); "COMMODORE 64"
```

Program 3-4. Center a message on the screen.

If we need to place the cursor on the first line, we must avoid executing the FOR loop at all. Remember that all FOR loops will execute at least once. So, we will use an IF test before our loop in the general case.

Printed messages are displayed without any effect on other parts of the screen. We can use this information to display novelty messages. For example, we might like to display a message backwards but in readable form. Such a message would be displayed from right to left, so that the final message is readable in the normal way. Program 3-5 is an example of this.

```
98 REM ** PRINT BACKWARDS
100 PRINT "⬜RT";
110 PRINT "▣"; TAB(21); "4"
120 PRINT "▣"; TAB(20); "6"
130 PRINT "▣"; TAB(19); " "
140 PRINT "▣"; TAB(17); "E"
150 PRINT "▣"; TAB(16); "R"
160 PRINT "▣"; TAB(15); "O"
170 PRINT "▣"; TAB(14); "D"
180 PRINT "▣"; TAB(13); "O"
```

```
190 PRINT "[S]"; TAB(12); "M"
200 PRINT "[S]"; TAB(11); "M"
210 PRINT "[S]"; TAB(10); "O"
220 PRINT "[S]"; TAB(9);  "C"
```

Program 3-5. Novelty backwards message.

Notice that we clear the screen only once but we use HOME for each component of the display.

We may apply a blank PRINT in a FOR loop along with TAB to place a die face anywhere on the screen. We use the loop to move the first line of the die to where we want it and use TAB in each PRINT statement for the die face to place the display horizontally. However, we must make sure that the values of X and Y place the entire die within the 40-by-25 graphics screen. That means that X may range from zero to 33 and Y is limited to values from zero to 21 for our seven-by-five-block die face. So, we first set values for X and Y. Next we GOSUB to a routine that moves the cursor to the desired line (let's put it at line 1000). And finally we GOSUB to a routine that actually displays the desired die face.

Now the final piece of the puzzle will fit into place as soon as we write six subroutines—one for each of the six possible faces of a die. Numbering the first line of each subroutine 1100, 1200, up to 1600 will help to identify the die it displays. Thus:

```
1098 REM ** DISPLAY "1"
1100 PRINT TAB(X); "[R]       "
1110 PRINT TAB(X); "[R]       "
1120 PRINT TAB(X); "[R]   ●   "
1130 PRINT TAB(X); "[R]       "
1140 PRINT TAB(X); "[R]       "
1190 RETURN
1198 REM ** DISPLAY "2"
1200 PRINT TAB(X); "[R]       "
1210 PRINT TAB(X); "[R]     ● "
1220 PRINT TAB(X); "[R]       "
1230 PRINT TAB(X); "[R] ●     "
1240 PRINT TAB(X); "[R]       "
1290 RETURN
          .
          .
          .
1598 REM ** DISPLAY "6"
1600 PRINT TAB(X); "[R]       "
1610 PRINT TAB(X); "[R] ● ● ● "
1620 PRINT TAB(X); "[R]       "
1630 PRINT TAB(X); "[R] ● ● ● "
1640 PRINT TAB(X); "[R]       "
1690 RETURN
```

Note that with the Commodore 64 screen editor you can create this code with very little actual typing. Just type one REM and one PRINT statement. The rest is easy to obtain with editing.

The display separates nicely into placing the cursor and displaying the dice.

These two functions are performed by distinct subroutines. GOSUB 1000 places the cursor. GOSUB 1100 through GOSUB 1600 may be used to display one to six spots on the die. We can set the colors independently. Once a die has been drawn on the screen, we may erase it with CLR/HOME.

...Another Visit with IF...THEN

It is clear that once we have a number such as R that tells us which die to display, we need a way to branch to the appropriate subroutine. Thus, we wish to execute just one of the following statements:

```
GOSUB 1100
GOSUB 1200
GOSUB 1300
GOSUB 1400
GOSUB 1500
GOSUB 1600
```

We could do that with the following logic:

```
910 IF R <> 1 THEN 920
912 GOSUB 1100
914 GOTO 990
        .
        .
        .
950 IF R <> 5 THEN 960
952 GOSUB 1500
954 GOTO 990
960 IF R <> 6 THEN 990
962 GOSUB 1600
964 GOTO 990
990 RETURN
```

However, that approach is cumbersome, requiring a lot of typing and 18 statements for a very simple decision. It is a good idea to simplify our programs whenever possible. We could eliminate the six GOTO 990 statements, as they are not essential. Only one of those IF statements will test out true for any given value of R. That would leave us with 12 statements, but we would still have a choppy structure that is unnecessarily long and difficult to read (for humans—the computer doesn't care). Alternatively, we can use another feature of IF...THEN statements to simplify the decision about which of the six die-display subroutines to execute. Any BASIC statement may follow THEN in an IF...THEN statement. This new feature makes it possible to achieve the same result with six simple BASIC program lines. We may execute just one of the die display subroutines with the following code:

```
910 IF R = 1 THEN GOSUB 1100
920 IF R = 2 THEN GOSUB 1200
930 IF R = 3 THEN GOSUB 1300
940 IF R = 4 THEN GOSUB 1400
950 IF R = 5 THEN GOSUB 1500
960 IF R = 6 THEN GOSUB 1600
```

Not only is this shorter to type, but it is much clearer to read. For any value of R in the range 1 to 6, just one of the IF...THEN tests comes out true. The other five come out false. Thus, the computer executes all six IF tests no matter what. But the computer is very fast and the five false results will not delay execution in any noticeable way for our present problem. Combining this approach with random numbers, we can program a wide variety of events.

Problems for Section 3-2 . . . .

1. Write a program to display a die face showing a six in the upper right corner of the graphics screen.

2. Write a program to display a random die face in the upper left corner of the screen.

3. Display a random die face, leave it for a few seconds, and then erase it.

4. Display two dice at random next to each other in the lower left corner.

5. Write a program to display a blinking die. Let it blink 10 times, then leave the display on the screen.

6. Display a few dice at random in random locations on the screen to simulate physically rolling the dice. Then display a pair of dice at random and leave them on the screen.

3-3...BASIC Multiple Features

...GOSUB Revisited

At first we saw how we might use 18 statements to branch to one of six die-display subroutines. We reduced this to six lines that were much easier to read by using an extended feature of IF...THEN—executing any statement if the tested expression is true. Now we can reduce the amount of code even further with a new feature of the GOSUB statement.

...ON...GOSUB

We can duplicate the effect of the six IF statements with BASIC's multiple GOSUB capability.

```
910 ON R GOSUB 1100,1200,1300,1400,1500,1600
```

Subroutines at lines 1100, 1200, . . . and 1600 are executed as the value of R is 1, 2, . . . and 6 respectively. Should the value of R be less than one or greater than six, statement 910 will be ignored. However, values less than 0 or greater than 255 will be rewarded with

```
?ILLEGAL QUANTITY  ERROR IN 910
```

Now, even the relatively simple six-statement logic used to branch to the proper die-plotting subroutine has been reduced to a single statement. Lest we get the idea that all programs can be reduced by at least one statement (and therefore eliminated entirely), be assured that there is a limit to the features available in

BASIC or any other computer language. Computers are finite and therefore limits do exist. Computers and computer languages are amazing, but they are not magic.

...**ON**...**GOTO**

GOTO has the same multiple line-number branching capability as GOSUB. Thus the single statement:

```
100 ON N1 GOTO 310,320,330,340,350,360,370
```

replaces seven IF...THEN statements. The same restrictions apply to the legitimate range for GOTO as for GOSUB.

Suppose we have a situation in which we want to execute line 1000 if $N1 = 3$, 1100 if $N1 = 6$, and 1200 if $N1 = 11$. Do not be tempted to use a multiple GOTO or GOSUB statement. In such a situation, it is much clearer to code three IF...THEN statements. Having 11 line numbers, only three of which are real, is very confusing to anyone reading your program. Don't do it! Even you won't understand it next week.

...**Multiple Statements (:)**

The ability to place several program statements on a single numbered line has many useful applications. Suppose we have a subroutine at 500 that needs values set for A, B, and C. This will require the following set of lines every time we use the subroutine:

```
100 A = 5
110 B = 9
120 C = 3
130 GOSUB 500
```

Where statements naturally belong together, it is helpful to place them all on the same line. Using the colon (:) to separate statements, we may use the following equivalent code:

```
100 A = 5 : B = 9 : C = 3 : GOSUB 500
```

While it can be very handy to place several statements on the same line, there may be good reasons not to. It may make the program harder to read when the statement lists on two lines. This capability should be used with caution.

It may also be desirable to annotate program lines by using the colon:

```
180 E1 = 0 : REM ** CLEAR ERROR COUNT
```

Line 180 here is described with a REM statement on the same line. Anyone reading this can see that the variable E1 is used to count errors and that at this point we are setting the count to 0.

Line numbers do require memory. Occasionally, a program grows to the point where it is too big for the available memory. One method for reducing the amount of memory a program requires is to use multiple statements on each line. In doing this with an existing program, you must be careful not to change the logic of the program by incorrectly combining lines that are referenced by a GOTO, IF...THEN, or GOSUB statement.

...Multiple Statements and IF...THEN

BASIC allows multiple statements following IF...THEN. So a statement such as:

```
100 IF A = 5 THEN B = 6 : C = 11
```

is perfectly legal. That statement will execute both B = 6 and C = 11 when A = 5, and neither B = 6 nor C = 11 when A does not equal 5.

3-4...Miscellaneous Character Graphics Features

...Border and Screen Background Colors

We have been looking at a blue screen background with a light blue border all this time. We know how to change the color of the characters as they are printed. Why not the screen and the border?

...POKE

Try this on your Commodore 64:

```
POKE 53281,0
```

Yes, go ahead and try it. The screen should instantly turn black. The number 53281 is a location in the memory of the Commodore 64 that controls the color of the screen background. The number 0 specifies Black.

The POKE statement is a BASIC instruction to set the value in location 53281 to 0. POKE may be used in immediate or deferred mode. The location we POKE to is determined by what we want to accomplish. We are interested here in the screen background color. Don't indiscriminately POKE values anywhere in memory—it is possible to change a value that will cause the computer to stop functioning in a rational manner. Turning the computer off and back on again will always restore it, but you will lose any program in memory at the time. Each location in memory holds a value in the range 0 to 255. This is because each location is limited to eight binary bits, which allows numbers only in this range. (For more about binary numbers see Chapter 7.)

To get the old color back type

```
POKE 53821,6
```

Try setting the background color to 14. Did everything disappear? The border color is 14 and so is the normal cursor color. At this point we might press STOP and RESTORE. Everything is back to normal.

If we want a black border, we simply key in

POKE 53280,0

There are 16 colors available for both border and screen backgrounds, so we have 256 possible combinations (16^2). Obviously some of them are more pleasing to the eye than others. If we combine this with the 16 possible colors for the characters we have a truly wide selection. In some programs we might want to key different colors to different functions in the program. It is very easy to just POKE the color number into 53280 for border and POKE into 53281 for screen color. The 16 colors we have already used in PRINT statements are numbered according to Table 3-2.

NUMBER	COLOR	NUMBER	COLOR
0	Black	8	Orange
1	White	9	Brown
2	Red	10	Light Red
3	Cyan	11	Gray 1
4	Purple	12	Gray 2
5	Green	13	Light Green
6	Blue	14	Light Blue
7	Yellow	15	Gray 3

Table 3-2. Color values for POKE.

Don't be confused by the fact that the colors numbered 0 to 7 here are found on the keys labeled 1 to 8 on the keyboard. Both systems are right.

...Character Colors

Each character position on the character screen is matched with a location in memory that can be used to control the color of the character displayed on the screen. The character screen begins with location 1024 and runs to 2023, totalling 1000 characters. The color memory begins at 55296 and runs to 56295. Location 55296 controls the color of the character at 1024, while location 55297 controls the color of the character at 1025. And 56295 controls the color of the character at 2023. The character screen positions are numbered from left to right and from top to bottom, as we would read a printed page. So, the first character position on the second line of the screen is numbered 1064; the color memory location is 55336. The screen location of any character is determined from its line number and position within the line by the formula

1024 + line°40 + position

where the lines are numbered from zero to 24 and the position within a line is numbered from zero to 39. The corresponding memory location for the color is given by

55296 + line°40 + position

Or, if we label the line and position as Y and X, respectively, the formulas become

character screen = 1024 + Y*40 + X
color memory   = 55296 + Y*40 + X

This conforms exactly to the screen layout in Figure 3-1. Notice that the screen position (0, 0) comes out 1024.

Once a character is displayed on the screen we can set its color with a POKE to the corresponding location of color memory. Try Program 3-6.

```
100 PRINT "⬜A"
110 POKE 55296,1
```

Program 3-6. Setting a character color in color memory.

This program clears the screen and places the letter A in the upper left corner with the PRINT statement. The POKE turns the letter A black. The value set in the range 55296 to 56295 has no effect on the PRINT statement. We must use the POKE after the character has been displayed with a PRINT statement.

...Characters with POKE

We can also POKE values into screen memory to display characters. We must also POKE a color value into color memory, or the character will be invisible. Even if we want the character to appear in the standard light blue, we must POKE a 14 into the corresponding color memory location. We can even POKE a character to the lower right corner of the screen without having it scroll the whole screen up one line. We simply POKE the correct character to 1024 + 999 and POKE the desired color number to 55296 + 999. All we need to know is what value produces what character. If we are looking for the value of a single character it is quick and easy to simply place that character on the screen and then use a new BASIC statement to read its value.

...PEEK

Let's clear the screen and type the letter A in the upper left character position. Use the cursor up to get there and cursor down to move to the third line of the screen. Now type

```
PRINT PEEK(1024)
```

The Commodore 64 responds with "1". That means that the value stored there is a "1". (This is not the famous ASCII system; we'll get to that in Chapter 5.) PEEK is a BASIC statement that reads the value stored in memory. We will always obtain a value between 0 and 255. So, we can display any character on the screen and PEEK at the corresponding memory location to determine its numeric value. These values are called *screen codes* for the Commodore 64. There are actually two character sets. One we get normally when the machine is turned on. The other we get by pressing the SHIFT and (⊑) keys simultaneously. You can watch the characters change on the screen. Mostly this affects the letters, but the pi key, the British pound key, the @ key, and the asterisk key are also affected. Let's get one complete character set on the screen to see what it looks like.

```
100 PRINT "□"
110 FOR I = 0 TO 255
120 POKE 1024  + 2*I, I
130 POKE 55296 + 2*I, 1
140 NEXT I
150 FOR I = 1 TO 11 : PRINT : NEXT I
```

Program 3-7. Display a character set.

Remember, we must POKE both the character and a color. White is used here. You might like to POKE a variety of colors to see the effect on the screen. We added 2*I rather than I here just to space the characters out a little.

Figure 3-4 shows the standard character set. Let's see the alternate one. We simply press (⬚) and SHIFT at the same time to produce Figure 3-5.

Notice in both character sets that every character is duplicated, appearing in both normal and reverse modes. The characters with screen codes in the range 128 to 255 are the reverse of characters in the range 0 to 127. It is important to realize that we cannot mix characters from the two sets on the screen at the same time. We can change from one to the other with another POKE.

```
POKE 53272,23
```

puts the Commodore 64 into the alternate character set, while

```
POKE 53272,21
```

restores the standard set. But, remember, one set completely replaces the other—no mixing is allowed. (See Appendix B for the two sets of screen codes. The advanced programmer can use features of the Commodore 64 to create individually tailored character sets.)

...Examples

Just for fun let's display some twinkling stars. Program 3-8 is an example.

```
     100 PRINT "□"
     110 FOR X = 0 TO 5
     120 FOR Y = 0 TO 5
-->130 POKE 1024 + 40*Y + X, 108
     140 NEXT Y
     150 NEXT X
     200 X = INT(RND(1)*6)
     210 Y = INT(RND(1)*6)
     220 SW = INT(RND(1)*100)
-->230 CL = 1 : IF SW > 5 THEN CL = 6
     240 POKE 55296 + 40*Y + X, CL
     250 GOTO 200
```

Program 3-8. Some twinkling stars.

We got the 108 in line 130 by printing the character generated by (⬚) -D on the screen and taking a PEEK at that location. We laid out a block in the upper left

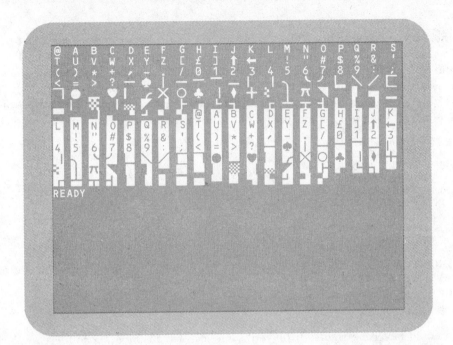

Figure 3-4. Execution of Program 3-7.

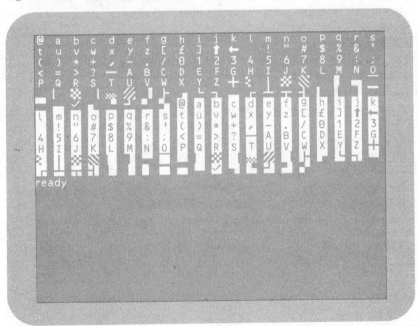

Figure 3-5. Execution of Program 3-7 with alternate character set.

corner of the screen. In line 230 we select color 1 to display a star or select color 6 to turn a star off. A star is turned off by setting it to the screen background color. You could change the screen background color to black and experiment with other things to create a realistic effect. Maybe you could program a sunset or a sunrise.

We can create crude animation with characters on the screen and a large dose of imagination. Program 3-9 lets us get our exercise without getting out of breath.

```
      100 PRINT "▫";
      110 PRINT " o"
      120 PRINT " ⌥⌐"
      130 PRINT "⌐ ⌐"
      140 GOSUB 500
      200 PRINT " o"
      210 PRINT "⌐⌐⌐"
      220 PRINT "⊓ ⊓"
      230 GOSUB 500
      240 GOTO 110
-->500 FOR I = 1 TO 200 : NEXT I
      510 PRINT "▫";
      590 RETURN
```

Program 3-9. Calisthenics.

You could have one figure displayed a line lower than the other to increase the appearance of motion. You might experiment with the timing in line 500. With creativity and imagination you can write fairly realistic animation with surprisingly little in the way of sophisticated programming technique.

...SUMMARY

The POKE statement can be used to place values from 0 to 255 in memory. The border color is controlled at memory location 53280. The screen background color is controlled at memory location 53281.

The character screen is located in memory from 1024 to 2023. This means that we can POKE values into those locations to place characters on the screen. In order for the characters to actually appear, we are required to also POKE a color in a corresponding location of color memory. Color memory is found in the range from 55296 to 56295.

We can determine the screen code of a character by displaying it on the screen in a known location and then reading the value with PEEK.

The rest is up to the creativity, imagination, and patience of the programmer.

Chapter 4

Miscellaneous Features and Techniques

Introduction . . . .

Certain calculations and other processes are required so frequently in programming that high-level languages like BASIC supply them in nice packages. Many of these packages are called *functions*. Some of them are called *operators*. And some are just plain features. These tools are a tremendous convenience in any computer language.

We have already used the INT function in some of our earlier programs in Chapter 2. Remember? INT(X) returns the greatest integer that is less than or equal to X, so that INT(5.699) = 5 and INT(−4.091) = −5. When we are working with decimal numbers it is often useful to round off results. We will explore this and some other uses for INT in this chapter.

RND is a package that gives us access to random numbers in a program. We used RND to good advantage in Chapter 2. RND may be used to add interest and variety to games. This function is invaluable for writing simulation programs. By randomly changing various factors in a proposed solution to a business problem, we can predict results without imposing poor judgment on a frustrated public. We may confine our failures to unpublicized runs of a computer program.

These BASIC packages and numerous others will reveal themselves as extremely useful. It is a good idea to learn about most of the features available to you early on, so that as the need arises you will be able to recall a convenient solution.

It takes several BASIC statements to determine whether a number is positive, negative, or zero:

```
890 REM ** DETERMINE +, 0, OR -
900 IF X > 0 THEN S = 1
910 IF X = 0 THEN S = 0
920 IF X < 0 THEN S = -1
930 RETURN
```

Having written such a subroutine, we should test it. Then, every time we need such a calculation in another program, we must type the entire subroutine. The SGN function does the same thing:

```
130 S = SGN(X)
```

In just the same way we can determine the absolute value of a number in BASIC with the ABS function.

```
140 A = ABS(X)
```

These functions are useful not only because they save us a lot of programming effort and typing time, but also because they indicate the meaning of the statement in which they appear. SGN(X) clearly conveys that we are interested in the sign of a number, while X = T : GOSUB 900 fails to convey just why we are invoking the subroutine at line 900 and that the result is returned in S. We would have to read the code beginning at line 900 or put in REM statements to understand the meaning.

The number in parentheses following the function name is called the *argument* of the function. This value is *passed* to the function and the result is returned in the entire expression.

Just as BASIC includes LET, GOSUB, END, IF...THEN, and FOR... NEXT, it includes features such as INT, RND, SGN, and ABS as elements of the language. This means that the necessary programming has already been taken care of for us and incorporated into BASIC. There are many advantages to this approach. The programming has been tested for us. The features will generally execute much faster than if we write the same calculations in BASIC. This is especially true for trigonometric and logarithmic functions.

...Prompted INPUT

Often we have printed messages as labels for our INPUT requests. This is always a good idea. BASIC provides a convenient way to include the prompting message right in the INPUT statement.

The statement

```
100 INPUT "ENTER HERE"; T1
```

will produce exactly the same results as:

```
100 PRINT "ENTER HERE"; : INPUT T1
```

Any message enclosed within quotes in an INPUT statement will be displayed exactly as typed. The message must be followed by a semicolon before the variable list, and the variables in the list must be separated with commas.

4-1...Numeric Functions

...ABS, SGN, RND, SQR, and INT

For general programming, the most common functions are ABS, SGN, RND, SQR, and INT. Functions that come with the language are sometimes called *built-in functions*.

As discussed earlier, ABS(X) returns the absolute value of X, and SGN(X) returns −1, 0, or +1, according to whether the value of X is negative, zero, or positive.

RND is the random-number generator. RND(X) returns random decimal numbers in the range from 0 to 1, including 0 and excluding 1. If X is negative, the number returned is the same for every occurrence of that negative value of X. If the value of X is positive, a different value is returned for each successive use of the RND function. We can repeat a random sequence by using a negative argument for the first value and a positive argument for all subsequent ones. Using a negative argument in this way is called *seeding* the random number generator. If X is zero, the random number generated will be independent of any seeding we might do.

SQR(X) returns the square root of X. We could also code X^.5, using the up-arrow to indicate an exponent, to represent X to the one-half power, but SQR is convenient and executes faster. Of course, the value of X must not be negative. A negative argument in the SQR function will incur the wrath of BASIC. If we insist on coding a statement such as:

```
100 PRINT SQR( -4 )
```

we will be subjected to the following message:

```
?ILLEGAL QUANTITY   ERROR IN 100
```

Once we gain familiarity with these functions, they will come to mind as they are needed.

Suppose we are interested in finding factors of integers. Right away INT should come to mind. We may program the computer to compare INT(N/D) to N/D. If they are equal, then D divides into N without remainder and D is a factor of N. If INT(N/D) does not equal N/D, then D is not a factor of N. For example:

```
INT(69/5) = 13
```

while

```
69/5 = 13.8
```

Clearly 13 and 13.8 are not equal, so 5 is not a factor of 69. On the other hand:

```
INT(69/23) = 3
```

and

69/23 = 3

Thus 23 is a factor of 69, and so is 3.

To find the largest factor of 1946, all that we have to do is write a program that tries all of the values from 1945 down to 2. The first one that is a factor is the largest factor. Display it and terminate the program. While we are at it, we might as well make this a more general program. Let's make our program request a value for testing.

```
    100 INPUT "FIND LARGEST FACTOR OF"; N
    120 FOR D = N - 1 TO 2 STEP -1
-->140 IF N / D <> INT(N / D) THEN 180
    150 PRINT D : END
    180 NEXT D
    200 PRINT N; "IS PRIME"
```

Program 4-1. Finding the largest factor.

Note line 140. If we have a remainder, then we perform the next test. If not, then we have the largest factor. Display it and quit.

```
RUN
FIND LARGEST FACTOR OF? 1946
973
```

Figure 4-1. Execution of Program 4-1.

There is something about this program that may not be obvious unless we witness the execution. The computer has to think for more than 10 seconds before producing the answer for N = 1946. And it would delay for over 20 seconds for N = 1949. The smaller the first factor, the longer the delay. Surely we could find the largest factor of 1946 faster by hand. So can the computer.

Decimal division on a computer takes time. We could save one division for each value of N by assigning N/D to an intermediate variable:

```
135 Q = N / D
140 IF Q <> INT(Q) THEN 180
```

The time saving is about 10%. While this might be worthwhile, we should also carefully examine the method we have chosen for solving this problem.

Take the case of 1946. The largest factor is 973 and the smallest factor is 2. We could simply test our factors beginning with 2. When we have found the smallest factor, the largest factor may be found by division. Thus we have gone from 973 trial values in the FOR...NEXT loop of Program 4-1 to a single trial for this particular value of N. We have also gone from 10 seconds to a small fraction of one second. That is an improvement worth working on. But what if we enter 1949? This new method will require 1947 trial values of D and just over 20 seconds to execute, because 1949 is a prime. So, this method only helps for values of N that have factors. We should be searching for an improved method that also works for prime integers.

Let's return to the observation that the largest factor of 1946 is 973 and the smallest is 2. How are the rest of the factors paired? See Figure 4-2.

2	973
7	278
14	139
139	14
278	7
973	2

Figure 4-2. Factor pairs of 1946.

There are six pairs of factors, each of which appears twice. How can we determine when we have found all of the unique pairs of factors? For every factor less than or equal to the square root of a number, the other factor will be greater than or equal to the square root. Once we are convinced of that the rest is easy; we need only test divisors up to the square root. Simply change

```
120 FOR D = N - 1 TO 2 STEP -1
```

to

```
120 FOR D = 2 TO SQR(N)
```

and change

```
150 PRINT D : END
```

to

```
150 PRINT N / D : END
```

This change in strategy reduces the number of tests for N = 1949 from 1948 to 43. That is significant and worth incorporating into our program. We can also use the intermediate variable Q to store N/D. Thus:

```
150 PRINT N / D : END
```

becomes

```
150 PRINT Q : END
```

See lines 120, 135, 140, and 150 of Program 4-2.

```
     100 INPUT "FIND LARGEST FACTOR OF"; N
-->120 FOR D = 2 TO SQR (N)
-->135 Q = N / D
-->140 IF Q <> INT(Q) THEN 180
-->150 PRINT Q : END
     180 NEXT D
     200 PRINT N; "IS PRIME"
```

Program 4-2. Finding the largest factor by using SQR(N).

...Rounding Decimal Results

Another use for INT comes up when we are working with dollars and cents and calculations come out in fractional cents. We would like always to round figures off to the nearest cent for printing. That is, 0.5 cents or more is rounded up and less than 0.5 cents is rounded down.

We can convert dollars and cents to cents by multiplying by 100. Then, if we add 0.5 cents, all values from 0.0 to 0.49 will become values in the range from 0.5 to 0.99, while all values in the range from 0.5 to 0.99 will become values in the range from 1.0 to 1.49. If we next apply INT, all decimal portions that were less than 0.5 disappear, and all values that were 0.5 or more result in one cent being added. Then we change from cents back to dollars and cents by dividing by 100. Thus we can round values to the nearest cent with a statement such as

```
200 D1 = INT( D * 100 + .5 ) / 100
```

Then we can easily write a test program to verify our solution for rounding values to the nearest cent (and incidentally for rounding any values to the nearest hundredth). See Program 4-3.

```
    100 REM ** DEMONSTRATE ROUNDING
-->130 PRINT "ROUNDED", "DATA"
    150 READ D
    160 IF D = -9999 THEN END
    200 D1 = INT(D * 100 + .5) / 100
    210 PRINT D1, D
    220 GOTO 150
    900 DATA   3.09123, 4.94561
    910 DATA      2390, -1.5102
    920 DATA     .0009, -1.4861
    990 DATA   -9999
```

Program 4-3. Rounding to the nearest hundredth.

We have included the labeling of line 140 to give the display some meaning.

```
RUN
ROUNDED    DATA
 3.09      3.09123
 4.95      4.94561
 2390      2390
-1.51     -1.5102
 0         9E-04
-1.49     -1.486
```

Figure 4-3. Execution of Program 4-3.

Note that this also handles negative values correctly. It is always a good idea to verify that our programs work properly for a wide variety of values. Even though the current problem doesn't require a particular class of values, it is desirable to test the program for them anyway. It is much easier to put the finishing touches on a routine while we are familiar with the problem than to return to it months later when we discover that we really do want to handle those previously unwanted values.

...Compound Interest

Suppose we have $100 in a savings account at 5.5% interest compounded daily. How much will that be at the end of one year? We can easily write a program to calculate that. There is a simple formula that gives the compound amount:

62

$$A = P(1 + I)^N$$

where

A = amount
P = principal
I = interest rate per interest period
N = number of interest periods

The raised N indicates "to the power." This formula is applied in Program 4-4.

```
100 REM ** CALCULATE COMPOUND INTEREST
200 P = 100
210 I = .055 / 365
220 N = 365
300 A = P * (1 + I) ^ N
310 PRINT A
```

Program 4-4. Compound interest by formula.

Note that the symbol ⌃ denotes "to the power" in BASIC. This symbol is found next to the RESTORE key; it is an up-arrow on the Commodore 64 keyboard.

```
RUN
105.653643
```

Figure 4-4. Execution of Program 4-4.

Now, since it is hard enough to buy anything with a whole cent, let alone 0.3643 cents, we might as well round that value off to the nearest cent. We can do that easily by replacing line 310 with:

```
310 PRINT INT( A * 100 + .5 ) / 100
```

Program 4-4 tells us what will be in our savings account at the end of the year. What this program doesn't tell us is what has happened to the buying power of our money because of inflation. It doesn't tell us of the federal, state, and even city income taxes we may have to pay on the interest. Still, earning interest is better than hiding the money in a mattress.

The compound interest formula works fine if we are going to put $100 in the bank and leave it there. But suppose we decide to put $20 into the account on the first of each month. For simplicity, let's consider that each month has 30 days and that a year has 360 days. Let's put $100 in the bank on January 1 and then put $20 in on the first of the month each month all year. We can handle this computation with a FOR...NEXT loop going from 1 to 12, as shown in Program 4-5.

```
    100 REM ** ADD $20 EACH MONTH
    200 P = 100
    210 I = .055 / 360
    220 N = 30
    300 FOR M = 1 TO 12
    310 P = P + 20
-->320 A = P * (1 + I) ^ N
-->330 P = A
```

```
340 NEXT M
350 PRINT "$100 PLUS $20 EACH MONTH $";
360 PRINT INT (A * 100 + .5) / 100
```

Program 4-5. Compound interest with money added each month.

Note that the amount at the end of each month becomes the principal for the next month, as indicated in lines 320 and 330 of Program 4-5.

```
RUN
$100 PLUS $20 EACH MONTH $ 352.94
```

Figure 4-5. Execution of Program 4-5.

...Programmer Defined Functions (DEF FN)

Often it is convenient to define a function of our own and use it at various places in our program. BASIC DEFined FuNctions serve this purpose. We can set up a rounding function at the beginning of a program and then use it wherever we need to perform the same calculation. Our rounding function R may be defined as follows:

```
110 DEF FNR(X) = INT( X * 100 + .5 ) / 100
```

To invoke our new function we code a line such as

```
360 PRINT FNR(A)
```

BASIC "knows" that we want the value of A in line 360 to be used wherever X appears in the function definition on line 110. The X's in line 110 simply hold places where values will be inserted whenever an FNR is encountered in an expression. The value of X at the time the function definition statement is executed has no effect on the outcome of the program. The variable used in parentheses in the defining statement is called a *dummy variable*, since no calculations ever use its value. The calculations are based on whatever replaces the dummy variable. We may code things like:

```
FNR(12345)      FNR(12 * .098)          FNR( RND(4) * 1000 )
```

Let's rewrite Program 4-3 to demonstrate rounding with a defined function. The result is Program 4-6.

```
    100 REM ** DEMONSTRATE DEFINED FUNCTION
-->110 DEF FNR(X) = INT(X * 100 + .5) / 100
    140 PRINT "ROUNDED","DATA"
    150 READ D
    160 IF D = -9999 THEN END
-->210 PRINT FNR(D), D
    220 GOTO 150
    900 DATA   3.09123, 4.94561
    910 DATA     2390, -1.5102
    920 DATA     .0009, -1.4861
    990 DATA   -9999
```

Program 4-6. Using DEF FN to round to the nearest hundredth.

64
...

In Program 4-6 we have defined the rounding function in line 110 and used it to display values rounded off to the nearest hundredth in line 210.

```
RUN
ROUNDED    DATA
 3.09      3.09123
 4.95      4.94561
 2390      2390
-1.51     -1.5102
 0         9E-04
-1.49     -1.485
```

Figure 4-6. Execution of Program 4-6.

Defined functions provide a way for us to put together packages of calculations in a convenient form. This is an ideal way to make conversions of all kinds. Programmer-defined functions are limited to one program statement, but that allows us a lot of leeway. Calculations and processes that cannot be coded in a single program statement are best handled as subroutines and invoked with a GOSUB statement.

Converting from Fahrenheit to Celsius and vice versa is easy with two defined functions:

```
100 DEF FNC(X) = 5/9 * ( X - 32 )
110 DEF FNF(X) = (9/5) * X + 32
```

Wherever we want to convert to Celsius from Fahrenheit, we simply code FNC (Fahrenheit temperature), and wherever we want Fahrenheit from Celsius, we code FNF (Celsius temperature). And if we want to round off the results, we can include:

```
120  DEF FNR(X) = INT( X * 100 + .5 ) / 100
```

Now, to display the Celsius temperature rounded off to the nearest hundredth, we code the following line:

```
210 PRINT FNR( FNC(T))
```

where T is the Fahrenheit temperature. We can even define one function in terms of another defined function. Thus:

```
130 DEF FNT(X) = FNR( FNC(X))
```

will calculate the rounded value with any reference to FNT(X).

One convenient use of DEF is to define a random number in terms of the range desired. A function to return a random number in the range 1 to X follows:

```
100 DEF FNR(X) = INT( RND(1) * X + 1 )
```

...SIN, COS, TAN, and ATN

The functions SIN(X), COS(X), and TAN(X) all return the trigonometric values we would expect, the sine, cosine, and tangent. The value of X must use radian measure. The inverse function ATN(X) is also provided for determining the arc tangent. ATN(X) returns radian values in the first and fourth quadrants.

From these trig functions all the others can be derived. It is up to the programmer to determine the correct quadrants where that is a problem.

...EXP(X) and LOG(X)

EXP(X) raises *e* (2.71828183) to the Xth power and LOG(X) finds the natural log of X.

...SUMMARY

ABS, SGN, RND, INT, and SQR are commonly used built-in functions. They have good mnemonic associations. We may also build our own functions with DEF FN, which allows us to define any function that will fit in a single program statement. More complex packages may be created with subroutines.

Problems for Section 4-1 . . . .

1. Write a program to find all prime factors of an integer by rewriting the guts of Program 4-2 as a subroutine and calling it repeatedly. Eliminate duplicates.

2. Write a program to determine the effect of considering the banking year to have 360 days instead of 365. Use interest rates of 5.5% and 12.5% on $100,000.

3. Compare daily compounding with monthly compounding for $1000 invested at 5.5% and 12.5% for one year.

4. Compound interest may also be calculated without the formula given in this section, by simply building a loop that adds the interest at the effective interest rate once for each period in the time that the money is on deposit. Write a program to calculate interest this way and compare your results with those in the programs of this section. Compare a 365-day year with a 360-day year.

5. Write a program to convert temperatures from Fahrenheit to Celsius. Request Fahrenheit temperatures from the keyboard. Be sure to have a way to stop. (Zero may not be the best value for terminating this program execution.)

4-2...More Goodies

...FRE

FRE(X) is a function that returns the amount of free memory in bytes. The value of X may be any legal number. It is handy to use FRE(9) or FRE(8) because the 8 and 9 are right there on the keyboard with the left and right parentheses. A byte corresponds to a single character in memory. It takes two bytes to store an integer and five to store a decimal value. BASIC keywords each require one byte. Arrays and strings require several bytes in addition to the space required for the data to be stored in them. If we are working with arrays and we want them to be as large as possible, this function will save a lot of trial and error. Be sure to run the program before determining the amount of free memory. Even then we should allow a margin of 50 or 100 bytes, because the program may use more memory during future executions with different data. Additional memory is used and relinquished during execution by such features as FOR loops and subroutines.

If more than 32767 bytes are available, the value of FRE(9) becomes negative. This is a result of the way the computer stores integers in memory, and will be explained further when we talk about binary numbering. To obtain the true value use

```
190 X = FRE(9) : IF X < 0 THEN X = X + 65536
```

or

```
190 X = FRE(9) - (FRE(9)<0) * 65536
```

The second example requires less memory than the first example.

If your program requires more memory than is available in the computer, BASIC will display the following message:

```
?OUT OF MEMORY  ERROR IN 90
```

where 90 is the line at which the computer ran out of space.

...CTRL

When the computer displays a lot of data, the screen may move too fast for us to read. We can slow it down by holding the CTRL key. Otherwise we can display one screenful at a time and use INPUT or GET (explained soon) to ask if the user is ready to proceed.

...SPC and TAB

SPC and TAB are functions that must appear in a PRINT statement.

```
231 PRINT TAB(X); "MESSAGE"
```

will display the M in MESSAGE in the Xth column of the current line. The first column is labeled 0. If X equals 40, then the rest of the display will begin in the first column of the next line on the normal screen. The TAB function cannot move the cursor to the left on the current line. The value of X may range from 0 to 255.

SPC(X) in a PRINT statement causes X spaces to be displayed. If X takes the display past the end of the current line, SPC moves to the next line and continues counting. The range for X is 0 to 255.

...POS

The POS(X) function may be used to determine where on the line the cursor lies. The argument of this function is a dummy and has no effect upon the function itself. Commodore 64 BASIC works with an 80-character line, so the positions on the line are numbered from 0 to 79. Positions 0 to 39 make up the first line and 40 through 79 occupy the second line on the screen.

...GET

The GET function provides a way to take input from the keyboard without displaying any text on the screen.

```
250 GET A
```

looks for a single digit from the keyboard. RETURN need not be pressed in this case. The program will not wait for us to press a key. If no key is pressed, BASIC sets A to zero. So, we might hold program execution up with

```
250 GET A : IF A = 0 THEN 250
```

This way, we must enter one of the digits 1 through 9. If any other key is pressed, BASIC delivers the

```
?SYNTAX  ERROR
```

message. Any digit entered before executing the GET statement will be read in and used. See Programmer's Corner 4 for an explanation of how to control this function.

The Commodore 64 has a keyboard buffer that stores up to 10 characters. Any characters beyond that number are lost. The GET statement can be executed over and over again to read as many characters as there are in the buffer.

We will explore how to read nonnumeric characters in Chapter 5.

...TIME

TIME is a reserved variable that keeps track of time in 60ths of a second. We call this unit of time a *jiffy*. Since TIME is a variable, we may access it with the first two letters of the variable name. The value of TI is set to 0 when we turn the Commodore 64 on. We cannot set the value of TI with an assignment statement. TI is a handy tool for comparing the time required by different ways of doing things. If we have a program with lots of long processes, timing becomes important.

Experienced programmers are aware of the relative amounts of time various processes require. This becomes very important for operations that appear within FOR...NEXT loops. Everything takes time. There are certain techniques that are more efficient than others. Let's look at a few examples.

You may have seen an expression such as

```
120 X = I*I
```

in a program and wondered why it wasn't written as

```
120 X = I^2
```

The reason is that raising to a power takes much more time than multiplying. Program 4-7 demonstrates the relative time required.

```
100 TO = TI
110 FOR I = 1 TO 100
120 X = I*I
130 NEXT I
140 PRINT "I*I"; TI - TO
196 :
200 TO = TI
210 FOR I = 1 TO 100
220 X = I^2
230 NEXT I
240 PRINT "I^2"; TI - TO
```

Program 4-7. Comparing time for I°I and I˚2.

We are going to multiply 100 times and raise to the second power 100 times.

```
I*I 31
I^2 318
```

Figure 4-7. Execution of Program 4-7.

Raising to the second power seems to take ten times longer. But a little further checking reveals that the difference is even more dramatic than that. The FOR . . . NEXT loop without anything in it requires about 10 jiffies. That means the times for I°I and I˚2 are more nearly 21 and 308, respectively. That is a factor of more than 14.

Often, it is faster to work with a variable than a constant. That is, it is faster to work with X than 342. Program 4-8 demonstrates this.

```
100 TO = TI
105 K = 342
110 FOR I = 1 TO 100
120 X = I + K
130 NEXT I
140 PRINT "  I + K"; TI - TO
196 :
200 TO = TI
210 FOR I = 1 TO 100
220 X = I + 342
230 NEXT I
240 PRINT "I + 342"; TI - TO
```

Program 4-8. Comparing time for I + K and I + 342.

```
  I + K 26
I + 342 43
```

Figure 4-8. Execution of Program 4-8.

We can see from Figure 4-8 that adding K requires 26 jiffies, while adding 342 takes 43. If we subtract the 10 jiffies for the loop to execute, we get 16 and 33. Running Program 4-8 with 123456789 instead of 342 reveals that more digits require more time.

We note that, while REM statements are not executed, they do require time to process. For programs with a lot of loops with a wide range, we could place REM statements outside the loop.

4-3...Logical Operators with IF...THEN

...AND

Often in a program there are several conditions that may determine the next course of action. We might want to execute a subroutine if AV >95 and SC<70. We can do this with AND.

```
300 IF AV > 95 AND SC < 70 THEN GOSUB 900
```

will do the job. AND is one of the three logical operators in BASIC. BASIC evaluates the expression AV >95. If that expression is true, BASIC sets its value to −1. If the expression is false, BASIC sets its value to 0. The same holds for SC<70. We can even assign logical values to variables:

```
290 L1 = AV > 95 : L2 = SC < 70
295 IF L1 AND L2 THEN GOSUB 900
```

This is equivalent to the single statement 300 above. In line 290 the value of L1 is set to −1 if AV >95 is true and 0 if AV >95 is false. Similarly, L2 becomes −1 or 0. Finally, in line 295, the value of the expression L1 AND L2 becomes −1 or 0. We can even assign L1 AND L2 to another variable if that suits our purpose.

...OR

OR does just what you would expect.

```
230 IF AV > 90 OR GR = 100 THEN PRINT "VERY GOOD"
```

If either AV > 90 or GR = 100, line 230 will display the message. If both of them are true, the message will still be displayed. Logical values assigned to variables work just fine with OR, too.

```
400 IF L1 OR L2 THEN PRINT "TRUE"
```

Line 400 prints TRUE if either L1 or L2 is true.

...NOT

NOT reverses the truth of an expression. If the truth value of an expression is 0, NOT sets it to −1. And if the truth value of an expression is −1, NOT sets it to 0.

```
NOT(A = 5 OR B = 6)
```

is the same as

```
A <> 5 AND B <> 6
```

We will take another look at AND, OR, and NOT when we study binary representation of numbers in Programmer's Corner 7.

PROGRAMMER'S CORNER 4

Controlling the Keyboard . . . .

So far, we have used the keyboard to interact with many of our programs. We have often used INPUT to request data from the keyboard. As long as we wait for the INPUT statement to actually execute, all's well. However, if we enter up to 10 characters during the delay, the INPUT statement will take those characters as part of our response. The Commodore 64 has a 10-character buffer, so that we can type as fast as we like without losing data—a helpful feature for fast typists. Sometimes we want to allow the user to type characters while the computer is doing something else. But sometimes we want to make sure that no spurious characters are entered. In this situation, we would like to take control of the input buffer. It turns out that the Commodore 64 stores the number of characters in the input buffer in location 198. We can fool the computer into thinking there are no characters by using POKE to put a zero value there. Before we do this, let's conduct an experiment to demonstrate the problem we are describing. Type in Program 4-9 on your Commodore 64.

```
100 FOR I = 1 TO 4000 : NEXT I
130 INPUT X
```

Program 4-9. Demonstrate keyboard buffer.

When you run this program, quickly type in at least 10 keystrokes. The delay in line 100 should allow you to complete this before the question mark from the INPUT statement appears. There should be a delay, and then the characters you typed will be displayed. Yet you stopped typing before this happened. At least INPUT waits for the RETURN key before going on. The GET statement doesn't wait. The value we might have inadvertently entered is not displayed and we have no idea what is going on. Even expensive, commercially available programs produce strange results through failure to recognize this as a potential problem: a whole screen of a menu can just flash by because a GET statement has grabbed our careless keystroke as a valid response.

The cure is simple. Line 120 of Program 4-10 does it all.

```
100 FOR I = 1 TO 4000 : NEXT I
120 POKE 198,0
130 INPUT X
```

Program 4-10. Curing the stray character problem for keyboard input.

We might even place the POKE and the INPUT on the same line so that we don't inadvertently add a BASIC statement between lines 120 and 130.

In a situation like this we might also set the value of X to some special value so that we can tell if just a RETURN was entered. Remember that Commodore 64 BASIC simply takes the previous value of X in that situation. So, we might routinely use a line such as

```
920 X=0 : POKE 198,0 : INPUT X
```

This will protect our programs against some common keyboard errors.

Chapter 5

Character Strings and String Functions

Most of our work has used numbers and calculations. However, we have printed messages and labels by enclosing them in quotation marks in PRINT statements. Handling nonnumeric data is important in working with computers. Such data are referred to as *string data*. String data may contain any of the letters, digits, and special characters available on the computer. This includes the vast supply of graphics characters on the Commodore 64. Thus, string data come in character strings.

Strings may be used for a mailing list, instructions telling how to use a computer program, labels to make displayed results more understandable, or as part identification labels in an inventory control system. We might simply use strings to make a game program more conversational. We can ask the player's name and use it in messages displayed later. BASIC provides a variety of features that make the handling of string data very convenient. There are string variables that enable us to store and manipulate character strings. Using string variables and string functions, we can manipulate individual characters and groups of characters. We can even print a string in reverse order just for fun.

5-1 ... Strings: An Introduction

BASIC provides string variables and a host of useful string manipulation functions. A string variable is distinguished from a numeric one by using a dollar sign ($) as the last character in the variable name.

We can work with string variables in many of the ways that we work with numeric variables. For instance, any of the following statements can appear in a program:

```
100 LET A$ = "FIRST"
100 A$ = "TESTING"
100 READ A$
100 INPUT A$
100 PRINT A$
```

Remember Quote Mode from Programmer's Corner 1? Now that we are working with strings, we are likely to run into it a lot. This means that we can place the cursor key functions, CLR/HOME, and DEL right in a string variable. It also means that we cannot use them to carry out their editing function after we have typed one quote. When we want to use them for editing, we simply type the closing quote mark or press RETURN and come back to edit the line.

String variables may contain from zero to 255 characters at a time. In order to execute READ A$ we must provide a corresponding DATA statement. If we want to include a comma in the string, then we should enclose the string in quotation marks. Without the use of quotation marks, any comma is interpreted as the end of the current DATA item. Program 5-1 reads string data and prints it for us to see.

In this program we introduce a technique for making programs more readable. It turns out that we may obtain a nearly blank line by entering a line number followed by a colon. This may be used to make a clear visual break between different parts of a program. Beginning with Program 5-1, we will use this technique often.

```
     100 READ A$
     120 PRINT A$
     130 GOTO 100
     495 :
-->500 DATA GEORGE M. COHEN, ABE LINCOLN
     510 DATA JOAN OF ARC
```

Program 5-1. READ...DATA with strings.

The comma in line 500 is interpreted as a data separator or delimiter. We could have provided the same data for this program by typing as follows:

```
500 DATA GEORGE M. COHEN, ABE LINCOLN, J
OAN OF ARC
```

Here the screen has automatically pushed characters to the next line as we type. In the interest of making our programs more readable, we will usually type DATA statements so that all the data fit on a single line. Doing this will take up additional memory. However, we are writing very short programs that don't require much memory. So, we won't worry about memory use until we are writing longer programs. The most readable form follows:

```
100 READ A$
120 PRINT A$
130 GOTO 100
495 :
500 DATA GEORGE M. COHEN
510 DATA ABE LINCOLN
520 DATA JOAN OF ARC
```

Program 5-2. Program 5-1 with reformatted DATA statements.

It is always worth a little effort to make programs more readable. As we gain experience with programming, this will come automatically.

```
RUN
GEORGE M. COHEN
ABE LINCOLN
JOAN OF ARC

?OUT OF DATA  ERROR IN 100
```

Figure 5-1. Execution of Program 5-2.

That "OUT OF DATA" message is a little disturbing. Well-written programs should never produce that message! In some situations, programs that end with an error message will fail to perform as desired. We should always provide for an orderly program termination. In this case we may simply add an artificial string data item to the data list. Such a data item is sometimes called a *dummy data* item. We will use this artificial data item as a signal to the program that all of the data have been read. After line 100 and before line 120 we compare A$ to the signal data. If we use STOP as the terminating signal the final program looks like Program 5-3.

```
      100 READ A$
-->110 IF A$ = "STOP" THEN 900
      120 PRINT A$
      130 GOTO 100
      495 :
      500 DATA GEORGE M. COHEN
      510 DATA ABE LINCOLN
      520 DATA JOAN OF ARC
-->599 DATA STOP
      900 END
```

Program 5-3. Using dummy data to terminate program execution.

Now our little demonstration program terminates in an orderly way. Of course, the actual signal is arbitrary, just so we select some value that will not be a real DATA item and test for that value.

BASIC permits us to compare strings for order in much the same way that we compare numbers with IF...THEN. The sequence used is known as ASCII (American Standard Code for Information Interchange). For strictly alphabetical strings, this code will alphabetize in the conventional order. ASCII places the digits 0 through 9 ahead of the letters of the alphabet. We can easily write a short program to demonstrate order comparison.

```
      95 REM ** COMPARE STRINGS FOR ORDER
      100 PRINT
-->110 PRINT "A$";
-->120 INPUT A$
      130 IF A$ = "STOP" THEN 990
      140 PRINT "B$";
-->150 INPUT B$
      160 IF A$ < B$ THEN 220
      170 IF A$ = B$ THEN 200
      175 :
      180 PRINT A$; " IS GREATER THAN "; B$
      190 GOTO 100
      195 :
      200 PRINT A$; " IS EQUAL TO "; B$
      210 GOTO 100
      215 :
      220 PRINT A$; " IS LESS THAN "; B$
      230 GOTO 100
      235 :
      990 END
```

Program 5-4. String comparison.

Lines 120 and 150 are string INPUT requests. We have the same option to include a message in quotes right in the INPUT statement itself for strings that we have for numeric input. Lines 110 and 120 may be replaced with the following single statement:

```
110 INPUT "A$"; A$
```

As with prompted INPUT requesting numeric data, the question mark is displayed. String INPUT also retains the previous value of the string variable if we simply press the RETURN key. We can first set the string equal to a null value if we are going to test for real input.

Combining a quoted message with an input request can be convenient, but if we want to use the same INPUT statement to ask different questions, we will still have to use a PRINT statement that displays a message stored in a string variable.

```
RUN

A$? WHAT'S THIS
B$? WHAT'S THAT
WHAT'S THIS IS GREATER THAN WHAT'S THAT

A$? WHAT'S THIS
B$? WHAT'S WHAT
WHAT'S THIS IS LESS THAN WHAT'S WHAT

A$? WHAT'S WHAT
B$? WHAT'S WHAT
WHAT'S WHAT IS EQUAL TO WHAT'S WHAT

A$? STOP
```

Figure 5-2. Execution of Program 5-4.

All of the comparison operators available for numeric comparisons are available for string comparisons.

We can manipulate strings in many ways. Consider the following statement:

```
200 C$ = A$ + B$
```

This does not perform numeric addition. Instead, it assigns a new string to the variable C$. The string variable assigned is the same as would be displayed by the following PRINT statement:

```
200 PRINT A$; B$
```

We can enter a space in C$ in the following way:

```
200 C$ = A$ + " " + B$
```

This device might be used in a situation where A$ contains a person's first name and B$ contains the last name. To print out the name last name first we might use a statement such as:

```
200 C$ = B$ + ", " + A$
```

Combining strings in this way is called *concatenation*, a very simple concept with a fancy name. There can be no more than 255 characters in the final string to be formed, or we will receive a message saying,

```
?STRING TOO LONG ERROR IN 200
```

and our program will stop dead. We can store up to 255 characters without any special provision; there is no way to put more in a single string variable. We can handle more characters by breaking the problem into segments, each requiring 255 or fewer characters.

...SUMMARY

BASIC provides string variables for storing character strings in a program. Strings may be assigned with INPUT, READ...DATA, or an assignment statement. The maximum number of characters in a string is 255. Strings may be compared for order in an IF...THEN statement. Strings may be concatenated by using a plus (+) sign.

Problems for Section 5-1 . . . .

1. Write a program that requests the user's name and responds with, "HELLO THERE [NAME]," using the entered name where [NAME] appears here.
2. Enter several words in DATA statements. Write a program that will display the data item that comes earliest in the alphabet. Be sure to use dummy data.
3. Enter several words in DATA statements. Write a program that will display only the word that is last in the list alphabetically.
4. Often in programs we want to ask the user questions for which "yes" or "no" are the only acceptable answers. Since we might want to do this at many

points in the same program, it is useful to write one subroutine that sets a numeric variable to 1 for "yes" and 0 for "no." Write such a subroutine.

5. When comparing strings for order, BASIC searches for the first pair of corresponding characters that are unequal. If we happen to enter 12 in one string and 6 in another, BASIC will report that 12 is less than 6 because the 1 is less than the 6. Write a program to overcome this problem.

5-2...String Functions

A variety of string functions are available:

    ASC
    CHR$
    LEFT$
    RIGHT$
    MID$
    LEN
    STR$
    VAL

...ASC

ASC is referred to as the ASCII function. ASC( ) returns a number from 0 to 255 that is derived from the ASCII (American Standard Code for Information Interchange) character set. ASCII is a standardized correlation between characters and the numbers used to represent them. For example, the numeric code for A is 65 and the code for Z is 90. The Commodore 64 uses a variation of the full standard.

Note that this code is different from the one we use to POKE characters to the character screen. If we PRINT the character A, whose ASC code is 65 on the character screen, and later PEEK the location where it is displayed, we will obtain a value of 1. Try not to be confused by this. We use Screen Codes for PEEK and POKE. We use ASC codes for strings. Any request for the ASC of a string of zero length brings forth

    ?ILLEGAL QUANTITY ERROR

...CHR$

CHR$(X) becomes the character whose ASC code is X. CHR$(90), for example, is Z, while the character for 32 is a space. The next time you get to a Commodore 64, run Program 5-5:

```
100 FOR I = 32 TO 127
110 PRINT CHR$(I);
120 NEXT I
196 :
200 FOR I = 160 TO 191
210 PRINT CHR$(I);
220 NEXT I
```

Program 5-5. Displaying the printing characters.

RUN

```
 !"#$%&'()*+,-./0123456789:;<=>?@ABCDEFG
HIJKLMNOPQRSTUVWXYZ[£]t←→⁄|┤├┬┴┤|Ⴙ|ΨLИ∨
┌┬●_┒ ⁄xO◆ |◆|⊦⊦| |π◥
```

Figure 5-3. Execution of Program 5-5 in upper-case mode.

Figure 5-3 shows the character set in upper-case mode. See Figure 5-4 for the lower-case character set.

RUN

```
 !"#$%&'()*+,-./0123456789:;<=>?@abcdefg
hijklmnopqrstuvwxyz[£]t←→RⓈ ▯◗◀|▨◸▧◪ ◳▤
◣◥ t←π◆ ⁄xO◆ |Ⴙ| ▨◥
```

Figure 5-4. Execution of Program 5-5 in lower-case mode.

We may display either mode, but only one at a time. This means, for example, that we cannot display a check mark and the graphics lower right corner symbol on the same screen. When we go to lower-case mode, we sacrifice 26 graphics characters and replace four. The characters from 0 to 31 and from 128 to 159 are invisible. Many of them cause some action. For example, an instruction to PRINT CHR$(5) is the same as pressing CTRL-2 on the keyboard—that is, further display will be in white.

The statement PRINT CHR$(8) cancels the ability to switch from one case to the other by pressing (Ⓒ) and SHIFT together; CHR$(9) restores it. CHR$(14) sets lower-case mode and CHR$(142) sets upper-case. Note that we don't need inverse characters in this set, because it is easy to set inverse mode with CHR$(18) and turn it off with CHR$(146). See Appendix C for a complete table of codes.

...LEFT$, RIGHT$

The LEFT$ function enables us to access the leftmost characters in a string. For example, LEFT$(A$,5) yields the first five characters in A$. If there happen to be fewer than five characters stored in the string, then this expression represents the full string. LEFT$(A$, X) represents the left X characters of A$, as long as the value of X is greater than zero. If we try something like

```
PRINT LEFT$(A$,-1)          or     PRINT LEFT$(A$,256)
```

we will see the following message:

```
?ILLEGAL QUANTITY  ERROR
```

The RIGHT$ function is exactly analogous to the LEFT$ function, but for the right end of the string.

...MID$

To print characters within a string, we use MID$. MID$(A$, X, Y) gives us the characters beginning with position X and continuing for Y characters. One way to describe the characters from position X and continuing through to the end of the string is with an expression such as MID$(A$, X). Note that this is not the same as RIGHT$(A$, X). We will create an error condition if we allow X to equal zero.

...LEN

LEN(A$) counts the number of characters actually stored in the string variable A$. LEN(X$) may be used anywhere a numeric expression is legal. For instance, we might code the line:

```
100 FOR X = 1 TO LEN(Y$)
```

if we want to perform some task for each character contained in the string Y$.

...STR$

The STR$ function converts a numeric value to string format. STR$(N) converts the internal binary code used to represent the numeric value of N into the ASCII code used for each of the digits. Let's examine the effect of a statement such as

```
200 T$ = STR$(N)
```

While N stores a numeric value that we may command the computer to use in arithmetic calculations, T$ stores the digits of the number N as string characters. Thus T$ permits us to manipulate the digits by using the string functions of BASIC. Note that the string T$ will include the leading space for positive numbers and the leading minus sign for negative values.

...VAL

VAL is the reverse of the STR$ function. VAL(A$) converts the character string of digits in A$ into the binary format used for storing numbers. If the first character could not be part of a number, then a 0 is returned. If the function is successful in converting the beginning of a string, then it continues until it finds an impossible character. When this happens VAL simply stops processing and returns the value up to that point. For example,

```
VAL("12 DAYS OF VACATION")
```

will convert to

```
12
```

This function handles scientific notation as well. The value will be converted into the standard form for BASIC. Thus

```
VAL("123E-1")
```

will convert to

```
12.3
```

80

There they are: ASC, CHR$, LEFT$, RIGHT$, MID$, LEN, STR$, and VAL. Now let's use some of them.

We begin by displaying the days of the week. We can make up a string using the common three-character abbreviations and select the individual day names with MID$. Our string will look like:

```
100 DA$ = "SUNMONTUEWEDTHUFRISAT"
```

To display the names, we need to loop through the string, printing three characters at a time, beginning with 1, 4, 7, etc. We could easily use a FOR loop such as FOR D = 1 to 19 STEP 3. It would be interesting, however, to relate the day number to the position in the string DA$. If we number the days 0 through 6 that is easy to do; we simply multiply the day number by 3 and add 1. See Program 5-6.

```
98 REM ** DISPLAY THE DAYS OF THE WEEK
100 DA$ = "SUNMONTUEWEDTHUFRISAT"
120 FOR D = 0 TO 6
-->130 J9 = 3*D + 1
140 PRINT D; MID$(DA$,J9,3)
150 NEXT D
```

Program 5-6. Displaying the days of the week.

Line 130 calculates the position in the string where the current day number begins.

```
RUN
 0 SUN
 1 MON
 2 TUE
 3 WED
 4 THU
 5 FRI
 6 SAT
```

Figure 5-5. Execution of Program 5-6.

We could deal with the full names of the days in a string such as

```
"SUNDAY MONDAY TUESDAY WEDNESDAY THURSDAY FRIDAY SATURDAY "
```

We can use loops and string functions to display selected portions of strings in an interesting variety of ways. For example, we can display a string in reverse order by using STEP − 1 in a FOR loop.

Suppose we are working on a program to prepare financial reports. This means that we will be printing numbers that represent money in dollars and cents (or yuan and fen or whatever). BASIC doesn't care what the units of our numeric values might be. As far as it is concerned, one dollar and 20 cents is 1.2; we however would like to show that quantity as 1.20. So, our first task is to write a routine that will convert numeric values like 1.2 to string values like 1.20. We must also write a routine to deal with values that come out with fractional cents, such as 381.2961. Fundamentally, we are faced with a formatting problem.

Let's write a subroutine that accepts a number in M1 and returns a string in D$. Then we can easily write a control routine to test it.

One way to make sure that a number like 1.2 has a trailing zero is to multiply it by 100. So, 1.2 becomes 120. Of course we must later insert the decimal point in the proper position. Our new number represents money in cents. Multiplying 381.2961 by 100 produces 38129.61. We need to round this off to the nearest cent. That can be done by adding 0.5 and eliminating the fractional portion of the resulting number. We saw in the last chapter that INT is made for just such a purpose. So, we may calculate the money values in cents with a statement such as

```
M9 = INT(M1 * 100 + .5)
```

Notice that we have left the value of M1 unchanged. It is a good idea to write subroutines that leave the input values intact.

Next, we can convert the number of cents from numeric to string data with

```
1010 X$ = STR$(M9)
```

Now, this string has no decimal point. We know that the two right digits represent cents and must appear to the right of a decimal point. Further, we know that the remaining digits represent dollars and must appear to the left of the decimal point. We may create the D$ string from these three pieces: dollars, decimal point, and cents. A decimal point may be included in one of two ways: enclosing a decimal point in quotes or using CHR$(46). We find the code for a decimal point by printing ASC("."). The number of digits in the dollar portion may be found by using the LEN function:

```
D9 = LEN(X$) - 2
```

Summing up:

Dollars	=	LEFT$(X$, D9)
Decimal point	=	"."
Cents	=	RIGHT$(X$, 2)

All that remains is to build the output string by concatenating these three portions. See Program 5-7.

```
 990 REM ** FORMAT DOLLARS AND CENTS
1000 M9 = INT(M1 * 100 + .5)
1010 X$ = STR$(M9)
1020 D9 = LEN(X$) - 2
-->1030 D$ = LEFT$(X$,D9) + "." + RIGHT$(X$,2)
1090 RETURN
```

Program 5-7. Formatting subroutine.

Now we can write a small control program to test our subroutine. This will require an INPUT statement to enter test values, with some dummy value to terminate, and a PRINT statement to display results. See Program 5-8.

```
90 REM ** TEST FORMATTER
100 INPUT "TEST VALUE"; M1
110 IF M1 = -9999 THEN END
120 GOSUB 1000
130 PRINT M1; "= "; D$
140 PRINT
150 GOTO 100
```

Program 5-8. Control routine to test Program 5-7.

It is a good idea to provide a special value of M1 that will allow us to exit the program without having to enter STOP-RESTORE. −9999 serves that purpose in this program.

```
RUN
TEST VALUE? 1.2
  1.2 =   1.20

TEST VALUE? -381.2961
-381.2961 =   -381.30

TEST, VALUE? 19
  19 =   19.00

TEST VALUE? 381.29499
  381.29499 =   381.29

TEST VALUE? -9999
```

Figure 5-6. Execution of Program 5-8.

Our program works well for the sample input values. However, consider what happens if the value of M1 is less than 10 cents. How could we add a dollar sign? How could we put commas in to mark off thousands? Accountants like to put negative numbers in brackets. How could we do this? These questions are left as problems.

...SUMMARY
The string functions ASC, CHR$, LEFT$, RIGHT$, MID$, LEN, STR$, and VAL have been presented. ASC(A$) returns the numeric code for the first character in A$, while CHR$(A) returns the character whose code is A. LEFT$, RIGHT$, and MID$ provide access to portions of strings. LEN(A$) returns the number of characters in A$. STR$(A) converts the numeric value of A to the string characters required to display it, while VAL(A$) converts the displayed characters to numeric representation.

Problems for Section 5-2 ....

1. Write a program to request a string from the keyboard and display it backwards.

2. Sometimes it is interesting to rearrange the contents of a string for display purposes. Write a program that enters the days of the week in a single string and displays them in the following format:

S	M	T	W	T	F	S
U	O	U	E	H	R	A
N	N	E	D	U	I	T
D	D	S	N	R	D	U
A	A	D	E	S	A	R
Y	Y	A	S	D	Y	D
		Y	D	A		A
			A	Y		Y
			Y			

3. Modify Program 5-7 to handle amounts less than 10 cents.

4. Modify Program 5-7 to place a $ to the left of the first digit in the formatted result.

5. Modify Program 5-7 to insert commas to mark off thousands.

6. Correct Program 5-7 to properly display 0.00 if the amount is zero.

7. Modify Program 5-7 to enclose negative values in angle brackets. That is, −1.43 should display as <1.43>.

8. Write a program to perform the reverse conversion, so that the string <$1234.51> would convert to the numeric value −1234.51. Hint: You'll want to use a FOR...NEXT loop and the MID$ function to pick out all of the possible special characters.

9. Problems 3 to 7 could be worked cumulatively, resulting in a program that performs all of the tasks described in the five problems. Write such a program.

10. Our formatter is a special case: it works only with hundredths. Extend this program to allow the user to specify the number of decimal places desired.

11. Given the date in yy/mm/dd form, display the date as Month dd, 19yy. That is, 82/12/31 becomes December 31, 1982. You may want to test for bad dates like 82/04/31.

12. Write a program to display messages on the screen so that they scroll horizontally across the screen. Use DATA statements to supply the messages.

13. Project: Write a program to justify text by inserting spaces between words to fill a specified line width.

5-3...String Goodies

...TIME$

The Commodore 64 has a clock. The variable TIME$ has been set aside to keep track of the time. In fact, we may use TI$, since BASIC really only uses the first two characters of variable names. When we turn the computer on, TI$ is set to 000000.

The digits are considered in pairs to count hours, minutes, and seconds, in that order. So, "010230" would tell us that the machine has been turned on for 1 hour, 2 minutes and 30 seconds. We can easily use the MID$ function to pick that string apart to display the time in any format we need. We can even set it so that we have the real time of day. Just realize that we are working with a 24-hour clock; the statement

```
275 TI$ = "130200"
```

would indicate that it is two minutes after one o'clock in the afternoon. Also note that the numeric variable TI is reset to correspond to TI$. So, line 275 would set TI to 2815200. On the other hand, we cannot directly set the value of TI. The Commodore 64 delivers a syntax error message in response to that. TI$ goes from 125959 to 130000 and from 235959 to 240000. The next time after 240000 is 000000.

The clock is turned off during access to the Datassette and during disk drive activity. So, TI$ will be inaccurate after any use of tape or disk.

...GET A$

We can use GET to accept single characters from the keyboard. The RETURN key is not needed for this. Nothing is displayed on the screen by the GET statement. Up to ten characters may be entered into the keyboard buffer and read later by repeated GET statements. If no keystroke has occurred, execution continues. The computer does not wait. In this case A$ is empty—its length is 0. GET is convenient for entering information without interfering with the screen display. GET A$ is usually more useful than GET A, as GET A will generate an error message if anything other than one of the digits is entered. Furthermore, with GET A we can't tell whether A is zero because we pressed 0 or because no key has been pressed.

We can require the user to press a key by repeating the GET statement until something happens:

```
210 GET A$ : IF LEN(A$) = 0 THEN 210
```

Pressing STOP will halt such a program line. Adding PRINT ASC(A$) to the above program gives the numeric values associated with the keystroke. If a key has been pressed inadvertently during a delay, GET A$ will take it and keep going. As described in Programmer's Corner 4, we can prevent this by inserting

```
POKE 198,0
```

just before the GET statement.

We may find that we can instruct the computer to answer our questions about itself faster than we can find the information in a manual. Suppose we want to find out the codes for the function keys 1 through 8 to the right of the keyboard. What we need is a program that will take characters from the keyboard and display the corresponding PRINT code. If we use INPUT, then we have to know to enter a quote as the first character to put the computer into quote mode. GET works without this extra ingredient. Program 5-9 does it in three lines.

```
210 GET A$ : IF LEN(A$) = 0 THEN 210
220 PRINT ASC(A$)
230 GOTO 210
```

Program 5-9. Using GET A$ to determine PRINT code.

...SUMMARY

The special variable TI$ is a 24-hour clock. The six digits report the hour, minute, and second of the current time. GET A$ reads a single keystroke. If no key is pressed, then A$ has zero length.

Problems for Section 5-3 ....

1. Write a subroutine that will display the time in the form hh:mm:ss from TI$.
2. Use the technique of Program 5-9 to determine the numeric codes for the cursor keys, the CLR/HOME key, and the INST/DEL key. Label each request so that the program will create a useful chart.
3. Use the technique of Program 5-9 to determine the numeric codes for the function keys 1 through 8. Label each request so that the program will create a useful chart.

PROGRAMMER'S CORNER 5

Colors from CHR$ ....

We can set the character color by putting the color character from the keyboard in quotes in a PRINT statement. We can also PRINT the CHR$( ) of the appropriate value. Let's find the numeric values that go with the colors. We can't do this with INPUT because the computer will take the keystroke as an instruction and change the color right away; we wouldn't learn the numeric code used for the color. We could type a quote to place the computer in quote mode. But, GET will find the value without this complication. Program 5-9 is what we need. We simply run the program and press the color keys in order. We will have the PRINT codes to go with the colors. See Figure 5-7.

```
RUN
 144   5   28   159   156   30   31   158   129
 149   150   151   152   153   154   155
BREAK IN 210
```

Figure 5-7. Execution of Program 5-9 for the color keys.

86

The BREAK message was caused by pressing STOP. This gives us the data we need to make the color chart of Table 5-1.

COLOR	VALUE	COLOR	VALUE
Black	144	Orange	129
White	5	Brown	149
Red	28	Light Red	150
Cyan	159	Gray 1	151
Purple	156	Gray 2	152
Green	30	Light Green	153
Blue	31	Light Blue	154
Yellow	158	Gray 3	155

Table 5-1. Color values for CHR$( ) in PRINT.

It is easy to see from the table that PRINT CHR$(5) will change the text display to white. The other colors may be generated in a similar manner. It may be a nuisance to learn all those color codes. They don't seem to be in any order and they are different from the 0 to 15 we are used to. One way to overcome this would be to create a string containing these 16 codes in the correct order so that we can just use the MID$ function to print the character in the color string needed to produce the desired color. This can be done by putting the 16 ASC codes in DATA statements in a program and reading them into the color string for later reference. Program 5-10 demonstrates this.

```
100 CO$ = ""
110 FOR X = 1 TO 16
120 READ I : CO$ = CO$ + CHR$(I)
130 NEXT X
200 FOR C = 0 TO 15
220 PRINT MID$(CO$,C+1,1);CHR$(18);"        "
230 NEXT C
900 DATA 144,   5,   28, 159
910 DATA 156,  30,   31, 158
920 DATA 129, 149, 150, 151
930 DATA 152, 153, 154, 155
```

Program 5-10. Store color codes in a string variable.

Note that the value 18 in line 220 is the PRINT code for ReVerSe ON.

The whole idea here is to have a color routine that will enable us to think in terms of the conventional color numbers that work for so many other things. We are going to find that the same 0 to 15 values are used for Hi-Res graphics and for Sprite graphics.

Chapter 6

Arrays

We have been using variables to store values one at a time. Such variables are referred to as *simple* variables. We have been able to perform marvelous feats on the computer with simple variables. We will accomplish even more with *array* variables. An array variable allows us to designate a collection of data values with a single variable name. Now, instead of designating the scores of the players in a five-player game with S1, S2, S3, S4, and S5, we can use an array variable. S(X) (read "S sub X") can be used to refer to the score of the Xth player. We can use the same variable name for an array as for a simple variable. You may want to avoid confusion by not doing this, though. The value in parentheses is called a *subscript*. Each data value in the array is called an *element*. Using an array, we would code the scoring for all five players with the same brief segment of our BASIC program.

Arrays are used for storing information that naturally belongs together. Tax tables, pricing structures, inventory information, and life insurance premiums are all appropriate for using arrays. There are many times that an array is useful for storing information about the workings of the program itself. We can use arrays for storing test scores, temperatures, random numbers, and lists of all kinds. If we are working with Fibonacci numbers, it might be nice to have them all in an array. (Fibonacci numbers are generated by adding the two previous numbers in the list. They go: 1, 1, 2, 3, 5, 8, 13 . . .) Even though we might be able to recreate a particular sequence, it is convenient to have it right there at the flick of a subscript.

6-1...One-Dimensional Numeric Arrays

We can immediately benefit from the array concept by simply referring to array variables as needed. If we want the sixth element of T to be 5, we simply code a statement such as:

```
200 T(6) = 5
```

We can readily use arrays in every way that we have been using simple variables.

We can write READ, PRINT, INPUT, and IF...THEN statements using array variables. When a program is executed, all elements of all arrays are set to zero.

To demonstrate the uses of arrays, in a given week we record the temperatures in Table 6-1.

Sunday	72
Monday	78
Tuesday	76
Wednesday	79
Thursday	85
Friday	85
Saturday	71

Table 6-1. Temperatures for a week.

There are any number of questions we might ask. We might want to know the average, the highest, and the lowest temperatures. By using an array we can easily find the answers. Let's read the data into Elements 1 through 7 of an array named W.

The average is easy. We just add up the seven temperatures and divide by seven. We can use T for the total. The first value of the total is the temperature for the first day.

We may find the highest and lowest temperatures by using two variables: H for high and L for low. Initially these variables may be set to the temperature of the first day, as it is at the same time the highest and lowest temperature.

The solutions for the three questions regarding temperatures each call for setting initial values and then performing some operation on each of the six days after the first (Monday through Saturday). So our program will have a section to set up all of these initial values and a section with a loop that performs some calculation for each of the three questions. See Program 6-1.

```
90 REM * ENTER THE TEMPERATURES IN ARRAY W
100 FOR J = 1 TO 7
110 READ W(J)
120 NEXT J
145 REM ** SET UP INITIAL CONDITIONS
150 T = W(1)
160 H = W(1) : L = W(1)
190 :
200 FOR J = 2 TO 7
210 T = T + W(J)
230 IF W(J) > H THEN H = W(J)
240 IF W(J) < L THEN L = W(J)
250 NEXT J
290 :
300 PRINT "AVERAGE TEMP:"; T / 7
320 PRINT "HIGHEST TEMP:"; H
330 PRINT " LOWEST TEMP:"; L
890 :
900 DATA 72,78,76,79,85,85,71
990 END
```

Program 6-1. Finding the average, highest, and lowest temperatures.

```
RUN
AVERAGE TEMP: 78
HIGHEST TEMP: 85
 LOWEST TEMP: 71
```

Figure 6-1. Execution of Program 6-1.

The next thing someone might ask is, "How many times did the temperature increase, decrease, and remain unchanged?" We might use the variables I, D, and U for this. We might want to know on what days the highest and lowest temperatures occurred. These questions are left as exercises.

Suppose we wish to simulate drawing numbers from a hat. We can easily do it with random numbers, provided that we may return each number to the hat before drawing the next one. If we must simulate drawing without replacement, then we must have a way of keeping track of what has been drawn. Here is an ideal application for an array. We simply set each element of an array equal to 1 and make the value 0 when that element has been selected. If the selected element is 1 then we know that it is available for use; use it and set it to 0. If a selected element is 0 then we know that it is not available for use and we must select again. Let's look at a program to draw five out of 10 numbers at random. See Program 6-2.

```
90 REM ** DRAWING FIVE NUMBERS AT RANDOM FROM AMONG TEN
95 :
100 FOR J = 1 TO 10
110 A(J) = 1
120 NEXT J
190 :
200 FOR J = 1 TO 5
210 R = INT( RND(1) * 10 + 1)
250 IF A(R) = 0 THEN 210
260 PRINT "   ";R;
270 A(R) = 0
280 NEXT J
290 PRINT
300 END
```

Program 6-2. Drawing five numbers at random from among ten.

```
RUN
  2  6  1  3  8
```

Figure 6-2. Execution of Program 6-2.

From all appearances our program works just fine. It might be interesting to evaluate how well it does work. One measure of quality is the number of unusable random numbers generated. We can easily insert a counting variable to determine this. This is left as an exercise.

Considering the problem set before us, the trial-and-error method of the above program does not contain any serious flaws in design. Drawing five numbers from among 10, or even drawing 10 from among 10, does not require major computer resources. However, what happens when we increase the numbers? Suppose we want to draw 100 from among 100? It is worth investing some effort to eliminate the trial-and-error approach entirely.

Here is a plan that allows us to use every random number selected. First initialize the elements of the array as follows:

```
100 FOR J = 1 TO 10
110 R(J) = J
120 NEXT J
```

This means that each element stores one of the numbers in the range 1 to 10 with no duplication. Next, select a random number in the range 1 to 10 and use that value as the subscript, say S. Now display R(S) and replace R(S) with R(10). Next, select a random number in the range 1 to 9. Since either we are on the first draw or we have replaced R(S), we do not need to decide whether or not R(S) has already been used: we know it has not. Since we have moved R(10) into a lower numbered element, we may select from among fewer elements and still include all of the remaining numbers in the next random selection. The second time through we move R(9) into the selected element. We simply repeat the select-display-replace sequence until the desired number of random draws have occurred.

We do need to calculate the number of elements remaining. As the draw number (J) goes from 1 to 5, the number of elements remaining goes from 10 to 6. Thus, we can calculate the last element with:

```
210 L = 10 - J + 1
```

See Program 6-3.

```
 90 REM ** DRAWING RANDOM NUMBERS WITHOUT
    REPLACEMENT AND WITH NO TRIAL AND ERROR
100 FOR J = 1 TO 10
110 R(J) = J
120 NEXT J
190 :
200 FOR J = 1 TO 5
-->210 L = 10 - J + 1
230 S = INT( RND(1) * L + 1)
-->240 PRINT R(S);
-->250 R(S) = R(L)
270 NEXT J
300 END
```

Program 6-3. Drawing without replacement efficiently.

Notice that the element is printed in line 240 and then replaced in line 250. The variable L is always the number of active elements in the array. Even if the Lth element happens to be the one selected at random, this method continues to function properly. The Lth element will be assigned to itself. No harm done.

```
RUN
 8   4   7   6   10
```

Figure 6-3. Execution of Program 6-3.

...DIM
The highest subscript we have used is 10. Whenever an array name is introduced, BASIC automatically provides for subscript values up to 10. We may use the

DIMension statement to set the highest subscript ourselves. We may want to do this to set either higher or lower limits.

```
100 DIM L(4), M(109), G3(1024)
```

This statement sets the highest subscript to 4 for array L, 109 for array M, and 1024 for array G3.

Every array we use allows the subscript to have a value of zero. This is true whether or not a DIM statement is used. Therefore, in the absence of a DIM statement we have 11 elements. In the sample statement above, L consists of five elements, M consists of 110 elements, and G3 provides for 1025 numbers. When we have no particular need for the zero element, we may simply ignore it.

...SUMMARY

An array enables us to manage a number of variables by using one variable name. DIM X(N) sets aside N + 1 elements in an array named X. Array elements may be used in program statements wherever a simple numeric variable may be used (with the exception that array variables may not be used as the loop variable in FOR... NEXT). With arrays we will often find it convenient to use FOR...NEXT loops to process all elements or a block of elements.

Problems for Section 6-1 ....

1. Modify the daily temperature program (Program 6-1) to tabulate the number of times the temperature increased, decreased, and remained unchanged.
2. Modify the daily temperature program (Program 6-1) to determine on which days the highest and lowest temperatures occurred.
3. In the first program that draws numbers from a hat (Program 6-2), insert a variable to count the number of unusable numbers generated. Run the program several times to get a range of values.
4. Do Problem 3, drawing 10 from among 10.
5. Modify Program 6-3 to select 100 numbers from among 100.
6. Write a program to find the largest value in a collection of data.
7. Write a program to find the smallest value in a collection of data and find which position that value occupies.
8. Fill a 20-element array with twice the value of the subscript. Display all of the elements in order and in reverse order.
9. Fill one array with the values 6, 3, and 9. Fill a second array with the values 2, 8, 6, and 5. Display all possible pairs that use one element from each array. (There are 12.)
10. Fill two arrays as in problem 9. Fill a third array with all elements from these two arrays with no duplicates.
11. Fill a 100-element array with random numbers. Count the number of increases, decreases, and the number of no changes. Calculate the average.

6-2...Multidimensional Numeric Arrays

We have seen that one-dimensional arrays may be used to organize data in a list. We may also use two or more subscripts to arrange data into tables of all kinds. We might be interested in the temperature at 6:00 am, 12:00 noon, and 6:00 pm for a week. For this we need an array with two subscripts, a two-dimensional array. We will use one dimension to represent the days of the week and the other to represent the three different times of day. And to tabulate several weeks, we might use a third dimension. Let's look at a program to find the average daily temperature using three readings a day. See Program 6-4.

```
    90 REM ** FIND AVERAGE TEMPERATURE
    100 FOR DA = 1 TO 7
    110 FOR RE = 1 TO 3
-->120 READ TE(DA,RE)
    130 NEXT RE
    140 NEXT DA
    175 :
    180 PRINT "        TEMPERATURE"
    190 PRINT "DAY 6AM 12N 6PM AVG"
    200 FOR DA = 1 TO 7
    210 PRINT DA;
    220 T = 0
    230 FOR RE = 1 TO 3
    240 T = T + TE(DA,RE)
    250 PRINT TE(DA,RE);
    260 NEXT RE
    270 PRINT T / 3
    280 NEXT DA
    980 :
    1000 DATA 76,79,75, 72,77,76
    1020 DATA 74,79,81, 75,80,83
    1040 DATA 80,77,70, 68,65,65
    1060 DATA 65,67,76
```

Program 6-4. Finding daily average temperature.

By naming two subscripts in line 120 we caused BASIC to automatically allow for 11 elements in each dimension. Since we only require values up to seven in one dimension and three in the other, we should use the statement

```
95 DIM TE(7,3)
```

It is good practice to include a DIM statement at the beginning of every program, even if it is not required for our application. The DIM statement reveals something about our program to the reader. Even if we want an array dimensioned to (10,10), we should do so with a DIM statement. In the absence of the DIM statement, the reader doesn't know that we are using an array until it appears in a statement of the program. Even then the reader has no idea how much of the array we are using.

```
RUN
        TEMPERATURE
DAY 6AM 12N 6PM AVG
  1   76   79   75   76.6666667
  2   72   77   76   75
  3   74   79   81   78
  4   75   80   83   79.3333334
  5   80   77   70   75.6666667
  6   68   65   65   66
  7   65   67   76   69.3333334
```

Figure 6-4. Execution of Program 6-4.

...Zero Subscripts

The zero subscript is always available. In many programming situations the zero subscript is a great convenience. The zero term of a polynomial is easily represented in this way. The positions reserved for the zero subscripts are there whether we use them or not. For most programs the impact of zero subscripts is minor. However, when writing large programs it may become necessary to use them just to get the program to fit.

...More Than Two Subscripts

The number of subscripts allowed in an array is limited by the amount of memory and the 80-character program line length on the Commodore 64. Three dimensions is often very convenient. As noted above, we should always include a DIM statement at the beginning of the program. For more than three dimensions we *must* include it, since a real array of 11 by 11 by 11 by 11 won't even fit in a 64K machine. Would you believe a 71.5K machine? Not only must we provide a DIM statement, but it must call for a smaller array than that.

...SUMMARY

We have multidimensional arrays in Commodore BASIC. The expression D(3,4) refers to the value in column 4 of row 3. Since 0 subscripts are included, column 4 is actually the fifth column and row 3 is actually the fourth row. We are not required to use 0 subscripts, but using them will conserve memory.

As with one-dimensional arrays, the DIM statement specifies the maximum subscript in each dimension. The statement

```
100 DIM X(6,3,8)
```

prepares for an array of three dimensions, seven by four by nine. Often we process data in arrays with loops and nested loops. Even though BASIC automatically provides 11 elements in each dimension, we should always include a DIM statement to help document our program.

Problems for Section 6-2 . . . .

1. In Program 6-4, write a routine to find the maximum temperature for each of the three reading times (6:00 am, 12:00 noon, and 6:00 pm).

94

2. In Program 6-4, write a routine to find the maximum temperature for each day.

3. In Program 6-4, write a routine to find the average temperature for each of the three reading times (6:00 am, 12:00 noon, and 6:00 pm).

4. Fill two four-by-five arrays with random numbers and display them. Then fill a third array with the sums of the corresponding entries from the first two arrays and display the result.

5. In a 10-by-10 array enter all ones in the upper left to lower right diagonal and the leftmost column, and all zeros elsewhere. Then beginning in the third row, second column, enter the sum of the entry in the same column of the row immediately above and in the column one to the left and the row immediately above, through the 10th row, 9th column. That is:

```
230 P(R,C) = P(R-1,C) + P(R-1,C-1)
```

for the described range. Display the resulting array.

6-3...String Arrays

The ability to use arrays to store alphabetic data is very convenient. The relationship between simple string variables and string arrays is exactly analogous to the relationship between simple numeric variables and numeric arrays. Each string array consists of a collection of string elements, all referred to by an array variable name and a subscript.

Each element of the string array has the same properties as a simple string variable. Each element may store up to 255 characters. We may read, input, assign, and print elements of string arrays. And we may apply all of the string functions discussed in Chapter 5: ASC, CHR$, LEFT$, RIGHT$, MID$, LEN, STR$, and VAL. Let's explore the convenience of using string arrays for labeling. Program 6-5 reads the names of the days of the week into an array and then displays them.

```
90 REM ** READ AND DISPLAY DAYS OF THE WEEK
95 DIM W$(7)
100 FOR DA = 1 TO 7
110 READ W$(DA)
120 NEXT DA
190 :
200 FOR DA = 1 TO 7
210 PRINT W$(DA)
220 NEXT DA
990 :
1000 DATA SUNDAY
1010 DATA MONDAY
1020 DATA TUESDAY
1030 DATA WEDNESDAY
1040 DATA THURSDAY
1050 DATA FRIDAY
1060 DATA SATURDAY
```

Program 6-5. Displaying the days of the week.

```
RUN
SUNDAY
MONDAY
TUESDAY
WEDNESDAY
THURSDAY
FRIDAY
SATURDAY
```

Figure 6-5. Execution of Program 6-5.

Once the string data are stored in the elements of the string array, we may manipulate them in many ways. It may be that on a report we want the days of the week spelled out in one place and abbreviated in another. We can easily do this with the LEFT$ function. We can demonstrate this with a simple change in line 210.

```
210 PRINT LEFT$(W$(DA),3); "  "; W$(DA)
```

```
RUN
SUN   SUNDAY
MON   MONDAY
TUE   TUESDAY
WED   WEDNESDAY
THU   THURSDAY
FRI   FRIDAY
SAT   SATURDAY
```

Figure 6-6. Execution of modified Program 6-5.

Recall that in Program 6-4, in order to average the three temperatures taken each day for a week we labeled the days of the week from 1 to 7. We now have the ability to produce a more readable report. We may modify that program to label each line with the day name. If we use the full day names, then we have to deal with the fact that not all names have the same number of letters. We can handle this by using comma spacing. The longest name contains nine letters. That is a handy fit for us as comma spacing creates 10-character columns. See Program 6-6.

```
     90 REM ** FIND AVERAGE TEMPERATURE
     95 DIM W$(7), TE(7,3)
    100 FOR DA = 1 TO 7
-->105 READ W$(DA)
    110 FOR RE = 1 TO 3
    120 READ TE(DA,RE)
    130 NEXT RE
    140 NEXT DA
    175 :
    180 PRINT "        TEMPERATURE"
    190 PRINT "DAY"," 6AM 12N 6PM AVERAGE"
    200 FOR DA = 1 TO 7
-->210 PRINT W$(DA),
    220 T = 0
    230 FOR RE = 1 TO 3
    240 T = T + TE(DA,RE)
    250 PRINT TE(DA,RE);
```

```
260  NEXT RE
270  PRINT T / 3
280  NEXT DA
990  :
1000 DATA SUNDAY,    76,79,75
1010 DATA MONDAY,    72,77,76
1020 DATA TUESDAY,   74,79,81
1030 DATA WEDNESDAY, 75,80,83
1040 DATA THURSDAY,  80,77,70
1050 DATA FRIDAY,    68,65,65
1060 DATA SATURDAY,  65,67,76
```

Program 6-6. Displaying average daily temperature with day names.

Look at the DATA section. We have included the days of the week right in with the temperature data. Doing it this way helps to clearly document which temperatures go with which day. Further, we have entered the temperature data neatly arranged in columns.

```
RUN
          TEMPERATURE
DAY          6AM 12N 6PM AVERAGE
SUNDAY       76  79  75  76.6666667
MONDAY       72  77  76  75
TUESDAY      74  79  81  78
WEDNESDAY    75  80  83  79.3333334
THURSDAY     80  77  70  75.6666667
FRIDAY       68  65  65  66
SATURDAY     65  67  76  69.3333334
```

Figure 6-7. Execution of Program 6-6.

This report is easy to read. We do not wonder whether Day 1 is Sunday or Monday. Four of the averages are displayed with nine digits. We might want to round those values off to the nearest tenth. If comma spacing doesn't work out for us, we can always use the TAB(X) function.

Suppose we have a record store and are using a computer to help calculate sales slips for us. Each record is marked with a letter, H through P. This letter is assigned according to the price of the record. Thus, H is the label on every $2.99 record and I is the label on every $3.45 record. We can easily write a program using arrays to calculate a total sale for us.

We can enter the correspondence between letters and prices into the program by using READ and DATA statements. Two arrays will be required—one string array for the letter codes, and one numeric array for the prices. It is a simple matter to arrange the data so that the letter codes and the prices are properly coordinated. Placing the data in DATA statements makes it easy to add new codes or change prices. We will use STOP as the signal to stop reading data. It is always a good idea to leave a gap in line numbers between the real data and the termination signal. See Program 6-7.

```
90 REM ** CALCULATE SALES SLIPS
100 DIM N$(26), P(26)
200 FOR I = 1 TO 26
210 READ N$(I),P(I)
220 IF N$(I) = "STOP" THEN 250
230 NEXT I
250 N1 = I - 1
285 :
290 REM ** REQUEST INPUT AND CALCULATE HERE
300 PRINT "('END' TO STOP)"
310 T = 0 : N = 0
320 INPUT "RECORD"; R$
330 IF R$ = "END" THEN 500
340 FOR J = 1 TO N1
350 IF R$ = N$(J) THEN 400
360 NEXT J
370 PRINT "NOT FOUND - REENTER"
380 GOTO 320
400 T = T + P(J)
410 N = N + 1
420 GOTO 320
490 :
500 PRINT
510 PRINT "RECORDS:"; N
520 PRINT "TOTAL: $"; T
900 END
990 :
1000 DATA H,2.99,  I,3.45
1010 DATA J,3.69,  K,3.99
1020 DATA L,4.49,  M,4.99
1030 DATA N,5.99,  O,6.99
1040 DATA P,7.99
1190 DATA STOP,0
```

Program 6-7. Total price in record store.

Program 6-7 is set up in four segments. The first segment, from 100 to 250, reads in the price data. The second segment, from 300 to 420, handles the entry of figures for each sale. Lines 500 to 520 display the final results. And the fourth segment is the data in lines 1000 to 1190.

```
RUN
('END' TO STOP)
RECORD? H
RECORD? P
RECORD? P
RECORD? O
RECORD? L
RECORD? A
NOT FOUND - REENTER
RECORD? END

RECORDS: 5
TOTAL: $ 30.45
```

Figure 6-8. Execution of Program 6-7.

98
. . .

...Geography

Let's write a program to play Geography, a simple game for two or more players. We will write a program for a person to compete with the computer. Each player says the name of a place such that the first letter is the same as the last letter of the name chosen by the previous player. Of course the first name can be any place at all. If I say Boston, then you might say New York. That fits the rule, because Boston ends with an "N" and New York begins with an "N." The next player might think of Kansas. No name may be used a second time. The first person unable to think of an appropriate name drops out.

We can easily program the computer so that it "remembers" all of the names used. The more games the computer plays, the tougher it will be to beat.

We need a string array to hold all of the names. We can use a numeric array to tell us if a specific name has been used. Let's set up a numeric array AV ( ) so that a one indicates that the name in the corresponding position of the NA$( ) names array is available for use and a zero means that the name has been used in this game. If AV (5) = 1, then NA$(5) may be used. We can enter a few names into the NA$( ) array by using DATA statements. This way the computer has some names to start with. Let's allow the computer to produce the first name.

It may sound like a big job to produce a program that performs as described. We can easily trim the job down to size by spending a little extra time organizing before we generate any BASIC program statements. Think about the steps in the game. There are six easily defined segments in our program:

1. Read the names into the NA$ array.
2. Display the instructions.
3. Initialize the AV array to all ones.
4. Have the computer begin the game.
5. Process the person's response;
     stop if person quits.
6. Prepare the computer's response;
     repeat step 5 if computer doesn't quit.

Each of these six jobs may be programmed as a subroutine. The advantages of doing it this way are tremendous. When we first test our completed program it will be easy to spot which subroutine is not performing properly. Once we are satisfied that our program is working well, it will be a simple matter to determine which subroutines we need to modify or replace to change the program so that the names are stored in a file on disk.

Let's begin by writing the control routine that will manage the six subroutines listed above. In thinking about this routine we need to handle the situation when the computer runs out of names in step 6. We can save the computer's response in a string variable and save "QUIT" when the computer quits. This leads us to think about letting the person quit at any time. Thus we select CP$ for the computer's response and PE$ for the person's response. Further, we may give players the option to play another game. We arbitrarily decide to provide for 500 names. See Program 6-8a.

99

```
20 DIM NA$(500), AV(500)
30 GOSUB 8000 : REM ** READ NAMES ARRAY
35 GOSUB 9000 : REM ** INSTRUCTIONS
40 GOSUB 4000 : REM ** INITIALIZE AVAILABLE NAMES ARRAY
45 GOSUB 7000 : REM ** COMPUTER STARTS
50 GOSUB 6000 : REM ** PERSON RESPONDS
58 IF PE$ = "QUIT" THEN 80
60 GOSUB 5000 : REM ** RESPONSE OF COMPUTER
65 IF CP$ <> "QUIT" THEN 50
80 INPUT "DO YOU WANT ANOTHER GAME"; A$
90 IF LEFT$(A$,1) = "N" THEN END
100 FOR I9 = 1 TO 1000 : NEXT I9
120 GOTO 35
```

Program 6-8a. Control routine to play Geography.

The six steps have become six subroutines at lines 8000, 9000, 4000, 7000, 6000, and 5000. The choice of line numbers is arbitrary. Now we are well prepared to write each individual subroutine.

We read the names at 8000. The place names are entered in DATA statements. We choose to provide the signal data DONE. See Program 6-8b.

```
    7996 :
    7998 REM ** READ NAMES
    8000 I9 = 1
    8010 READ NA$(I9)
    8020 IF NA$(I9) = "DONE" THEN 8080
    8030 I9 = I9 + 1 : GOTO 8010
-->8080 N0 = I9 - 1
    8090 RETURN
    8096 :
    8100 DATA NEW YORK, CHICAGO, PHILADELPHIA, BOSTON
    8590 DATA "DONE"
```

Program 6-8b. Reading names into an array for Geography game.

Notice that line 8080 saves the number of names in the array, using the numeric variable N0.

Instructions are simple enough to provide—we can just display a description on the screen. Think about that. How fast do people read? We must provide a way for the fast reader to move on while allowing the slow reader a chance to finish. We can do this by asking the person to tell the program when they are ready. See Program 6-8c.

```
    8996 :
    8998 REM ** INSTRUCTIONS
-->9000 PRINT CHR$(147); : REM ** CLEAR THE SCREEN
    9005 PRINT "THIS PROGRAM WILL PLAY A GEOGRAPHY GAME" : PRINT
    9010 PRINT "WITH YOU.  YOU WILL TAKE TURNS WITH THE" : PRINT
    9015 PRINT "COMPUTER.  EACH OF YOU WILL BE TRYING TO"; : PRINT
    9020 PRINT "THINK OF NAMES OF PLACES SUCH THAT THE" : PRINT
    9025 PRINT "FIRST LETTER OF YOUR NAME IS THE SAME AS"; : PRINT
    9030 PRINT "THE LAST LETTER OF THE PREVIOUSLY USED" : PRINT
    9035 PRINT "PLACE NAME." : PRINT
    9045 INPUT "ARE YOU READY? "; A$
```

```
     9065 IF LEFT$(A$,1) <> "Y" THEN 9045
     9070 FOR I9 = 1 TO 1000 : NEXT I9
-->9080 PRINT CHR$(147); : REM ** CLEAR THE SCREEN
     9090 RETURN
```

Program 6-8c. Geography game instructions.

The wording of instructions is somewhat subjective. Instructions should tell the user what to expect. Note that we use PRINT CHR$(147) to clear the screen and place the cursor at the top left corner in lines 9000 and 9080.

The initialization of the AV array beginning at line 4000 is very straightforward. See Program 6-8d.

```
3996 :
3993 REM ** INITIALIZE AVAILABLE NAMES ARRAY
4000 FOR J9 = 1 TO NO
4010 AV(J9) = 1
4020 NEXT J9
4090 RETURN
```

Program 6-8d. Initializing the available names array.

To start the game, at line 7000, we have the computer select a name at random from the names array. The place must be recorded as used and the CP$ string variable is loaded with the name selected. See Program 6-8e.

```
6996 :
6998 REM ** COMPUTER BEGIN THE GAME
7000 X9 = INT( RND(1) * NO + 1)
7010 CP$ = NA$(X9) : AV(X9) = 0
7020 PRINT "FIRST PLACE : "; CP$
7090 RETURN
```

Program 6-8e. Beginning the Geography game.

Once the computer has produced a place name, the program proceeds to the person response subroutine.

We agreed to have the person's response stored in PE$. The person's response must pass a number of tests. It ought to have at least two characters. That is handled with the LEN( ) function. The first letter of the person's response must match the last letter of the computer place name. We take care of that with the RIGHT$( ) and LEFT$( ) string functions. If PE$ passes these two tests then we must see if it is in the list of names stored in the NA$( ) array. If PE$ is in the list, has it been used during this latest game? If it is not in the list, then we put it in the list. See Program 6-8f.

```
5996 :
5998 REM ** PERSON GO
6000 PRINT
6010 INPUT "    YOUR TURN"; PE$
6012 IF PE$ = "QUIT" THEN 6190
6015 IF LEN (PE$) > 1 THEN 6030
6020 PRINT "NAME TOO SHORT" : GOTO 6010
6030 IF LEFT$(PE$,1) = RIGHT$(CP$,1) THEN 6040
```

101

```
6035 PRINT "NO MATCH" : GOTO 6010
6040 FOR I9 = 1 TO NO
6045 IF PE$ = NA$(I9) THEN 6100
6050 NEXT I9
6055 IF NO < 500 THEN  6065
-->6060 PRINT "NO ROOM FOR MORE NAMES" : GOTO 6010
6065 NO = NO + 1
6070 NA$(NO) = PE$ : AV(NO) = 0
6080 GOTO 6190
6096 :
6098 REM ** "FOUND NAME"
6100 IF AV(I9) = 1 THEN 6150
6110 PRINT "USED ALREADY" : GOTO 6010
6150 AV(I9) = 0
6190 RETURN
```

Program 6-8f. Person response subroutine in Geography.

In the event that someone runs enough games to build the names array up to 500 names, line 6060 of this subroutine will display a message rejecting any additional names.

Finally, the computer response subroutine at line 5000 completes the program. We simply search the NA$( ) array for a place name with the proper first letter that has not been used in this latest game. If no such name is found we save the word QUIT in CP$. See Program 6-8g.

```
4996 :
4998 REM ** COMPUTER RESPOND
5000 FOR I9 = 1 TO NO
5010 IF LEFT$(NA$(I9),1) = RIGHT$(PE$,1) AND AV(I9) = 1 THEN 5050
5015 NEXT I9
5020 PRINT : PRINT " I HAVE RUN OUT OF NAMES"
5025 CP$ = "QUIT"
5030 GOTO 5090
5050 CP$ = NA$(I9) : AV(I9) = 0
5060 PRINT "    I CHOOSE: "; CP$
5090 RETURN
```

Program 6-8g. Computer response subroutine for Geography.

The program does not verify that the names are actually legitimate place names. That is left to the honor of the player. This same program allows the player to change the rules of the game. We could just as well use people's names or a computer glossary. In that case, we would want to change the instructions and the DATA statements. Notice that in the computer response subroutine at line 5000 the entire list is scanned for names. Since every name that is added to the list during the game is by definition not available for the remainder of this game, the program need not do this. We could establish another variable to hold the number of names at the beginning of the current game. We could also have the computer begin at a random place in the NA$( ) array instead of beginning with the first name every time. This change would add variety to the game.

We list the complete program here for your convenience.

```
      20 DIM NA$(500), AV(500)
      30 GOSUB 8000 : REM ** READ NAMES ARRAY
      35 GOSUB 9000 : REM ** INSTRUCTIONS
      40 GOSUB 4000 : REM ** INITIALIZE AVAILABLE NAMES ARRAY
      45 GOSUB 7000 : REM ** COMPUTER STARTS
      50 GOSUB 6000 : REM ** PERSON RESPONDS
      58 IF PE$ = "QUIT" THEN 80
      60 GOSUB 5000 : REM ** RESPONSE OF COMPUTER
      65 IF CP$ <> "QUIT" THEN 50
      80 INPUT "DO YOU WANT ANOTHER GAME"; A$
      90 IF LEFT$(A$,1) = "N" THEN END
     100 FOR I9 = 1 TO 1000 : NEXT I9
     120 GOTO 35
    3996 :
    3998 REM ** INITIALIZE AVAILABLE NAMES ARRAY
    4000 FOR J9 = 1 TO NO
    4010 AV(J9) = 1
    4020 NEXT J9
    4090 RETURN
    4996 :
    4998 REM ** COMPUTER RESPOND
    5000 FOR I9 = 1 TO NO
    5010 IF LEFT$(NA$(I9),1) = RIGHT$(PE$,1) AND AV(I9) = 1 THEN 5050
    5015 NEXT I9
    5020 PRINT : PRINT " I HAVE RUN OUT OF NAMES"
    5025 CP$ = "QUIT"
    5030 GOTO 5090
    5050 CP$ = NA$(I9) : AV(I9) = 0
    5060 PRINT "    I CHOOSE: "; CP$
    5090 RETURN
    5996 :
    5998 REM ** PERSON GO
    6000 PRINT
    6010 INPUT "   YOUR TURN"; PE$
    6012 IF PE$ = "QUIT" THEN 6190
    6015 IF LEN (PE$) > 1 THEN 6030
    6020 PRINT "NAME TOO SHORT" : GOTO 6010
    6030 IF LEFT$(PE$,1) = RIGHT$(CP$,1) THEN 6040
    6035 PRINT "NO MATCH" : GOTO 6010
    6040 FOR I9 = 1 TO NO
    6045 IF PE$ = NA$(I9) THEN 6100
    6050 NEXT I9
    6055 IF NO < 500 THEN   6065
-->6060 PRINT "NO ROOM FOR MORE NAMES" : GOTO 6010
    6065 NO = NO + 1
    6070 NA$(NO) = PE$ : AV(NO) = 0
    6080 GOTO 6190
    6096 :
    6098 REM ** "FOUND NAME"
    6100 IF AV(I9) = 1 THEN 6150
    6110 PRINT "USED ALREADY" : GOTO 6010
    6150 AV(I9) = 0
    6190 RETURN
    6996 :
    6998 REM ** COMPUTER BEGIN THE GAME
```

```
      7000  X9 = INT( RND(1) * NO + 1)
      7010  CP$ = NA$(X9) : AV(X9) = 0
      7020  PRINT "FIRST PLACE : "; CP$
      7090  RETURN
      7996  :
      7998  REM ** READ NAMES
      8000  I9 = 1
      8010  READ NA$(I9)
      8020  IF NA$(I9) = "DONE" THEN 8080
      8030  I9 = I9 + 1 : GOTO 8010
-->8080  NO = I9 - 1
      8090  RETURN
      8096  :
      8100  DATA NEW YORK, CHICAGO, PHILADELPHIA, BOSTON
      8590  DATA "DONE"
      8996  :
      8998  REM ** INSTRUCTIONS
-->9000  PRINT CHR$(147); : REM ** CLEAR THE SCREEN
      9005  PRINT "THIS PROGRAM WILL PLAY A GEOGRAPHY GAME" : PRINT
      9010  PRINT "WITH YOU.  YOU WILL TAKE TURNS WITH THE" : PRINT
      9015  PRINT "COMPUTER.  EACH OF YOU WILL BE TRYING TO"; : PRINT
      9020  PRINT "THINK OF NAMES OF PLACES SUCH THAT THE" : PRINT
      9025  PRINT "FIRST LETTER OF YOUR NAME IS THE SAME AS"; : PRINT
      9030  PRINT "THE LAST LETTER OF THE PREVIOUSLY USED" : PRINT
      9035  PRINT "PLACE NAME." : PRINT
      9045  INPUT "ARE YOU READY? "; A$
      9065  IF LEFT$(A$,1) <> "Y" THEN 9045
      9070  FOR I9 = 1 TO 1000 : NEXT I9
-->9080  PRINT CHR$(147); : REM ** CLEAR THE SCREEN
      9090  RETURN
```

Program 6-8h. Playing a Geography game.

...SUMMARY

String arrays are very convenient for maintaining a collection of string data in memory while our program is running. String arrays may be declared in a DIM statement. Zero subscripts may be used if required.

We have seen in the sample programs that it is easy to coordinate numeric values with string data by using a string array in tandem with a numeric array. Thus, the Kth element in the numeric array contains information about the string stored in the Kth element of the string array.

Problems for Section 6-3 ....

1. In Program 6-8h the Geography program, notice that the loop beginning at line 5000 scans every name in the list. None of the names that have been added in this most recent game may be used by the computer, because they have all been used by the human player. Fix this so that the computer scans only those names that it "knows" at the start of the most recent game. (Suggestion: Establish a new variable N2 that represents the number of names at the beginning of the current game.) Don't be tempted to change line 6040.

2. Modify the computer response subroutine (Program 6-8g) so that the computer randomly selects a starting point in the names array. Be sure that if no name is found that the computer scans from the beginning of the array to the random starting point.

3. Sometimes it is interesting to simply rearrange strings for display purposes. Write a program that enters the days of the week in a string array and displays them in the following format:

```
S   M   T   W   T   F   S
U   O   U   E   H   R   A
N   N   E   D   U   I   T
D   D   S   N   R   D   U
A   A   D   E   S   A   R
Y   Y   A   S   D   Y   D
        Y   D   A       A
            A   Y       Y
            Y
```

4. Write a program to enter a collection of names in a string array. Find the element that comes first alphabetically. Display it and its position in the array.

PROGRAMMER'S CORNER 6

Integer Variables . . . .

Generally, we use conventional variables to work with numeric values. This gives us up to nine decimal digits for calculation and display. These numbers are referred to as *real numbers*. While one of the desirable features of the Commodore 64 is its capability for real arithmetic, there may be times when we can solve our problem with integer arithmetic. This is especially significant when we are working with large arrays. Each of the numbers allocated in an integer array occupies two-fifths of the memory of each number allocated to a real array.

We set up conventional arrays by simply naming ordinary variable names. Commodore 64 BASIC distinguishes real and integer variables by requiring us to append a percent sign to indicate integer values.

```
100 DIM A%(100,100)
```

allocates 10201 integers in a 101-by-101 integer array. We can't even dimension such a real array on a Commodore 64.

Simple variables may be established for integers in the same way. For example,

```
100 B%=1.234
```

will result in storing the integer 1 in the integer variable B%.

105

...A Word About Zero Subscripts and Space

If we are working on a program that requires arrays and we are having problems fitting into the available memory, we may be able to gain some space by using the zero subscripts. Suppose we have a 100-by-100 array, because we really want 10,000 elements. We may simply dimension the array with

```
100 DIM A%(99,99)
```

and subtract one from all subscript references in the program. This saves the memory required by 201 integer values or 402 bytes.

This effect increases as the number of dimensions in the array increases. Suppose we require an array to be 10 by 10 by 10. That comes to 1000 elements. If we dimension the array 10 by 10 by 10, we provide for 11 by 11 by 11, which is 1331 elements. That would be 331 more elements than the problem requires, a 33.1% excess.

Chapter 7

Miscellaneous Applications

7-1...Looking at Integers One Digit at a Time

In general, the more detailed the control we have over a number in the computer, the more complex the problems we might expect to be able to handle. We also will find that as we learn more about what goes on inside the computer, we will be able to apply more elegant solutions to problems. It is common to store a different piece of information in each digit of a number. It is also common to group digits in twos or threes for this purpose. Part numbers, serial numbers, and course numbers are just a few examples of this. We have expressed the date in yymmdd form. In this section we will simply develop methods of breaking up numeric values into their separate digits.

...Using Successive Division

Consider the number 2789. The 2 means two thousand, which may be written $2 * 10^3$; the 7 means seven hundred, which may be written $7 * 10^2$; the 8 means eight tens, which may be written $8 * 10^1$; and the 9 means nine units, which may be written $9 * 10^0$. Looking at the numbers step by step,

$$2789 = 2 * 10^3 + 789$$
$$789 = 7 * 10^2 + 89$$
$$89 = 8 * 10^1 + 9$$
$$9 = 9 * 10^0 + 0$$

This is an example of the general relationship:

```
N = I * 10^E + R
```

where I is the integer quotient found by

$$I = INT(N / 10^E)$$

and an iterative process whereby the new N is the old R and the value of E is decreased by one for each iteration. Solving for R we get

$$R = N - I * 10^E$$

For nine-digit integers the value of E will have to begin at eight and go to zero in steps of minus one. Carefully study Program 7-1.

```
 90 PRINT CHR$(147);
100 PRINT "INPUT AN INTEGER";
110 INPUT N
120 IF N = 0 THEN END
130 FOR E = 8 TO 0 STEP -1
-->140 T = 10 ^ E
150 I = INT(N / T)
160 PRINT I;
-->170 R = N - I * T
180 N = R
190 NEXT E
200 PRINT : PRINT
210 GOTO 100
```

Program 7-1. Accessing digits by successive division.

Note line 140. In that line we simply save the value of 10^E. Exponentiation is a slow process and there is no need to have the computer do it twice for each value of E.

```
RUN
ENTER AN INTEGER?123456789
 1  2  3  4  5  6  7  8  8

ENTER AN INTEGER?999
 0  0  0  0  0  0  9  9  8

ENTER AN INTEGER?0
```

Figure 7-1. Execution of Program 7-1.

A quick look at the display (shown in Figure 7-1) of the execution of our seemingly simple program reveals that something is terribly wrong.

We have created a situation where the computer is rounding things off internally in such a way that accuracy is lost. Even 999 comes out 998. If we insert a statement at line 175 to display the values for R, we will see that it is just a little low. The easiest way to fix this is to calculate the value of R by rounding off to the nearest unit. This is left as an exercise.

...Using STR$

A very easy method of accessing the individual digits of a number is provided by the STR$ function. Once we store a number as a string, we can use the LEFT$, MID$, and RIGHT$ functions to pick numbers apart as we see fit. It becomes very easy to pick out any starting point and any number of digits. We can scan the number to look for a decimal. We can use the LEN function to find how many characters it takes to display the number. For demonstration purposes, let's write a program to display each digit of a number individually.

```
90 PRINT CHR$(147);
100 PRINT "ENTER A NUMBER";
110 INPUT N
120 IF N = 0 THEN END
130 A$ = STR$(N)
140 FOR I = 1 TO LEN(A$)
150 PRINT MID$(A$,I,1); " ";
160 NEXT I
170 PRINT : PRINT
180 GOTO 100
```

Program 7-2. Using STR$ to separate numeric digits.

```
RUN
ENTER A NUMBER?695.32147
  6 9 5 . 3 2 1 4 7

ENTER A NUMBER?147896325523698741
  1 . 4 7 8 9 6 3 2 6 E + 1 7

ENTER A NUMBER?0
```

Figure 7-2. Execution of Program 7-2.

Note the second number entered in Figure 7-2. Since it is represented in exponential notation for display purposes, that is the format used by STR$( ). In the case of decimal numbers and exponential notation we will have to construct more logic to determine the actual numeric value represented by a particular digit according to its position in the number.

...SUMMARY

We have seen two methods for picking apart numbers digit by digit in a computer. Either successive division or the STR$( ) function may be used. We discovered that we had to round off the value we obtained after removing the leftmost digit each time we used successive division. Using the STR$( ) function, we can easily access any individual digit in any order.

Problems for Section 7-1 . . . .

1. Write a program that requests a number without any decimals. Enter each digit of the value into an element of an array. Display the contents of the resulting array.
2. Rewrite line 170 of Program 7-1 so that the value in R is rounded to the nearest unit. This will eliminate the errors we experienced.
3. Modify Program 7-1 so that leading zeros are not displayed. Be careful that you don't eliminate all zeros!

4. Write a program to construct an integer by reversing the digits of an entered integer. Place the result in a numeric variable and print its value.

5. Find all three-digit integers that are prime. Form new integers by reversing the digits and see if the new number also is prime. Print a number only if it and its reverse number is prime. There are 43 such pairs of numbers, some of which appear twice.

6. Do Problem 5, but eliminate duplicates.

7-2...Number Bases

The day-to-day world of business, commerce, and general communications reckons in the familiar base ten number system. The ultimate reckoning of the computer is in base two. Base two requires only the two digits 0 (zero) and 1 (one). Computers may represent a 1 with a positive voltage level or a magnetized state and a 0 with a zero voltage level or a demagnetized state. Therefore, it is useful to be familiar with the base two number system. The base two number system is also referred to as the *binary number system*. A number is a number is a number is a number. The number does not change by virtue of being expressed in a different number system. As we change from one base to another, we may be using different symbols to name the same number. In the binary number system, there are only two possible digits.

Addition in base two is very simple. Either there is a "carry" as the result of two ones being added or there is not. Thus,

$$0 + 0 = 0 \qquad 0 + 1 = 1 \qquad 1 + 1 = 10$$

Multiplication is also simplified by the two-digit structure. When multiplying by one the digits shift according to the position of the one; when multiplying by zero the result is zero. When multiplying by one in the rightmost position the shift is zero. When multiplying by one in the second position from the right, the shift is one place. If we choose to number the positions from right to left as 0, 1, 2, 3, . . . N, then the shift is equal to the position of the 1.

$$
\begin{array}{ll}
1 * 101001 = 101001 & \text{(shift of 0)} \\
10 * 101001 = 1010010 & \text{(shift of 1)} \\
1000 * 101001 = 101001000 & \text{(shift of 3)}
\end{array}
$$

Thus:

```
    10          11011
 *  10       *    101
   ---         ------
   100          11011
               00000
              11011
             --------
             10000111
```

Note that in the second multiplication example, there is a carry across several positions.

One disadvantage of the binary number system is that it takes so many digits to represent numbers. For instance, 15 base ten is written as 1111 in binary and 127 base ten is written 1111111 in binary. However, this is a disadvantage only to humans, not computers. In fact, computers are very good at accessing individual bits and turning them on or off one at a time. This is discussed further in Programmer's Corner 7. The number 255 base ten is written 11111111 in binary. It requires eight binary digits to represent the number 255. Each binary digit is referred to as a *bit*. Bits are collected into groups of eight to form *bytes*. The Commodore 64 is an eight-bit machine. That is, it uses electronic circuits in sets of eight to represent numbers and instructions in memory. Everything that the computer does is stored in a byte or a group of bytes. This is why a number of the limits for the Commodore 64 are 255.

Each digit of any integer represents an integral power of the base. So the digits in binary represent 1, 2, 4, 8, 16, 32, 64, 128, 256, 512, etc., in base ten, corresponding to bit positions 0, 1, 2, 3, 4, 5, 6, 7, 8, 9, etc., in binary. On the Commodore 64 the largest true integer value allowed is 32767, while the smallest is −32768. That is 65536 numbers. Zero base ten is zero in binary. The number 65535 base ten is represented by 1111111111111111 in binary notation. That is 16 binary digits. We get 16 binary digits by grouping two bytes together. It takes two bytes to represent integers from 0 to 65535. In practice, however, the leftmost binary bit is used to designate whether the integer stored in the other 15 bits is positive or negative. A 1 indicates that the number is negative, while a 0 indicates that it is positive. Thus for two-byte storage, we are limited to the range of −32768 to +32767 as mentioned above. Values from 0 to 32767 are stored as we would expect. Values from 32768 to 65535 are translated into values in the range −1 to −32768. The 16th bit is used to determine the sign of the number.

...Decimal to Binary

Let's begin by writing a program to convert decimal to binary. If the base ten number we have is odd, then the first base two digit on the right is a one. If we have an even base ten number, then the first base two digit on the right is a zero. Now, to move the base two decimal point one to the left, we divide our base ten number by two and ignore the decimal part. (We can ignore the decimal part by simply chopping it off.) This process for eliminating the decimal part of a number is called *truncation*. If the truncated result is zero, then we are finished. If the truncated result is nonzero, then we repeat the process for the next binary digit. Consider the process for 53:

	53	is odd	1
divide by 2 and truncate	26	is even	01
divide by 2 and truncate	13	is odd	101
divide by 2 and truncate	6	is even	0101
divide by 2 and truncate	3	is odd	10101
divide by 2 and truncate	1	is odd	110101
divide by 2 and truncate	0	We have finished;	

53 base ten = 110101 base two.

Now we simply need to work out a way to print the results and a program will be forthcoming. The method we use is to store the digits in a 16-element array as we determine them. We store the rightmost (or lowest order) digit in the 16th element, the second digit in the 15th element, and so forth until we are finished. Later this can easily be expanded to accommodate larger numbers.

For any base ten number, if division by two comes out even, then the corresponding base two digit is 0. If division by two leaves a decimal portion, then the corresponding base two digit is 1. This we can easily describe with two lines of BASIC code:

```
310 IF I / 2 =  INT(I / 2) THEN A(J) = 0
320 IF I / 2 <> INT(I / 2) THEN A(J) = 1
```

Line 310 enters a zero in the Jth element if the integer is divisible by two, while line 320 enters a one in the Jth element if the integer is not divisible by two. Examine Program 7-3.

```
100 REM ** CONVERT DECIMAL TO BINARY
110 DIM A(16)
200 INPUT "ENTER AN INTEGER"; I
210 IF I <= 0 THEN 999
220 IF I < 65536 THEN 300
230 PRINT "TOO LARGE" : PRINT : GOTO 200
296 :
298 REM ** LOAD THE ARRAY
300 FOR J = 16 TO 1 STEP -1
310 IF I / 2 =  INT(I / 2) THEN A(J) = 0
320 IF I / 2 <> INT(I / 2) THEN A(J) = 1
340 I = INT(I / 2)
360 NEXT J
396 :
398 REM ** DISPLAY RESULTS
400 FOR J = 1 TO 16
410 PRINT STR$(A(J));
420 NEXT J
455 PRINT : PRINT
460 GOTO 200
999 END
```

Program 7-3. Converting decimal to binary by using successive division.

```
RUN
ENTER AN INTEGER? 127
 0 0 0 0 0 0 0 0 0 1 1 1 1 1 1 1

ENTER AN INTEGER? 32512
 0 1 1 1 1 1 1 1 0 0 0 0 0 0 0 0

ENTER AN INTEGER? 53
 0 0 0 0 0 0 0 0 0 0 1 1 0 1 0 1

ENTER AN INTEGER? 32767
 0 1 1 1 1 1 1 1 1 1 1 1 1 1 1 1
```

```
ENTER AN INTEGER? 32768
 1 0 0 0 0 0 0 0 0 0 0 0 0 0 0 0
```

Figure 7-3. Execution of Program 7-3.

Program 7-3 does not handle negative numbers.

Commodore 64 BASIC uses *two's complement* form to store negative integers in the range −1 to −32768. Once we have the binary form of the absolute value of our negative number, the rule for finding two's complement is to change every zero to a one, change every one to a zero, and add one. Let's look at an example. Running Program 7-3 for 32000 gives us

0111110100000000 = 32000

According to the rule we change ones to zeros, zeros to ones, and add one, like this:

1000001011111111
$$\frac{+\ 1}{1000001100000000} = -32000 \text{ in two's complement}$$

...**Binary to Hexadecimal**

The hexadecimal number system reckons in base sixteen, because hex uses 16 possible digits. The hex digits are 0, 1, 2, 3, 4, 5, 6, 7, 8, 9, A, B, C, D, E, and F. So 10 in hex is 16 in base ten and EF in hex is 14°16 + 15°1 or 239 base ten. While the place values for binary representation are 1, 2, 4, and 8, the place values for hexadecimal representation are 1, 16, 256, and 4096. (NOTE: In all numbering systems the place values are really 1, 10, 100, and 1000, when expressed in the notation of the numbering system itself. The numbers 1, 10, 100, and 1000 in hex are written as 1, 16, 256, and 4096 in base ten notation.) It takes four binary digits to form a hex digit:

```
1011  0001      binary
 B    1   =   B1 hex
```

So, two hexadecimal digits may be used to represent any number stored in one byte and four hexadecimal digits may represent two bytes. This is very convenient for use with an eight-bit machine.

The hexadecimal numbering system offers some advantages when working with a computer. The term B1 is more compact and much easier to read than 10110001. There are some parameters associated with computers that are just plain easier to remember in hex than in base ten. Computer memory is often blocked off in segments containing 16384 bytes each. That is 16 times 1024 or 4000 bytes in hex. One common unit of measure for computer memory is the "K." One K is 1024 bytes. So, for a 64K machine, the four 16K segments begin at 0000H, 4000H, 8000H, and C000H. Those numbers are much easier to remember than 0, 16384, 32768, and 49152.

...Hexadecimal to Decimal

The conversion from decimal to hex is exactly analogous to the conversion from decimal to binary, except that we have to work out how to get the extra digits A through F into the picture. Since the extra digit problem also occurs in the hex to decimal conversion, this is where we start.

Let's convert 1B3A Hex to Decimal:

The digit	A	in the 1's	column represents	10
The digit	3	in the 16's	column represents	48
The digit	B	in the 256's	column represents	2816
The digit	1	in the 4096's	column represents	4096

1B3A hex equals 6970 base ten

To work in hex, our programs must have a way to accept hex input and display hex output. Obviously this cannot be done with numeric variables. We may store the 16 hex digits in a string variable. All hex input should be checked to verify that no invalid digits have been entered. Let's start by writing a program that simply requests hex input, verifies it, and displays the verified number.

```
100 REM ** DEVELOP HEX INPUT/OUTPUT
130 H$ = "0123456789ABCDEF"
140 GOSUB 400 : REM ** REQUEST & VERIFY
150 PRINT N$
190 GOTO 140
396 :
398 REM ** REQUEST & CALL VERIFY
400 PRINT : INPUT "HEX NUMBER"; N$
410 L = LEN(N$)
420 IF L = 0 THEN END
430 IF L < 5 THEN 440
432 PRINT "TOO MANY DIGITS"
434 GOTO 400
440 GOSUB 700
450 IF FL = 0 THEN 490
460 PRINT "BAD FORMAT" : GOTO 400
490 RETURN

696 :
698 REM ** VERIFY HEX STRING
700 FL = 0 : REM ** GOOD INPUT
710 FOR J = 1 TO L
720 FOR K = 1 TO 16
-->730 IF MID$(H$,K,1) = MID$(N$,J,1) THEN 760
740 NEXT K
750 FL = 1 : REM ** BAD INPUT
755 GOTO 790
760 NEXT J
790 RETURN
```

Program 7-4. Hex input/output.

```
RUN

HEX NUMBER? ABCD
ABCD

HEX NUMBER? AFAF
AFAF

HEX NUMBER? HEX
BAD FORMAT

HEX NUMBER? FF
FF

HEX NUMBER?
```

Figure 7-4. Execution of Program 7-4.

Now, how do we get the computer to "know" that an A is 10, a B is 11, and so on? Since the digits are not numeric, we have this problem even for 0, 1, etc., as well.

This is not so tough as it might seem at first. Line 730 of Program 7-4 gives us all the information we need. The value of K there tells us which digit in the sample string H$ matches the Jth digit of the input string. If K = 1 then the digit in H$ is a zero, while if K = 16 then we come up with F. So, subtracting one from K gives us the values from 0 to F corresponding to 0 to 15. Then, knowing which digit we are on tells us which place that digit represents, so we know what power of 16 to use.

The digit value is K − 1. The place is L − J. So the base ten value is:

$$(K-1) * 16 \char94 (L-J)$$

We simply need a numeric variable in which to accumulate this information. Using this information, the subroutine at line 700 could easily return the base ten value of the hex input. Simply set a numeric variable to zero at about line 705 and accumulate at line 760, while moving NEXT J to line 770. This is left as an exercise.

...SUMMARY

We have seen that the rationale for base two or binary notation is that the digits 0 and 1 can be represented as electrical states of one sort or another. The hexadecimal number system is convenient because it correlates so nicely to data as it is stored in computer memory. While it takes eight digits to represent a byte of computer memory in binary, it requires only two hexadecimal digits. All conversion techniques rely on determining the position of a particular digit and its actual value.

Problems for Section 7-2 . . . .

1. Write a program to convert binary to hex.
2. Modify Program 7-3 to eliminate leading zeros and display the result with no spaces.

3. Modify Program 7-4 to perform the conversion as described in this section.

4. Rewrite Program 7-3 to display two's complement form for integers in the range -1 to -32768.

7-3...Writing a Program Menu

It is common practice where programs are run on a fast video display to present the user with a list of options. Usually the options are numbered and the user simply enters the number of the preferred option followed by a carriage return.

A sample menu might look like Figure 7-5.

1) PLAY TIC TAC TOE

2) SUPER LO-RES DEMO

3) QUIT

Figure 7-5. Sample menu.

Note option 3. This is very important. By providing this option right in the menu we give the user proper control of the program. Many of the programs for sale in computer stores and by mail order are *menu-driven*—that is, they include a menu. The quality of menus is not consistent. One of the most common problems is the failure to include an option to terminate the program. We have to press STOP to do that. Sometimes we even have to shut the machine off and back on again to run other programs. In some cases this is done to make it difficult for the user to make unauthorized copies of a program.

Another common affliction is that entering something not in the list of choices produces a messy display. In some cases the menu even begins to disappear from the screen if we enter several out-of-range choices. With some programs pressing an extra key before the menu even appears on the screen produces surprising results. We will endeavor to write a menu program that avoids all of these problems.

...Developing the Menu Routine

Each of the options in the menu may be a subroutine in a single program, or each may be a separate program. That doesn't matter much. What we are about to do here is to develop a good menu processing routine.

First of all, PRINT CHR$(147); should be used to clear the text screen.

Next, we should give some thought to how we take the choices from the keyboard. We may use an INPUT request or we can use GET A$ to process the keystrokes directly.

INPUT is quick and easy to code. However, if we code:

```
940 INPUT X
```

and the user enters anything other than a numeric value, BASIC takes over, displaying error messages and rerequesting data. This results in a messy screen and may cause the menu to scroll out of sight. We could use

```
940 INPUT X$
```

and then convert the response to numeric data with the VAL function. This nicely handles the situation where the user fails to enter a numeric response. In any program where we may expect the user to know enough to press the RETURN key this is a good method to use.

GET A$ and POKE 198,0 give us the ultimate in control. We can request a character from the keyboard and not worry about whether or not the user knows to press the RETURN key. Programming with GET and POKE 198,0 will require a little more effort to write the BASIC routine. But it seems worth doing. Once we have written a menu routine that works, we may plan future programs so that they use it, too. All we will have to change are the names of the options and the control routine. Program 7-5 does it all.

```
98 REM ** TEST THE MENU SUBROUTINES
100 DIM A$(10)
200 GOSUB 9400
210 GOSUB 9000
220 IF S = NO THEN END
230 PRINT "YOU CHOSE - "; A$(S)
240 FOR I = 1 TO 1200 : NEXT I
290 GOTO 210
8994 :
8996 REM ** "DO THE MENU"
8998 REM     RETURN SELECTION IN S
9000 PRINT CHR$(147);
9002 PRINT : PRINT TAB(18); "MENU"
9004 PRINT : PRINT
9006 FOR I = 1 TO NO
9008 PRINT STR$(I); ") "; A$(I) : PRINT
9010 NEXT I
9020 PRINT "YOUR CHOICE: ";
9022 POKE 198, 0
9024 GET A$ : IF LEN(A$) = 0 THEN 9024
9026 S = VAL(A$)
9030 IF S >= 1 AND S <= NO THEN 9080
9036 PRINT TAB(19); "NOT OFFERED"
9038 FOR I = 1 TO 1200 : NEXT I
9040 GOTO 9000
9080 PRINT S : PRINT
9090 RETURN
9394 :
9396 REM ** READ MENU OPTIONS
9398 REM     NUMBER OF OPTIONS IN NO
9400 READ NO
9405 IF NO < 10 THEN 9410
9407 PRINT "TOO MANY OPTIONS" : STOP
9410 FOR I = 1 TO NO
9420 READ A$(I)
9430 NEXT I
9490 RETURN
9496 :
```

```
9500 DATA 9
9510 DATA PLAY TIC TAC TOE
9515 DATA SUPER LOW-RES DEMO
9520 DATA SWELL SOUNDS
9525 DATA GOLF EXTRA
9530 DATA COMPLICATED ARITHMETIC
9535 DATA NEXT OPTION
9540 DATA ANOTHER ONE
9545 DATA THIS IS THE LAST OPTION
9555 DATA QUIT
```

Program 7-5. Processing a menu.

We have set up this menu program so that the options are entered in data statements. Lines 9000 to 9090 take care of displaying the menu and accepting a response from the keyboard. Note that line 9022 clears the character count before line 9024 reads the character buffer. In this way, no stray characters will be read in before the user is ready. Remember that VAL returns zero for any character other than the digits 1 through 9. We have even arranged to display the message "NOT OFFERED" on the same line as the question.

We might want more than nine options. One method for handling this is to break the selections into categories so that each category has nine or fewer options. This is not a bad idea anyway—it makes the selection process easier for the user. Simply include an earlier question that tells the program which category to offer. This structure can be extended to provide various levels of menu, where some selections bring forth another menu offering another selection. Finally, a selection takes the user into the process or program desired.

If you simply must have more than nine options, then you might try using hex digits to get up to 15 options, or using the alphabet. Alternatively, it is very easy to use INPUT with a string variable and VAL to get any number of options. This is fine as long as it is acceptable to expect the user to press the RETURN key.

7-4...Miscellaneous Problems for Computer Solution

We offer a few interesting problems for computer application here. Do not limit yourself to the problems suggested here. You should be bringing your own problems to the computer. While it is important to have problem suggestions in any book, you will find a tremendous satisfaction comes with developing your own ideas on the computer.

...Problems of General Interest

1. There is an old number puzzle about cows, pigs, and chickens that lends itself nicely to computer solution. A farmer has exactly $100 to spend on animals. He wants to buy at least one cow, at least one pig, and at least one chicken. Cows are $10 each, pigs are $3 each, and chickens are $0.50 each. How many of each must he buy to have exactly 100 animals?

118

At first, this looks like an easy algebra problem. Soon, however, we find that we have only two equations with which to solve a problem having three unknowns. This is where the computer comes in. We simply try all combinations of cows, pigs, and chickens until these equations are satisfied:

$$10 * CO + 3 * PI + CH / 2 = 100$$
$$CO + PI + CH = 100$$

Observing that there must be many more chickens than either pigs or cows we could solve this by hand using trial and error. But we still might become frustrated with the number of calculations required.

The key to this problem is to realize that each of the three numbers we are looking for must be an integer. We could easily write a program with three nested FOR...NEXT loops where CO goes from 1 to 10, PI goes from 1 to 33, and CH goes from 2 to 100 by twos. If we do that, we will find that the program has to "think" for some time. We can greatly speed things up by using more of the information available to us. Clearly, if there must be at least one of each animal, there cannot be 10 cows or 33 pigs or 100 chickens. There could be no more than 9 cows, no more than 29 pigs, and no more than 98 chickens. We can derive the greatest speed improvement by using the fact that once the number of pigs and cows to try has been established, we can find the number of chickens from:

$$100 - CO - PI$$

Next we check this number to see that it is even, since the price is $0.50.

Write a program to solve this puzzle.

2. Sometimes it is fun to try to guess a number that someone else is thinking of. It is fairly easy to program a computer to play this simple game. Have the computer request the largest number from the user. Then the program should compute a random number in the range from one to the largest number entered earlier. Next the program should ask for guesses from the user. Each guess should be checked. If the number is less than one, or greater than the upper limit, a message should put the user back on the right track. If the number is a correct guess, the program should say so. The program should also note whether the actual number is higher or lower than the most recent guess.

3. There are many famous chess puzzles from antiquity that are appropriate for computer solution. A notable one is the eight queens problem. How many ways can eight queens be placed on a chess board so that no queen attacks another?

This puzzle may be solved by using one eight-element array. Placing a queen in a position of the array assures that no two queens occupy the same row. A queen may be placed in the row by entering her column number there. Now we assure that no two queens occupy the same column by avoiding duplicate column numbers in the eight-element array. Finally, we check for diagonal attack by noting that for two queens at positions (X,Y) and (X',Y'), one diagonal is shared if $X - X' = Y - Y'$, while the other diagonal is shared if $X + X' = Y + Y'$. We need to have the computer test this for each queen in every column of one row. Write a program to print the positions of all queens for each solution.

For more about the eight queens problem see the October 1978 and February 1979 issues of *BYTE* magazine.

4. It is always instructive to learn about the cost of homeownership. Aside from the ongoing costs of painting, fixing the roof, real estate taxes, and insurance, there is the ever-present mortgage interest. Most mortgages are set up so that the monthly payment stays constant. In the beginning, there is a large interest payment and a small payment toward the principal. At the end, the interest payment is small and more goes toward the principal. The following formula may be used to calculate the monthly payment PA:

$$PA = P \, \frac{I\,(1 + I)^{N}}{(1 + I)^{N} - 1}$$

where

P is the principal
I is the monthly interest rate
N is the number of months

Write a program to request the principal, annual interest rate, and number of years. Have the program display the monthly payment, the total amount paid, and the total interest paid.

...Math Oriented Problems

1. Every positive integer may be expressed as the sum of the squares of four integers. Zero may be included as one or more of those integers to be squared. For example:

$$1 = 0^2 + 0^2 + 0^2 + 1^2$$

Write a program to find all sets of four such integers for a requested integer. Be careful about efficiency in this one. Test your solution with small integers before trying large ones!

2. Suppose you have to find the greatest common factor of 23902 and 15096. What would you do? The famous mathematician Euclid would have found the remainder after dividing 23902 by 15096, which is 8806. Then he would have found the remainder after dividing 15096 by 8806, which is 6290. Then he would have continued this pattern as follows:

$$23902 = 1 \,^{\circ}\, 15096 + 8806$$
$$15096 = 1 \,^{\circ}\, 8806 + 6290$$
$$8806 = 1 \,^{\circ}\, 6290 + 2516$$
$$6290 = 1 \,^{\circ}\, 2516 + 1258$$
$$2516 = 2 \,^{\circ}\, 1258 + 0$$

Next, Euclid would have reasoned that since the remainder of the last division was zero, the greatest common factor must be the last divisor, in this case 1258. This method required only five iterations. How many would it have taken using other methods?

3. The sieve of Eratosthenes is an ingenious method for generating prime integers. Write down all the integers from two to the desired upper limit. Keep the first prime number—two—and cross out all of its multiples. Now keep the next uncrossed out number and cross out all of its multiples. Repeat this process until there are no more numbers to cross out. The remaining numbers are prime.

There are two areas in this algorithm that are potential pitfalls for unnecessary extra processing. First, if the first multiple in any case has already been crossed out, then so will all other multiples have been crossed out. Second, we only have to check for uncrossed out integers up to the square root of the largest number in the original range.

This algorithm can easily be implemented in an array. First, enter the integers from two to the upper limit into the array elements two through the upper limit. Next, use a FOR...NEXT loop to access the multiple positions in the array. Set the contents of any element to be crossed out to zero. Finally, print all subscript positions for which the element is not zero.

4. *Perfect numbers* are integers the sum of whose proper factors is the integer itself. The proper factors of 15 are one, three, and five. The sum of the factors of 15 is nine. Therefore 15 is not a perfect number. The proper factors of six are one, two, and three. The sum of the proper factors of six is six. Thus six is called a perfect number. Write a program to find the first four perfect numbers. Since the fifth perfect number is 33,550,336, and there is a significant amount of execution associated with determining "perfectness," we would be unwise to test each integer up to that one! It turns out that there don't seem to be any odd perfect numbers, so let's test only even numbers.

5. Euclid was an active mathematician! He concluded that all possible even perfect numbers are of the form

$$N = 2^{(E-1)} * F$$

where

$$F = 2^E - 1$$

and F is an odd prime.

Using Euclid's algorithm, write a program to calculate perfect numbers. Try a range of two to 12 for E.

6. Pythagorean triples are sets of three integers that can be the lengths of the sides of a right triangle. Thus, the sum of the squares of the two smaller integers must equal the square of the largest one. The first Pythagorean triple is 3, 4, 5. Write a program to generate Pythagorean triples.

7. The number π has fascinated mathematicians for many many centuries.

Values for π may be calculated in a variety of ways. The following sequence is known to approach the value of π:

$$4(1 - 1/3 + 1/5 - 1/7 + 1/9 - 1/11 \ldots)$$

Write a program to evaluate this sequence for several large numbers of terms.

8. There are many sequences that approach π as the number of terms increases. Here is another one.

$$2 + 16 \left(\frac{1}{1 * 3 * 5} + \frac{1}{5 * 7 * 9} + \frac{1}{9 * 11 * 13} + \ldots \right)$$

Write a program for this sequence. If you also did problem 7, which sequence converges faster?

9. One method for approximating the value of π derives from the fact that the area of a circle with radius r is known to equal πr^2. A circle having a radius of 1 unit has an area of π. Thus, if we inscribe a circle in a square having a side of 2 units and examine one quarter of the figure, we have a quarter circle inscribed in a smaller square with a side of 1 unit.

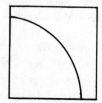

The area of the square is 1 unit and the area of the quarter circle is $\pi/4$. If we have some way of measuring the area of the quarter circle, then we simply multiply that number by four to get an approximation of π.

If we generate random values between 0 and 1 for the coordinates X and Y, we will always obtain a point in the square. Sometimes we will obtain a point in the circle. The ratio of the number of times the point falls in the circle to the number of points selected is proportional to the areas of the quarter circle and the square. If we find 80 points in the circle out of 1000 points selected, then the approximation of π we come up with is 4 ° (80/100) or 3.2. Write a program to calculate π in this way for 100, 500, 100, and 5000 random points. Assume that if a point lands on the circle then it counts as part of the circle.

You might experiment to see whether or not excluding the points that fall on the circle has an impact on how fast the value you get approaches the known value of π. ($\pi = 3.1415926536 \ldots$)

PROGRAMMER'S CORNER 7

Bits of AND, OR, and NOT

We have used the logical operators AND, OR, and NOT in IF...THEN statements to evaluate the truth of an expression in BASIC. Logical expressions as used with IF...THEN have two states: true or false. The values assigned are 0 for false and −1 for true. In addition, the logical operators can perform operations on any integer values. This is done on a bit-by-bit basis. The result of any logical operation is always an integer. Remember, integers are whole numbers in the range −32768 to 32767 on the Commodore 64.

The idea of working with numbers on a bit-by-bit basis is common in computer work, where we use various collections of bits to control the computer. This makes it easy to work with a byte as eight little switches. When this approach is used in conjunction with PEEK and POKE, we gain lots of power in a small space. We will discuss this in detail when we work with graphics in Chapters 9 and 10, and with sound in Chapter 11.

The bits of a byte are numbered from 0 to 7, while their values go from 1 to 128. We can refer to them as the 1 bit, 2 bit, 4 bit, etc., up to the 128 bit. When we want to refer to the position, we call them bit 0, bit 1, bit 2, etc., up to bit 7. The value of a bit is derived by raising 2 to the power of the bit number. So bit 5 has a value of 2^5 or 32.

Where we need more than 256 values we place two bytes together and work with them as a unit. The result is a 16-bit storage package. This is exactly what the Commodore 64 does to obtain integer values in BASIC. We call the byte that contains bits 0 through 7 the *low byte*, and the byte that contains bits 8 through 15 the *high byte*.

For some purposes, we break a byte into two groups of four bits. These groups are commonly called *nibbles*. In this situation, the nibble containing bits 0 through 3 is called the low nibble and the other 4 bits are referred to as the high nibble.

...AND

The operator AND produces a value that has all bits turned on that were turned on in both of two numbers. For example

    5 AND 6

is 4. It is 4, because the 4 bit is turned on in both the number 5 and the number 6. It is the only one turned on in both values.

    5 = 101
    6 = 110

Suppose we are using bit 5 to control some function. There are two considerations. We might want to know if bit 5 is turned on, or we might want to set it. We can easily look at the condition of bit 5 with an expression such as the following:

```
310 IF SW AND 2^5 = 2^5 THEN PRINT "BIT 5 IS ON"
```

Suppose we want to turn off bit 5. In this case we want to preserve the status of all bits except bit 5. What we need is the value of the number 11011111. If we link it by AND to the value of SW the result will have bit 5 turned off and all others unaffected. We could convert 11011111 to decimal, or we could realize that the value of 11111111 is 255 and the value of 11011111 is $255 - 2^5$. We can easily calculate that to be 223 or we could leave it in the form $255 - 2^5$ so that the purpose of the BASIC statement is clear right in the program.

```
420 SW = SW AND (255 - 2^5)
```

In line 420, if SW is an integer in the range 0 to 255, we turn bit 5 off. If SW is larger than 255, then we turn off bits 8 through 15 as well.

What happens when the value of SW in line 240 exceeds 32767? All the logical operators are designed to work with integers. 32768 is not a true integer, so, we will produce

```
?ILLEGAL QUANTITY  ERROR
```

There must be some way to examine the low byte of a number in the range 32768 to 65535. All we need to do is subtract any number that has none of the bits in the low-order byte turned on. The result will have the same low-order byte as the original number. The smallest value to do that is 256. Try it. The statement 256 AND 255 equals 0. So for a number N, we could obtain the low-order byte with

```
(N - 256) AND 255
```

Now we can obtain numbers up to 33023. The next larger value with all zeros in the low-order byte is 512 or 2^9. Continuing this process, we find that for just bit 15 on, we get 32768 or 2^{15}. This is ideal for moving values in the range 0 to 65535 to the range from -32768 to 32767.

How do we obtain the high byte of a two-byte integer? This is done by dividing by 256. The expression

```
INT(N/256)
```

gives the high byte as an integer. Note that if we happen to be using POKE to place that value into memory, we don't even have to use the INT function.

So, to obtain the low byte of any integer in the range 0 to 65535, use the following expression:

```
(N - 32768) AND 255
```

If we will never see a value greater than 32767, we don't even need to subtract 32768. And to obtain the high byte use

```
N / 256        or       INT(N/256)
```

...**OR**

OR produces a value that has all bits turned on that were turned on in either or both of two numbers. Earlier, we used AND to turn bit 5 off in variable SW. It is very easy to turn bit 5 on in variable SW with

```
420 SW = SW OR 2^5
```

It is as simple as that. If bit 5 was already on, it stays on. Suppose we want to turn on bit 5 and bit 7. Then we would use $2^5 + 2^7$ or 160. Often we would put an expression such as $2^5 + 2^7$ right in the final program so that the meaning of the BASIC statement is clear.

...**NOT**

The operator NOT works on a single value. The NOT operator simply reverses all of the bits in a value. Since numbers are stored in two's complement form, it may take a minute to get used to this. For example, NOT $0 = -1$. And NOT $-1 = 0$.

Think about the two's complement form for -1. Referring to Section 7-2, we take the binary form for $+1$, reverse all the bits, and add 1.

$$
\begin{array}{ll}
1 = & 0000000000000001 \\
\text{reverse} & 1111111111111110 \\
\underline{\text{add 1}} & \underline{\hspace{3em} +1} \\
\text{yields} & 1111111111111111 \text{ which is the two's complement form of } -1.
\end{array}
$$

Minus one has all bits turned on. That is exactly what we should expect from NOT 0.

It turns out that for any number N

```
NOT N = -(N + 1)
```

Chapter 8

Sequential Files

8-1...DOS

DOS stands for *Disk Operating System*. The disk is contained in the little square envelope that we insert into the disk drive. The disk drive is the machinery required to read and write the disk itself. DOS is a program, just as BASIC is a program. DOS and BASIC together make it possible for us to work with data files in programs that we write. It is DOS that allows us to save programs on a disk. This single capability often justifies the purchase of a disk drive. With a disk system we may save many programs on one disk and retrieve them later by using program names. The Commodore Datassette is a cassette tape recorder that makes it possible for us to save programs and data on tape cassettes. The disk is much faster than tape. See Appendix D for a discussion of the various commands available for managing programs on disk.

The ability to store data on a disk turns our computer into a powerful data processing system. We can now use a Commodore 64 to handle a name-and-address list. We can enter statistical data with one program and use one or more other programs to perform a variety of analytic processes. It will not be necessary to enter the data separately for each program. With text stored on a disk we can use a word processing program for writing of all kinds. Data for many Sprites in Sprite graphics can be stored on disk for easy access with a graphics program. There are many uses for disk-based programs.

Data stored on a disk are referred to as a *data file*. There is a set of BASIC keywords that we may use to manipulate data on a disk. These may be used in programs to create files, write data, read data, and delete files.

You should read Appendix D before proceeding further in this chapter.

8-2...Introduction to Sequential Files

...What Is a File?

A *file* is simply some area of the disk where we may save data. As stated earlier, we may save programs on disk, too. When we save a program on disk, DOS does everything for us. When we save data in a data file, it is up to us to organize the data.

One of the aspects about data files that encourages mystery is that they are invisible. Well, so are programs during execution. We have found that we could perform fantastic feats with programs even though we could see nothing of what was going on until the final printed result. We will now expand our capabilities tremendously by using programs to create and access data files. We can LIST a program, but we are going to have to write programs to LIST any data file we create.

All programs in this chapter were developed on the Commodore 1541 single disk drive.

Sequential files are easy to set up and use. We simply do everything beginning at the beginning. If we want to place 15 items in the file, then we simply write them in order from 1 to 15. We are not concerned with the relative space required by the various entries. We need to be aware that there is space on the disk for the data that we want to store there, but DOS decides where to store things. If we later wish to read the 14th item, then we read them all in order, beginning with item 1, and stop when we get to item 14. Structurally, data in sequential data files are just like data in the DATA statements of a program. There is no skipping around.

OPEN, PRINT#, INPUT#, and CLOSE are the four most commonly used commands required for performing any useful work with data files. For some purposes, the GET# command is also very helpful. Let's discuss them all before we attempt our first example.

...OPEN

OPEN establishes a communications channel between our program and the data file on the disk. OPEN creates the link between the file and the program and points to the beginning of the file. The OPEN statement must specify a file number, a device number, and a channel number. The OPEN statement must also declare the file type. We are working with SEQuential files. We need to open sequential files in either READ or WRITE mode. All of this is done in a single statement.

```
100 OPEN 3,8,2,"TEST FILE,SEQ,WRITE"
```

Three is the file number, the eight is our familiar value for the disk drive, and two is the channel number. (You did read Appendix D, right?) We can have up to three sequential files open at the same time. We may have any number in a single program, it is just that we can only open three of them at once. You might like to use the same value for file number and channel number. TEST FILE is the name of the file. SEQ indicates a sequential file, and WRITE indicates that we wish to write to the file. We may abbreviate the SEQ and WRITE, so we might use a statement such as

```
100 OPEN 3,8,2,"TEST FILE,S,W"
```

As time goes on, we may want to replace the data stored in a disk file. If we execute an OPEN statement on an existing file we will have the same experience that we had resaving a program. The program seems to be all right, but the red light keeps blinking. In order to replace an existing file, we need to declare our intention right in the OPEN statement. Again, we use the at symbol (@), here.

```
100 OPEN 3,8,2,"@:TEST FILE,S,W"
```

is what we need. The at symbol may also be used to create a new file.

Any of the values in an OPEN statement may be expressed as variables.

```
80 F = 3 : C = 2 : A$ = "@:TEST FILE,S"
100 OPEN F,8,C,A$ + ",W"
```

has the same effect as the last OPEN statement above. We may use file numbers in the range from 1 to 127, while channel numbers for files are limited to the range from 2 through 14.

Channel 15 is special. It is used to send commands to the disk itself. Channel 15 is used for things like the SCRATCH command, and for reading the error channel to look for disk errors. (We'll get to errors.)

...PRINT#

PRINT# X writes data to file number X. PRINT# performs exactly like PRINT. It has to be PRINT#; PRINT # (with a space) won't do.

```
240 PRINT# 3, A$; X; Z1
```

sends data out to file 3 on the disk in exactly the same format that the data would appear in on our video screen. Numbers are preceded by a space or a minus sign and followed by a space. Semicolons and commas generate the same spacing in a file as they do on the screen. Even a carriage return goes out to the file at the end of any line where it would do so on the screen.

For general purpose programs, it is usually best to simply PRINT# each item, one to a PRINT# statement. Then the file will look very much like a collection of data in the DATA statements of a program. We can even separate each data item in the file with a comma by using a statement such as

```
240 PRINT# 3, A$; ",";
```

The advantages of having the data in a file are numerous. We can use the same data for several programs. The data do not have to be in memory, so we save lots of program space. Eventually, we can write a program to edit data in a file to deal with typing errors and such. One program can process data from one file and write the results to another file for further processing. All this provides tremendous flexibility.

...INPUT#

Data are retrieved from a file with the INPUT# statement. This is a variation of the INPUT statement used for requesting input from the keyboard. It is important that we use INPUT# and not INPUT #.

```
300 INPUT# 3, A$, B$, X
```

will attempt to read three separate items—two strings and a numeric value. In order for that to work, the three items must be separated by either commas or carriage returns in the file.

...GET#

Just as GET accepts data from the keyboard one character at a time, GET# accepts data from a file one character at a time.

```
GET# 3, A$
```

takes a single character from file 3. This is especially useful for programmers. If we have a file with mysterious contents, simply put GET# F, A$ with PRINT A$ in a loop. Many a program error can be solved by examining the contents of a file in this way. If a file contains more than 255 characters without a comma or a carriage return, this is the only way we can read it.

...CLOSE

Just as important as opening files is closing them.

```
180 CLOSE 3
```

This CLOSE statement takes care of all of the management associated with disconnecting our program from the file. If we omit the CLOSE statement, we will encounter strange situations. We may lose all of the data in the file. END will not close files for us. If the little red light stays on and you are sure that the program is completed, then it may be that the CLOSE statement is missing. Files must be closed one at a time. We cannot use CLOSE 2, 3; file 2 will be closed, but file 3 will not and no error message will be displayed.

Strange things can happen. Especially for the new programmer, it may be difficult to retrace just how we got to some strange error condition. If after we use CLOSE on all the files we know about, the red light still will not go out, then we may have to use the INITIALIZE command. (See Appendix D.) Many unexplainable errors are cured by

```
OPEN 15,8,15,"I"
CLOSE 15
```

Or, if you have C-64 WEDGE in place, @I will do it just as well.

So, we have OPEN, PRINT#, INPUT#, GET#, and CLOSE. Any program accessing files must have an OPEN and a CLOSE statement. In addition, for it to be useful, we must use at least one of the other three statements.

...Errors

We all strive to write error-free programs. The ability to detect errors is especially important when we are working with the disk drive on the Commodore 64. The 1541 drive is called an *intelligent peripheral*. It can accept an instruction and go off on its own while BASIC continues on its merry way. That is wonderful, as long as the disk drive is able to carry out our wishes. Usually it can and will. But, sometimes the unexpected happens. The disk runs out of space, we have forgotten to insert the disk, we have the wrong disk, the file we need is not there, a file that shouldn't be there is there—the list goes on and on. In order to benefit from this intelligent peripheral we must be responsible for checking disk errors at all times.

We are going to need to check for errors in all of our file programs. We should check for an error after every file operation. So, let's take time now to examine a subroutine that will help us in every program. Program 8-1 is what we need.

```
800 INPUT# 15, E,E$,T,S
810 IF E < 20 THEN 890
820 PRINT E$
830 STOP
890 RETURN
```

Program 8-1. Error reading subroutine for files.

This program takes some explaining. File 15 must be opened to the command channel. So, the main program must have an OPEN statement such as

```
100 OPEN 15,8,15
```

As mentioned in Appendix D, there are four parameters available to help us analyze errors. Line 800 reads them for us. The E is the error number. These numbers are keyed to a table in the user's manual supplied with each 1541 disk drive. Values less than 20 do not reflect an error. Therefore, in line 810 we ignore them and RETURN. The E$ is a character string that describes the error. Usually this expression is enough for us to determine the cause of the trouble. For many purposes, it is enough for a program to simply halt with a display of the error. As we gain more programming experience we find that we can perform some corrective operations in some situations—and we will have fewer errors anyway. As beginners, we just stop right there upon encountering any error. The values of T and S are the *track* and *sector* on the disk where the difficulty occurred. Usually this is not important. But, if the error is due to a damaged disk, a truly advanced programmer may be able to use the track and sector to bypass the problem and recover valuable data. We won't attempt that here.

Let's look at an example. Program 8-2 is a simple program that does nothing but open a sequential file in write mode.

```
100 OPEN 15,8,15
110 OPEN 3,8,2,"TEST FILE,S,W":GOSUB 800
180 CLOSE 3 : CLOSE 15
190 END
800 INPUT# 15, E,E$,T,S
810 IF E < 20 THEN 890
```

```
820 PRINT E$
830 STOP
890 RETURN
```

Program 8-2. Demonstration of how to read file errors.

Running this program will produce a simple READY message. The red light will come on briefly and go off. All's well. Notice in line 180 that we CLOSE the data file channel and then the file on the error channel. That is the order in which they should be closed. Suppose we run it again. Now we have a different story. See Figure 8-1.

```
RUN
FILE EXISTS

BREAK IN 830
READY.
```

Figure 8-1. Execution of Program 8-2 a second time.

What we do about this depends on whether we want to replace the file named TEST FILE or not. If we don't want to replace it, then we may have run the program by mistake and we have saved ourselves from the possibility of erasing valuable data. If we do want to replace it, then we have a programming error and line 110 in Program 8-2 should read as follows:

```
110 OPEN 3,8,2,"@:TEST FILE,S,W":GOSUB 800
```

The "@:" will cause the already existing file to be replaced. The old data will be lost.

Whenever a files program is halted by an error, we are in danger of losing data. BASIC and DOS are not coordinated at this point. If you expect data to be written to a file, then it is important to use the INITIALIZE command to minimize the damage.

We have covered all the information needed to work with sequential files. It is best to know everything before we begin to actually write useful programs: Now we can work on a project in the next section.

8-3... Using a File: The Geography Game

Remember the program we wrote to play Geography in Chapter 6? We wrote that program using subroutines so that it would be easy to convert to store the names in a disk file. This way, we can arrange to have the computer "remember" place names from one day to another. Let's first write a program to store the four beginning names, Program 8-3.

```
98 REM ** INITIALIZE GEOGRAPHY FILE
100 OPEN 15,8,15
110 F$ = "PLACES,S,W"
120 OPEN 2,8,2,F$ : GOSUB 800
130 READ NO
140 PRINT#2, NO
```

```
150 FOR I9 = 1 TO N0
160 READ P$ : PRINT#2, P$
170 NEXT I9
180 GOSUB 800
190 CLOSE 2 : CLOSE 15
190 GOSUB 800
290 END
796 :
798 REM ** READ ERROR CHANNEL
800 INPUT# 15, E,E$,T,S
810 IF E < 20 THEN 890
820 PRINT E$
830 STOP
890 RETURN
896 :
898 REM ** A FEW CITIES
900 DATA 4
902 DATA NEW YORK
904 DATA CHICAGO
906 DATA LOS ANGELES
908 DATA PHILADELPHIA
```

Program 8-3. Writing initial names to a file for Geography game.

When we run this program, we will have a file containing five items. The first item will be a 4 and the next four items will be four city names. If we try to run it a second time, it will fail with the error message

FILE EXISTS

That prevents us from accidentally reinitializing the names file after we have built it up to a hundred or so names. A good idea.

It is important to note that the number we wrote to the file will be converted to the characters of the number, just like STR$. Thus, if N0 = 25, then there will be a space, a 2, and a 5 in the file. However, we may retrieve the value with INPUT# X, N0, just the same. Or in some special situation we might want to retrieve that number in a string variable. INPUT# behaves the same way that it does at the keyboard. Any leading spaces will be ignored. So, "25" in the file will appear in the resulting string as "25".

As the value representing the number of names increases from one to two digits, the space required to store it in the file goes from three characters to four. So when we rewrite the entire file, each of the place names will be located one character position further along in the file. We can program solutions to many problems without even realizing this. As we seek more elegant solutions, however, information of this kind will be important to have.

Let's now convert the Geography game from Chapter 6 to store names in a file. We simply need to replace the READ...DATA concept with a subroutine that reads the place names from the file into the array. We also need to provide a subroutine that writes out all of the names to the file at the end of a series of games.

The array version reads the names from DATA in a subroutine at line 8000. So we may simply replace that subroutine with a new one that reads the names from a file. Of course, we will still need the error reading subroutine of Program 8-1. That means that we should note that the control routine needs to OPEN the command channel on file 15. See Program 8-4a.

```
7996 :
7998 REM ** READ NAMES FILE
8000 OPEN 2,8,2, F$ + ",S,R" : GOSUB 800
8010 INPUT# 2, NO
8030 FOR I9 = 1 TO NO
8040 INPUT# 2, NA$(I9)
8050 NEXT I9
8060 CLOSE 2
8090 RETURN
```

Program 8-4a. File reading subroutine for Geography game.

We have checked the error channel just once in this subroutine. In a crucial file process, we might be more cautious and check it in lines 8010 and 8040 as well. On the other hand, writing the number of items at the beginning of the file helps to limit the possibilities for error here.

At the end of a series of games in this file version, we want to write all the names to the sequential file. Since there was nothing special to do at the end of the array version, our new routine to write the names to the file at the end will be a new subroutine rather than a replacement. Let's put it at 8500. Then the two files subroutines will be near each other in the final program. It is a good idea to isolate the files handling portion of any program when that is a practical thing to do. See Program 8-4b.

```
      8496 :
      8498 REM ** UPDATE NAMES FILE
-->8500 OPEN 2,8,2,"@:" + F$ + ",S,W" : GOSUB 800
      8520 PRINT# 2, NO
      8530 FOR I9 = 1 TO NO
      8535 PRINT# 2, NA$(I9)
      8540 NEXT I9
      8580 CLOSE 2
      8590 RETURN
```

Program 8-4b. Writing names to the file in the Geography game.

Notice in line 8500 that we incorporate the at sign (@) because we are always going to replace the contents of an existing sequential file. In this subroutine we might include a GOSUB 800 in lines 8520 and 8535. This routine writes data to a file. In this situation, the program could run out of disk space. So, that might be a good idea.

We can easily incorporate these two subroutines into the array Geography program. In addition, we need to be sure to include the subroutine of Program 8-1. Next, we must assign the file name in F$ and modify the end-of-game logic to execute the subroutine at 8500 if the game just ended will be the last. And we need to make sure the error channel is opened on file 15. All of this is accomplished by the six lines of Program 8-4c.

```
   10 F$ = "PLACES"
   15 OPEN 15,8,15
   90 IF LEFT$(A$,1) = "N" THEN 140
  140 GOSUB 8500 : REM ** REWRITE THE NAMES FILE
  150 CLOSE 15
  190 END
```

Program 8-4c. Changes in the control routine to convert array Geography to file Geography.

It might be a good idea to include a GOSUB 800 just before line 150 in Program 8-4c as a catch-all error checker. We present the complete program here for your convenience as Program 8-5.

```
-->10 F$ = "PLACES"
-->15 OPEN 15,8,15
   20 DIM NA$(500), AV(500)
   30 GOSUB 8000 : REM ** READ NAMES ARRAY
   35 GOSUB 9000 : REM ** INSTRUCTIONS
   40 GOSUB 4000 : REM ** INITIALIZE AVAILABLE NAMES ARRAY
   45 GOSUB 7000 : REM ** COMPUTER STARTS
   50 GOSUB 6000 : REM ** PERSON RESPONDS
   58 IF PE$ = "QUIT" THEN 80
   60 GOSUB 5000 : REM ** RESPONSE OF COMPUTER
   65 IF CP$ <> "QUIT" THEN 50
   80 INPUT "DO YOU WANT ANOTHER GAME"; A$
-->90 IF LEFT$(A$,1) = "N" THEN 140
  100 FOR I9 = 1 TO 1000 : NEXT I9
  120 GOTO 35
-->140 GOSUB 8500 : REM ** REWRITE THE NAMES FILE
-->150 CLOSE 15
-->190 END
-->796 :
-->798 REM ** READ ERROR CHANNEL
-->800 INPUT# 15, E,E$,T,S
-->810 IF E < 20 THEN 890
-->820 PRINT E$
-->830 STOP
-->890 RETURN
  3996 :
  3998 REM ** INITIALIZE AVAILABLE NAMES ARRAY
  4000 FOR J9 = 1 TO NO
  4010 AV(J9) = 1
  4020 NEXT J9
  4090 RETURN
  4996 :
  4998 REM ** COMPUTER RESPOND
  5000 FOR I9 = 1 TO NO
  5010 IF LEFT$(NA$(I9),1) = RIGHT$(PE$,1) AND AV(I9) = 1 THEN 5050
  5015 NEXT I9
  5020 PRINT : PRINT " I HAVE RUN OUT OF NAMES"
  5025 CP$ = "QUIT"
  5030 GOTO 5090
  5050 CP$ = NA$(I9) : AV(I9) = 0
  5060 PRINT "    I CHOOSE: "; CP$
  5090 RETURN
```

```
 5996 :
 5998 REM ** PERSON GO
 6000 PRINT
 6010 INPUT "   YOUR TURN"; PE$
 6012 IF PE$ = "QUIT" THEN 6190
 6015 IF LEN (PE$) > 1 THEN 6030
 6020 PRINT "NAME TOO SHORT" : GOTO 6010
 6030 IF LEFT$(PE$,1) = RIGHT$(CP$,1) THEN 6040
 6035 PRINT "NO MATCH" : GOTO 6010
 6040 FOR I9 = 1 TO NO
 6045 IF PE$ = NA$(I9) THEN 6100
 6050 NEXT I9
 6055 IF NO < 500 THEN  6065
 6060 PRINT "NO ROOM FOR MORE NAMES" : GOTO 6010
 6065 NO = NO + 1
 6070 NA$(NO) = PE$ : AV(NO) = 0
 6080 GOTO 6190
 6096 :
 6098 REM ** "FOUND NAME"
 6100 IF AV(I9) = 1 THEN 6150
 6110 PRINT "USED ALREADY" : GOTO 6010
 6150 AV(I9) = 0
 6190 RETURN
 6996 :
 6998 REM ** COMPUTER BEGIN THE GAME
 7000 X9 = INT( RND(1) * NO + 1)
 7010 CP$ = NA$(X9) : AV(X9) = 0
 7020 PRINT "FIRST PLACE : "; CP$
 7090 RETURN
-->7996 :
-->7998 REM ** READ NAMES FILE
-->8000 OPEN 2,8,2, F$ + ",S,R" : GOSUB 800
-->8010 INPUT# 2, NO
-->8030 FOR I9 = 1 TO NO
-->8040 INPUT# 2, NA$(I9)
-->8050 NEXT I9
-->8060 CLOSE 2
-->8090 RETURN
-->8496 :
-->8498 REM ** UPDATE NAMES FILE
-->8500 OPEN 2,8,2,"@:" + F$ + ",S,W" : GOSUB 800
-->8520 PRINT# 2, NO
-->8530 FOR I9 = 1 TO NO
-->8535 PRINT# 2, NA$(I9)
-->8540 NEXT I9
-->8580 CLOSE 2
-->8590 RETURN
 8996 :
 8998 REM ** INSTRUCTIONS
 9000 PRINT CHR$(147); : REM ** CLEAR THE SCREEN
 9005 PRINT "THIS PROGRAM WILL PLAY A GEOGRAPHY GAME" : PRINT
 9010 PRINT "WITH YOU.  YOU WILL TAKE TURNS WITH THE" : PRINT
 9015 PRINT "COMPUTER.  EACH OF YOU WILL BE TRYING TO"; : PRINT
 9020 PRINT "THINK OF NAMES OF PLACES SUCH THAT THE" : PRINT
 9025 PRINT "FIRST LETTER OF YOUR NAME IS THE SAME AS"; : PRINT
 9030 PRINT "THE LAST LETTER OF THE PREVIOUSLY USED" : PRINT
```

```
9035 PRINT "PLACE NAME." : PRINT
9045 INPUT "ARE YOU READY? "; A$
9065 IF LEFT$(A$,1) <> "Y" THEN 9045
9070 FOR I9 = 1 TO 1000 : NEXT I9
9080 PRINT CHR$(147); : REM ** CLEAR THE SCREEN
9090 RETURN
```

Program 8-5. File-oriented Geography game.

Once again we have reaped tremendous benefits from good program organization and extensive use of subroutines. By segmenting the array Geography program we made it a relatively simple exercise to convert to operate with a data file. We replaced one subroutine, added two subroutines, and made minor changes in the control routine. By making minor changes in a well-structured program we have made major changes in that program's behavior. It is important to realize that we have isolated all possible sources of error to small areas of the resulting program. If the first program had been badly put together, we would have found ourselves tinkering in numerous places to create the new program. The tinkered program would have contained many more potential sources of error.

Problems for Section 8-3 . . . .

1. Write a program that will list the place names in the Geography game file.

2. Try as people will, somebody will misspell a name in a game of Geography. Write a program that enables us to edit place names.

3. Write a program that will enable you to eliminate a place name from the Geography names file.

4. The Geography game logic for the computer response scans the names array from the first item every time. Modify the game so that the scan begins at some random point. Don't forget to come around to the beginning of the list after checking the last name.

5. The scan for the computer's turn in Geography covers the entire names array. That unnecessarily includes the names that have been added during the current game. Modify the program so that the scan for the computer's turn covers only those place names that came from the names file at the beginning of the current game.

8-4 . . . Miscellaneous Information

Let's explore sequential files behavior in a little more detail. It is important to be familiar with the use of commas and carriage returns in sequential files. Generally, the carriage-return character is used to separate data items in sequential files. This character is automatically sent to the file by a PRINT statement with no trailing semicolon or comma.

. . . Comma Separators

Commas also act as a kind of separator. Consider Program 8-6.

```
100 OPEN 2,8,2,"TEST,S,W"
140 PRINT#2, "THIS, AFTER ALL, IS THE MAIN POINT."
150 CLOSE 2
```

Program 8-6. Demonstration of commas in a PRINT# statement.

Some special things happen when a comma is used (or we wouldn't be discussing it). The comma in the quoted string will be written into the file. If we try to read this with an INPUT statement each comma will be interpreted as the end of a data item. We cannot read those data with three separate INPUT# statements. INPUT# statements used to read data from a file behave in the same manner as they behave reading data from the keyboard. We will need three string variables in a single INPUT# statement to read the file. See Program 8-7.

```
100 OPEN 2,8,2,"TEST,S,R"
110 INPUT#2, A$, B$, C$
120 CLOSE 2
130 PRINT A$
140 PRINT B$
150 PRINT C$
```

Program 8-7. Demonstration of multiple INPUT# from a file.

```
RUN
THIS
AFTER ALL
IS THE MAIN POINT
```

Figure 8-2. Execution of Program 8-7.

Contrast this with what happens when we use the following statement to write to a sequential file:

```
100 OPEN 2,8,2,"TEST,S,R"
130 A$ = "ONE" : B$ = "TWO"
140 PRINT#2, A$, B$
160 CLOSE 2
```

Program 8-8. Demonstration of comma in PRINT# A$, B$.

Just as the comma separating A$ and B$ would cause spaces to be inserted in the display for a PRINT statement, they will be inserted in the file. Program 8-9 demonstrates the result.

```
100 OPEN 2,8,2,"TEST,S,R"
140 INPUT#2, A$
150 CLOSE 2
190 PRINT A$
```

Program 8-9. Reading file data written by Program 8-8.

```
RUN
ONE            TWO
```

Figure 8-3. Execution of Program 8-9.

As you can see, A$ reads in the entire string "ONE   TWO." It should be clear that

137

the reading of data from a sequential file must be carefully coordinated with the writing, and vice versa. For many purposes, it is best to use PRINT# statements to enter data items into the file one at a time. Let DOS provide the carriage return.

...Updating a Sequential File

In the Geography game program, we updated the sequential file by reading the whole file into an array in memory at once. Then we simply recreated the entire file at the end of a game. For very large files that is not possible because the data will not fit in memory at once. Here is another way.

OPEN a second file in write mode. INPUT# each item from the first file and immediately PRINT# it to the second file. Develop the necessary logic to make the necessary changes on the way. Once the updated information is in the new file, scratch the old file and rename the new one. We are relying here on knowing how many items are in the file. We could save an item count as the first item in the file, as we did in the Geography game, or we could even OPEN another sequential file to hold just that number. The method of using a separate file for the item count is useful for situations when the count is not known until the program has already written the data out to the file. Once we have begun to write a sequential file, it is not possible to back up. Alternatively, it is possible to read the error channel and stop reading when the error number is equal to 50. That error number tells us that we have read the last record of the file. In general, anything we can do in our programs to control the contents of a file is good. It is better to know the number of items than to risk triggering errors in our programs. This method limits us to files half the size of a disk. That ought to allow us to work on some reasonable projects before we buy a second disk drive.

Chapter 9

Bit-Map Graphics: Hi-Res

In Chapter 3 we worked with the display screen, using some of the built-in graphics characters. The screen accommodates 1000 text and/or graphics characters, intermixed as we choose. Sixteen colors are available, individually selectable by character. All of the color character graphics features are accessible by including the appropriate information and symbols in PRINT statements. Alternatively, characters and colors can be controlled individually by using POKE.

Bit-map graphics is a whole new world that offers a bit-map screen grid 320 dots wide by 200 dots high. This means that the screen contains 64,000 individually accessible dots. Sometimes these dots are referred to as *pixels*. The bit-map screen is laid out in a grid similar to the character screen. We may think in terms of an X, Y position on the screen for each dot. Values for X may range from 0 to 319, while Y goes from 0 to 199. The point (0, 0) is in the upper left corner and the point (319, 199) is in the lower right corner. We may create images on this screen in 16 colors.

The bit-map screen occupies a portion of memory in the Commodore 64 containing 8000 bytes. Each byte holds eight bits. Each bit represents a dot on the screen. Therefore we will be creating images on the screen by actually turning bits on and off in memory. We will do this by using the commands PEEK, POKE, AND, and OR.

The 8000 bytes of bit-mapped memory are coordinated with the 1000 bytes of the character screen beginning at memory address 1024. One byte of the character screen is used to control the colors possible in an eight-byte block of the bit-map screen. Bits 4 to 7 are used to set the color of any bit turned on, while bits 0 to 3 are used to set the color of any off bit. In other words, the high nibble is used to set the color of the on bits, and the low nibble is used for the color of the off bits. That provides four bits to determine each color. Four bits are all we need for numbers in the range 0 to 15. A perfect fit!

9-1...Introduction to Bit-Map Graphics

...The Bit-Map Graphics Screen

Bit-map graphics is controlled by directly changing values in memory using the POKE command. Often we desire to change only a single bit in memory without changing the rest of the bits in the same byte. So, once we know the memory address of the byte and the bit position of the bit within the byte, we will use a statement such as:

```
1250 POKE MA, PEEK(MA) OR (2^BP)
```

to turn that bit on. To turn it off we could use

```
POKE MA, PEEK(MA) AND (255 - 2^BP)
```

Refer to Programmer's Corner 7.

The color is determined by setting values in a corresponding location of memory. But we'll get to that. For now, we need to examine the layout of the Hi-Res screen in detail.

The Hi-Res screen is structured just like the character screen. (So we can use the character screen to set colors.) Each character position is coordinated with an eight-byte portion of bit-map memory. Each byte consists of eight bits, so we have the 64000 dots on the screen we need for the 320-by-200 grid. The character position in the upper left corner of the screen is made up of bytes numbered 0 through 7. The character position next to it is made up of bytes 8 through 15. The character position to the extreme right on that line is made up of bytes 312 through 319. The character position in the lower right corner of the screen is made up of bytes 7992 through 7999. This is the way in which the 40-by-25 character screen is related to the 320-by-200 Hi-Res screen. See Figure 9-1. What we need here is a formula that will enable us to begin with an X, Y position on the screen and come up with a byte and bit-within-byte in bit-mapped memory.

Given a Y position in the range 0 to 199, we can determine which of the 25 text character lines it falls within on the character screen by dividing by eight.

```
1200 TL = INT(Y/8)        : REM ** FIND TEXT LINE
```

The eight comes from 200 divided by 25. This gives a value in the range from 0 to 24. Since each text line requires eight bytes, TL * 8 bytes are accounted for and Y − TL * 8 is the one byte within this text line we need. We can arrive at the same value by using the logical AND operator to determine which of the bits 0, 1, and 2 are set. Note that $2^0 + 2^1 + 2^2 = 7$. Thus, Y and 7 yields the same information.

```
1210 BL = Y AND 7         : REM ** FIND BYTE WITHIN TEXT LINE
```

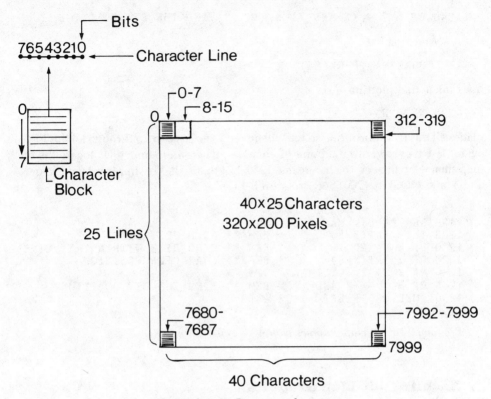

Figure 9-1. Hi-Res screen layout.

Similarly, we can determine which character position we want on the 40-character text line from the value of X in the range 0 to 319 by

```
1220 CP = INT(X/8)       : REM ** CHARACTER POSITION
```

This eight comes from 320 divided by 40. Now we have the eight-byte block and the byte within that block identified.

All this tells us how far from the beginning of the bit-map screen our byte is. For general purposes we may begin the screen at memory address 8192. That is the 8K boundary and is easily accessible. BASIC programs begin at 2049, which is the 2K boundary. So, this leaves 6K for BASIC programs. Programmer's Corner 9 tells how to provide for larger programs. We assign the actual memory address for plotting a dot with

```
1230 MA = 8192 + TL*320 + CP*8 + BL
```

All that remains is to determine the bit position. We can use AND 7 to examine bits 0, 1, and 2 in the value of X, as we did to find the byte from the value of Y. But the bits within the byte are numbered from right to left, so we need to subtract that bit position from 7.

```
1240 BP = 7 - (X AND 7) : REM ** FIND THE BIT POSITION
```

does it. And finally,

```
1250 POKE MA, PEEK(MA) OR 2^BP
```

does the actual plotting. Adding

```
1290 RETURN
```

places all this in a subroutine so we will never, ever have to go through all this logic again. If we ever get to the point of changing where in memory we locate the bit map then we will need to change line 1230, but that's all. We simply set values for X and Y and GOSUB 1200. See Program 9-1a.

```
1196 :
1198 REM ** BIT MAP PLOTTING
1200 TL = INT(Y/8)        : REM ** FIND TEXT LINE
1210 BL = Y AND 7         : REM ** FIND BYTE WITHIN TEXT LINE
1220 CP = INT(X/8)        : REM ** CHARACTER POSITION
1230 MA = 8192 + TL*320 + CP*8 + BL
1240 BP = 7 - (X AND 7) : REM ** FIND THE BIT POSITION
1250 POKE MA, PEEK(MA) OR 2^BP
1290 RETURN
```

Program 9-1a. Bit-map graphics plotting routine.

...Enabling Bit-Map Graphics

We need to turn bit-map graphics on. This is controlled by a single bit at memory address 53265. Bit 5 on turns bit-map graphics on, bit 5 off turns it off. Memory address 53265 controls other things as well, so we want to change only bit 5.

```
POKE 53265, PEEK(53265) OR 2^5
```

turns bit 5 one, and

```
POKE 53265, PEEK(53265) AND (255-2^5)
```

turns it off.

Bit-map graphic occupies 8000 bytes of memory. Setting bit 3 at 53272 in memory to 1 sets the bit map to begin at 8192.

```
POKE 53272, PEEK(53272) OR 2^3
```

We need to clear out memory beginning at 8192. Otherwise, we will be looking at whatever happens to be in that segment of memory at the time. We clear this out by setting all 8000 memory addresses to 0. In BASIC it takes a few seconds. In general, bit-map graphics is slow in BASIC. But Sprite graphics (see Chapter 10) is quite fast. Many of the fancy graphics games are programmed in machine language. Program 9-1b sets up bit-map mode and clears out the Hi-Res memory.

```
1000 POKE 53265, PEEK(53265) OR 2^5 : REM ** BIT-MAP MODE ON
1010 POKE 53272, PEEK(53272) OR 2^3 : REM ** SET MEMORY
```

```
    1020 FOR I9 = 8192 TO 16191        : REM ** CLEAR MEMORY
-->1030 POKE I9, 0
    1040 NEXT I9
```

Program 9-1b. Setting up the Hi-Res screen.

Notice that in line 1030 we zero out all eight bits of a memory byte with a single POKE. Let's go on.

...Colors on the Hi-Res Screen

We use the 1000 bytes of the character screen beginning at 1024 to set colors in the 8000 byte Hi-Res screen. The byte at 1024 controls bytes 0 to 7, 1025 controls bytes 8 to 15, and so on up to 2023, which controls bytes 7992 to 7999. The byte in the character screen sets the color of both on and off bits within the eight bytes of the Hi-Res screen. The high four bits set the color for on and the low four bits set the color for off. We arrive at the value of the color byte by multiplying the on color value by 16 and adding the off color value. The color values are the same as for the character screen. See Table 9-1.

COLOR	VALUE	COLOR	VALUE
Black	0	Orange	8
White	1	Brown	9
Red	2	Light Red	10
Cyan	3	Gray 1	11
Purple	4	Gray 2	12
Green	5	Light Green	13
Blue	6	Light Blue	14
Yellow	7	Gray 3	15

Table 9-1. The color values.

Thus, a value of 1 establishes white for off and black for on. We would never select the same color for on and off; that would produce a blank screen. Some combinations are better than others. Try to select contrasting colors. It is fairly easy to experiment. Let's look at a few sample values in Figure 9-2.

ON COLOR		OFF COLOR		7654	3210	VALUE	
Black	(0)	White	(1)	0000	0001	1	(0*16 + 1)
White	(1)	Black	(0)	0001	0000	16	(1*16 + 0)
Green	(5)	Gray 3	(15)	0101	1111	96	(5*16 + 15)
Gray 3	(15)	Green	(5)	1111	0101	245	(15*16 + 5)

Figure 9-2. Sample color values for controlling bit-map screen.

Program 9-1c sets the whole screen to white for off and black for on.

```
1050 FOR I9 = 1024 TO 2023        : REM ** SET BIT MAP COLOR
1060 POKE I9, 1
1070 NEXT I9
```

Program 9-1c. Setting bit-map color in character screen area.

143

The best way to handle setting up and clearing the screen is to create a subroutine to use as needed. For this subroutine we should be able to specify the value to be poked into the character screen to set the two colors. Let's use C, as in line 1060 of Program 9-1d.

```
996 :
998 REM ** BIT-MAP SCREEN SETUP
1000 POKE 53265, PEEK(53265) OR 2^5 : REM ** BIT-MAP MODE ON
1010 POKE 53272, PEEK(53272) OR 2^3 : REM ** SET MEMORY
1020 FOR I9 = 8192 TO 16191           : REM ** CLEAR MEMORY
1030 POKE I9, 0
1040 NEXT I9
1050 FOR I9 = 1024 TO 2023            : REM ** SET BIT-MAP COLOR
-->1060 POKE I9, C
1070 NEXT I9
1090 RETURN
```

Program 9-1d. Bit-map screen setup subroutine.

This subroutine allows us to select a color pattern for the whole screen by setting a value for C and using GOSUB 1000. We do not have to think about the detail again.

Similarly, we may create a subroutine to restore the normal character screen. Besides undoing the POKE commands, we should clear the character screen. Remember, we used that area of memory for the colors on the Hi-Res screen. The statement PRINT CHR$(147); clears the screen for us and leaves the cursor in the upper left corner. See Program 9-1e.

```
1096 :
1098 REM ** RESTORE NORMAL CHARACTER SCREEN
1100 POKE 53265, PEEK(53265) AND (255-2^5)
1110 POKE 53272, PEEK(53272) AND (255-2^3)
1120 PRINT CHR$(147);
1190 RETURN
```

Program 9-1e. Restoring the normal character screen.

We have created three subroutines. GOSUB 1000 sets up the Hi-Res screen for us. GOSUB 1200 plots the point (X, Y). GOSUB 1100 restores the normal character screen.

...A Simple Border

Finally, we can begin to draw figures on the screen. Let's first write a routine to display a border around the screen. We need four straight lines. Here is a line on the left edge of the screen:

```
X = 0
FOR Y = 0 TO 199
GOSUB 1200
NEXT Y
```

We might write three similar routines for the other edges, or we might combine them and create a subroutine as follows:

144

```
      196 :
      198 REM ** PLOT A BORDER
      200 FOR Y = 0 TO 199 : REM ** LEFT AND RIGHT
      210 X = 0    : GOSUB 1200
      220 X = 319  : GOSUB 1200
      230 NEXT Y
      250 FOR X = 0 TO 319 : REM ** TOP AND BOTTOM
      260 Y = 0    : GOSUB 1200
      270 Y = 199  : GOSUB 1200
      280 NEXT X
      290 RETURN
```

Program 9-1f. Routine for displaying a border at the edge of the screen.

Program 9-1f displays a border at the very edge of the Hi-Res screen. It is easy to change this routine to display a box anywhere on the screen. This is left as an exercise.

All we need now is a control routine and our first Hi-Res graphics program is complete. See lines 100 to 190 of Program 9-2.

```
      100 C = 1         : REM ** WHITE ON BLACK
      110 GOSUB 1000 : REM ** SET UP
      120 GOSUB 200  : REM ** PLOT A BORDER
-->130 GET A$ : IF LEN(A$) = 0 THEN 130
      140 GOSUB 1100 : REM ** RESTORE CHARACTER SCREEN
      190 END
      196 :
      198 REM ** PLOT A BORDER
      200 FOR Y = 0 TO 199 : REM ** LEFT AND RIGHT
      210 X = 0    : GOSUB 1200
      220 X = 319  : GOSUB 1200
      230 NEXT Y
      250 FOR X = 0 TO 319 : REM ** TOP AND BOTTOM
      260 Y = 0    : GOSUB 1200
      270 Y = 199  : GOSUB 1200
      280 NEXT X
      290 RETURN
      996 :
      998 REM ** BIT-MAP SCREEN SETUP
      1000 POKE 53265, PEEK(53265) OR 2^5 : REM ** BIT-MAP MODE ON
      1010 POKE 53272, PEEK(53272) OR 2^3 : REM ** SET MEMORY
      1020 FOR I9 = 8192 TO 16191         : REM ** CLEAR MEMORY
      1030 POKE I9, 0
      1040 NEXT I9
      1050 FOR I9 = 1024 TO 2023          : REM ** SET BIT-MAP COLOR
      1060 POKE I9, C
      1070 NEXT I9
      1090 RETURN
      1096 :
      1098 REM ** RESTORE NORMAL CHARACTER SCREEN
      1100 POKE 53265, PEEK(53265) AND (255-2^5)
      1110 POKE 53272, PEEK(53272) AND (255-2^3)
      1120 PRINT CHR$(147);
      1190 RETURN
      1196 :
      1198 REM ** BIT MAP PLOTTING
```

145
• • •

```
1200 TL = INT(Y/8)       : REM ** FIND TEXT LINE
1210 BL = Y AND 7        : REM ** FIND BYTE WITHIN TEXT LINE
1220 CP = INT(X/8)       : REM ** CHARACTER POSITION
1230 MA = 8192 + TL*320 + CP*8 + BL
1240 BP = 7 - (X AND 7) : REM ** FIND THE BIT POSITION
1250 POKE MA, PEEK(MA) OR 2^BP
1290 RETURN
```

Program 9-2. Plotting a black border on a white screen.

Look at line 150. We simply freeze the drawing on the screen until someone hits any key at all.

...Point-to-Point Plotting

Program 9-2 shows how to plot horizontal and vertical lines. That is fine, but what about lines on a diagonal? Let's develop a routine for plotting a line between any two given end points. The two end points may be expressed as (X1, Y1) and (X2, Y2). Using the equation

$$y = mx + b$$

for each point, we may solve simultaneous equations to obtain values for m and b. We get

$$m = (Y2 - Y1)/(X2 - X1) \quad \text{and} \quad b = Y1 - mX1$$

The result is that for a given value of X, the corresponding value of Y is given by

$$Y = Y1 + m(X - X1)$$

Putting this all together yields the routine of Program 9-3a.

```
400 M = (Y2-Y1)/(X2-X1)
410 FOR X = X1 TO X2 STEP SGN(X2-X1)
420 Y = Y1 + M*(X-X1)
430 GOSUB 1200 : REM ** PLOT ROUTINE
440 NEXT X
490 RETURN
```

Program 9-3a. Plotting a line from (X1, Y1) to (X2, Y2).

This program works well (slowly, to be sure) for most lines. But suppose we feed this subroutine two points such as (20, 2) and (20, 191). Line 400, where we divide by (X2 − X1), causes an error because we are trying to divide by zero. We need another routine that avoids dividing by 0. We need another routine that avoids dividing by (X2 − X1). Further, suppose we feed this subroutine two points such as (10, 2) and (11, 190). We get only two plotted dots on the screen. Both flaws can be solved by writing a second subroutine that scans Y and solves for X. Program 9-3b does this.

```
500 M = (X2-X1)/(Y2-Y1)
510 FOR Y = Y1 TO Y2 STEP SGN(Y2-Y1)
520 X = X1 + M*(Y-Y1)
530 GOSUB 1200 : REM ** PLOT ROUTINE
540 NEXT Y
590 RETURN
```

Program 9-3b. Plotting a line from two points for (X2 − X1) = 0.

Notice that Program 9-3a cannot plot vertical lines and Program 9-3b cannot plot horizontal lines. If we simply select Program 9-3a (GOSUB 400) when (Y2 − Y1) is greater than (X2 − X1) and Program 9-2b (GOSUB 500) otherwise, we will get a reasonable number of dots on the screen. When (Y2 − Y1) = (X2 − X1) it doesn't matter which we select. Now we have the pieces of a program to plot any straight line in a fixed color. We can easily prepare DATA statements to draw any figures we care to design. Program 9-3c does the job of reading data and controlling which plotting routine to use.

```
296 :
298 REM ** READ DATA AND PLOT THE LINE
300 READ X1,Y1,X2,Y2
310 IF X1 = -1 THEN 390
320 IF ABS(X2-X1) >  ABS(Y2-Y1) THEN GOSUB 400
330 IF ABS(X2-X1) <= ABS(Y2-Y1) THEN GOSUB 500
340 GOTO 300
390 RETURN
```

Program 9-3c. Reading plotting data and controlling plotting.

The control routine is the shortest of all. We need to set up the bit-map screen, do the plotting from data, provide a delay, and restore the screen to normal. Just like Program 9-1. See Program 9-3d.

```
90 REM ** CONTROL GRAPHING FROM DATA
100 C = 1
110 GOSUB 1000 : REM ** BIT-MAP SETUP
120 GOSUB 300  : REM ** PLOT FROM DATA
140 GET A$ : IF LEN(A$) = 0 THEN 140
150 GOSUB 1100 : REM ** TURN OFF BIT-MAP MODE
190 END
```

Program 9-3d. Control routine for graphing from data.

Now we have a complete program in Program 9-4.

```
90 REM ** CONTROL GRAPHING FROM DATA
100 C = 1
110 GOSUB 1000 : REM ** BIT-MAP SETUP
120 GOSUB 300  : REM ** PLOT FROM DATA
140 GET A$ : IF LEN(A$) = 0 THEN 140
150 GOSUB 1100 : REM ** TURN OFF BIT-MAP MODE
190 END
296 :
298 REM ** READ DATA AND PLOT THE LINE
300 READ X1,Y1,X2,Y2
310 IF X1 = -1 THEN 390
320 IF ABS(X2-X1) >  ABS(Y2-Y1) THEN GOSUB 400
330 IF ABS(X2-X1) <= ABS(Y2-Y1) THEN GOSUB 500
340 GOTO 300
390 RETURN
396 :
398 REM ** DRAW A NON-VERTICAL LINE
400 M = (Y2-Y1)/(X2-X1)
410 FOR X = X1 TO X2 STEP SGN(X2-X1)
420 Y = Y1 + M*(X-X1)
```

147

```
430 GOSUB 1200 : REM ** PLOT ROUTINE
440 NEXT X
490 RETURN
496 :
498 REM ** DRAW A NON-HORIZONTAL LINE
500 M = (X2-X1)/(Y2-Y1)
510 FOR Y = Y1 TO Y2 STEP SGN(Y2-Y1)
520 X = X1 + M*(Y-Y1)
530 GOSUB 1200 : REM ** PLOT ROUTINE
540 NEXT Y
590 RETURN
996 :
998 REM ** BIT-MAP SCREEN SETUP
1000 POKE 53265, PEEK(53265) OR 2^5 : REM ** BIT-MAP MODE ON
1010 POKE 53272, PEEK(53272) OR 2^3 : REM ** SET MEMORY
1020 FOR I9 = 8192 TO 16191         : REM ** CLEAR MEMORY
1030 POKE I9, 0
1040 NEXT I9
1050 FOR I9 = 1024 TO 2023          : REM ** SET BIT-MAP COLOR
1060 POKE I9, C
1070 NEXT I9
1090 RETURN
1096 :
1098 REM ** RESTORE NORMAL CHARACTER SCREEN
1100 POKE 53265, PEEK(53265) AND (255-2^5)
1110 POKE 53272, PEEK(53272) AND (255-2^3)
1120 PRINT CHR$(147);
1190 RETURN
1196 :
1198 REM ** BIT MAP PLOTTING
1200 TL = INT(Y/8)      : REM ** FIND TEXT LINE
1210 BL = Y AND 7       : REM ** FIND BYTE WITHIN TEXT LINE
1220 CP = INT(X/8)      : REM ** CHARACTER POSITION
1230 MA = 8192 + TL*320 + CP*8 + BL
1240 BP = 7 - (X AND 7) : REM ** FIND THE BIT POSITION
1250 POKE MA, PEEK(MA) OR 2^BP
1290 RETURN
```

Program 9-4. Drawing a figure by using line data.

We could even use this routine to plot a border. The data for the four lines would look like:

```
9000 DATA   0,  0,319,  0
9005 DATA 319,  0,319,199
9010 DATA 319,199,  0,199
9015 DATA   0,199,  0,  0
9900 DATA -1,0,0,0
```

...SUMMARY

An 8000-byte segment of the Commodore 64 memory, beginning at 8192, may be used for direct high-resolution graphics. Each bit of every byte represents a dot on the screen, making available a grid 320 dots wide and 200 dots high. The color is controlled in eight-byte blocks by each byte of the regular character display screen. Bits 4 to 7 set the color of an on bit and bits 0 to 3 set the color of an off bit in the Hi-

Res screen. The Hi-Res screen is enabled by setting bit 5 of memory location 53256 and bit 3 of memory location 53272 both on. Turning them both off and clearing the character screen with CHR$(147) restores things to normal. We have developed subroutines to make the job easier. Program 9-1d sets up and clears the Hi-Res screen. Program 9-1a plots a dot at the point (X, Y). Program 9-3c reads data for the end points of a line and controls drawing the line. Program 9-1e restores the conventional character screen.

Problems for Section 9-1 ....

1. Modify the border-plotting subroutine of Program 9-2 so that it may also be used to plot a border at any distance from the edge of the screen by setting the value of a variable DI before calling it.
2. Modify the border-plotting subroutine of Program 9-2 so that it will draw a box anywhere on the screen, given the (X, Y) coordinates of the four corners.
3. Supply data for Program 9-4 to draw a box using the midpoints of the four edges of the screen as the four corners.
4. Supply data for Program 9-2 to draw a tic-tac-toe board.

9-2...A Graphics Example: A Lighthouse

Just for fun, let's draw a lighthouse. We should do the drawing on graph paper so that we can easily read the X, Y coordinates for each end of each straight line in the drawing. See Figure 9-3.

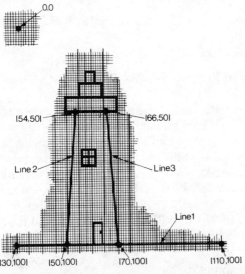

Figure 9-3. Drawing of a lighthouse on graph paper.

149
· · ·

The first three lines are numbered as examples in Figure 9-3. Line 1 is represented by DATA 30, 100, 110, 100. Line 2 is represented by DATA 50, 100, 54, 50. And line 3 is represented by DATA 70, 100, 66, 50. In a similar fashion we obtain the rest of the DATA statements shown in Program 9-5a. When we have so much data in a program like this, it is a good idea to insert REM statements to separate it into sensible groups.

```
996 :
998 REM  * THE TOWER
9000 DATA  30,100,110,100
9005 DATA  50,100, 54, 50
9010 DATA  70,100, 66, 50
9018 REM ** TOP OF TOWER
9020 DATA  50, 50, 70, 50
9025 DATA  50, 50, 50, 45
9030 DATA  70, 50, 70, 45
9035 DATA  50, 45, 70, 45
9040 DATA  55, 45, 56, 40
9045 DATA  65, 45, 64, 40
9050 DATA  56, 40, 64, 40
9055 DATA  58, 40, 58, 35
9060 DATA  62, 40, 62, 35
9065 DATA  58, 35, 62, 35
9078 REM ** THE DOOR
9080 DATA  60,100, 60, 92
9085 DATA  60, 92, 64, 92
9090 DATA  64, 92, 64,100
9095 DATA  63, 96, 63, 96
9118 REM ** THE WINDOW
9120 DATA  56, 70, 62, 70
9125 DATA  56, 67, 62, 67
9130 DATA  56, 64, 62, 64
9135 DATA  56, 70, 56, 64
9140 DATA  59, 70, 59, 64
9145 DATA  62, 70, 62, 64
9900 DATA  -1,  0,  0,  0
```

Program 9-5a. Data for drawing a lighthouse.

All we have to do is supply the data of Program 9-5a for Program 9-4 to draw our lighthouse.

As long as we have gone this far with the lighthouse, what with a door and a window, we really ought to have a blinking light, don't you think? One of the nice things about working with subroutines is that we can easily add new elements to our programs. We can go into the main routine of Program 9-4 and insert a subroutine call to a light blinking subroutine at line 600. Now, in order for the light to blink on, we can call our subroutine at 1200, but for it to blink off, we need a statement to turn off the bit that GOSUB 1200 turns on. We could write a whole new subroutine, or we could use the fact that the value of MA and BP are all we need, and they are available from when we turned the light on. See Program 9-5b.

```
596 :
598 REM ** BLINKING LIGHTHOUSE LIGHT
600 X = 59 : Y = 37
610 FOR I2 = 1 TO 150
```

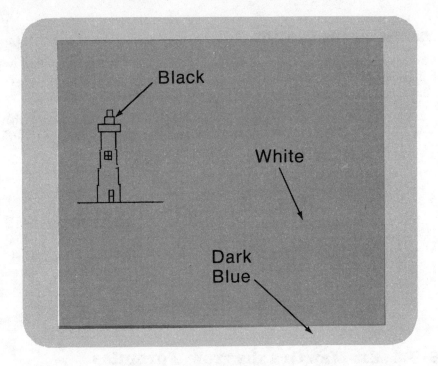

Figure 9-4. Execution of Program 9-4 with data from Program 9-5a.

```
620 GOSUB 1200 : REM ** PLOT
625 FOR I9=1TO600 : NEXT I9 : REM ** DELAY
630 POKE MA, PEEK(MA) AND (225-2^P)
635 FOR I9=1TO200 : NEXT I9 : REM ** DELAY
640 NEXT I2
690 RETURN
```

Program 9-5b. Blinking light for the lighthouse.

This is hard to show with a figure in a book. You will have to type this one in to see it work. Be sure to add a line

```
130 GOSUB 600 : REM ** THE BLINKING LIGHT
```

to Program 9-4 when you do this.

There is always room for improvement. The program we have put together can draw only one lighthouse of one size at one spot on the screen. We might convert the data so that every point is calculated in terms of a single starting point. That way we will be able to move the lighthouse to any point that keeps the entire figure on the screen. Our border drawing subroutine could be used to frame our picture. Or you might prefer to plot the border from data. We could determine the data for many figures and save it in data files on disk. Then we will have a whole library of figures to use for later graphics applications. The possibilities are truly unlimited.

You might want to work with figures on the screen and incorporate more than two colors by including color data with the line data. This will require partitioning your drawings to allow for the fact that only two colors are available in any 8-by-8 bit block.

151

Problems for Section 9-2 . . . .

The possibilities for drawing figures on the screen are literally unlimited. We can only begin to make some suggestions leading you into problems of interest. Let your imagination lead you into exciting graphics demonstrations.

1. Adjust the DATA statements in the lighthouse drawing program so that each set of data is calculated in terms of a fixed starting point. Using (X0, Y0) as (30, 100), the first three DATA lines will be

```
9000 DATA    0,  0, 80,  0
9005 DATA   20,  0, 24,-50
9010 DATA   40,  0, 36,-50
```

   Now the control routine can select a variety of starting points and draw the lighthouse anywhere on the screen with just one plotting subroutine.
2. Supply data to draw a sailboat on the screen by using Program 9-4.
3. Supply data to draw a simple TV set on the screen by using Program 9-4.

9-3 . . . Bit-Map Graphs from Formulas

Figures that can be described by using a formula are easy to graph. We simply use a FOR loop to scan one variable and use the formula to calculate the other. If the formula is given in terms of X and Y then we have our points to plot (provided we are not attempting to plot a vertical line). If not, then we convert to X and Y. There are many many examples from mathematics.

. . . Cartesian Coordinates

Let's develop a method for adjusting X and Y values in the conventional Cartesian coordinate system for plotting on the Commodore 64 screen. We would like to move the (0, 0) point nearer the center of the screen and alter the orientation for Y values so that they increase upwards instead of down. Given the 320-by-200 Commodore 64 bit-map screen, the point (160, 100) is as close to the center as we can get. So, that corresponds to the point (0, 0) in a Cartesian system. The X conversion is easy: we simply want to move each plotted point to the right on the screen. The Y conversion requires that we turn the graph "upside down." So the point:

   (X1, Y1)

in the conventional Cartesian coordinate system becomes

   $(160 + X1, 100 - Y1)$

on the Commodore 64 screen.

   Plotting points that fit a formula is straightforward enough. We replace the subroutine that reads data with one that determines values of X and Y by using the formula. For our first graphs we might use only functions. This is a good application for a DEFined function. Our subroutine will scan all possible values for X and determine if the Y value is on the screen. With $(0, 0)$ at $(160, 100)$ on the Commodore 64 screen, the value of X will range from -160 to 159. We must assure that the Y value is restricted in the range from -100 to 99. If Y is in range, then the routine should do the plotting. If not, then the routine should simply try the next X value. Parabolas are nice, so let's draw a graph of

$$y = 0.1x^2 - 3x - 57$$

It would also be nice to have the axes displayed. Since we are not going to use the logic of the point-to-point graphing we did earlier, we will use a separate plotting routine for this. See Program 9-6.

```
100 C = 1
110 GOSUB 1000 : REM ** BIT MAP SETUP
120 GOSUB 200  : REM ** PLOT AXES
120 GOSUB 300  : REM ** PLOT A FUNCTION
130 GET A$ : IF LEN(A$) = 0 THEN 130
140 GOSUB 1100 : REM ** RESTORE CHARACTER SCREEN
190 END
196 :
198 REM ** PLOT AXES
200 Y = 100
210 FOR X = 0 TO 319 : GOSUB 1200 : NEXT X
220 X = 160
230 FOR Y = 0 TO 199 : GOSUB 1200 : NEXT Y
290 RETURN
296 :
298 REM ** DEFINE THE FUNCTION
300 DEF FNA(X) = .1*X^2 - 3*X - 57
310 GOSUB 600  : REM ** DO THE PLOT
390 RETURN
596 :
598 REM ** SCAN THE SCREEN FOR FNA(X)
600 FOR X1 = -160 TO 159
610 Y1 = FNA(X1)
620 X = 160 + X1 : Y = 100 - Y1
630 IF Y < 0 OR Y > 199 THEN 650
640 GOSUB 1200
650 NEXT X1
690 RETURN
996 :
998 REM ** BIT-MAP SCREEN SETUP
1000 POKE 53265, PEEK(53265) OR 2^5 : REM ** BIT-MAP MODE ON
1010 POKE 53272, PEEK(53272) OR 2^3 : REM ** SET MEMORY
1020 FOR I9 = 8192 TO 16191         : REM ** CLEAR MEMORY
1030 POKE I9, 0
1040 NEXT I9
1050 FOR I9 = 1024 TO 2023          : REM ** SET BIT MAP COLOR
1060 POKE I9, C
1070 NEXT I9
1090 RETURN
```

```
1196 :
1198 REM ** BIT MAP PLOTTING
1200 TL = INT(Y/8)        : REM ** FIND TEXT LINE
1210 BL = Y AND 7         : REM ** FINE BYTE WITHIN TEXT LINE
1220 CP = INT(X/8)        : REM ** CHARACTER POSITION
1230 MA = 8192 + TL*320 + CP*8 + BL
1240 BP = 7 - (X AND 7) : REM ** FIND THE BIT POSITION
1250 POKE MA, PEEK(MA) OR 2^BP
1290 RETURN
```

Program 9-6. Plotting a function in bit map.

We could easily change this program to place the axes anywhere on the screen.

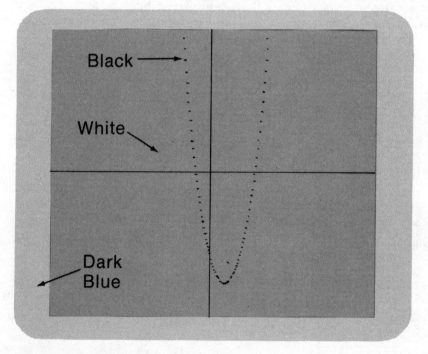

Black

White

Dark
Blue

Figure 9-5. Execution of Program 9-6.

...Polar Graphs

Polar equations often produce interesting graphs. One of the reasons we don't draw many polar graphs is that they take too much tedious calculation involving trigonometric functions. We can easily produce the graphs without the tedium by using computer graphics and letting BASIC perform the calculations. While the slow plotting of BASIC may be disappointing for many purposes, the effect is very well suited to polar graphing. We can see the sequence in which points are drawn.

We may use

$$R = 1 - 2 \cos (G)$$

as a sample equation. Using sines and cosines we obtain the X and Y coordinates as follows:

$$X = R \cos (G) \qquad \text{and} \qquad Y = R \sin (G)$$

where G is the central angle in radians. To obtain a full graph the central angle must sweep through a full 360 degrees or 2π. That is about 6.29. We can get about 60 points by using STEP .1 in a FOR...NEXT loop. Since the point (0, 0) is in the corner of the Commodore 64 Hi-Res screen we need to adjust the starting point, just as we did with the parabola. All points (X1, Y1) will become $(160 + X1, 100 - Y1)$ on the screen.

It would be nice to display a polar axis right on the screen with the graph. We can easily plot a line beginning at the point (0,0) and extending to the right edge of the Commodore screen. Placing the polar axis on the screen will clearly locate the graph for us.

Once we have a working program, it will be a simple matter to plug in other equations. In this way we can look at dozens of graphs in the time it would take to draw a single graph by hand. It is interesting to watch the figures as they are formed on the screen. Drawing a polar graph by hand, like typing a 100-page paper on a portable typewriter, is one of those things everybody ought to do once in a lifetime.

Our program divides nicely into three packages: the control routine, the polar axis plotting routine, and the graph plotting routine. Let's work on them in that order.

In the control routine we establish the Hi-Res screen in the usual manner, by setting a value of C and calling the subroutine with GOSUB 1000. Next, we define the X and Y axes and call a polar axis plotting subroutine. Polar graphs plotted true size are usually very small. So we should provide a scaling factor to produce a larger graph. We define the radial scale in RS. In the actual plotting subroutine we will be arranging for the central angle to range through a full rotation of 2π. But we might like to control the step size in the control routine. Thus we set the value of SP here. Finally, we call the plotting subroutine. When it is all over, we freeze the Hi-Res screen. Any input from the keyboard allows the program to restore the normal character screen. And that's all there is to it. See Program 9-7a.

```
100 C = 6 : GOSUB 1000    : REM ** PREPARE HI-RES SCREEN
110 YO = 100 : XO = 160 : REM ** PLACE THE POINT (0,0)
120 GOSUB 300             : REM ** PLOT A POLAR AXIS
130 RS = 25 : ST = .1     : REM ** SET SCALE AND STEP
140 GOSUB 200             : REM ** PLOT THE GRAPH
150 GET A$ : IF LEN(A$) = 0 THEN 150
160 GOSUB 1100 : REM ** RESTORE CHARACTER SCREEN
190 END
```

Program 9-7a. Control routine for polar graphing.

The easy section is the polar axis plotting routine. All we do is draw a line from the point (X0, Y0) to the right edge of the screen, as in Program 9-7b.

```
396 :
398 REM   * PLOT POLAR AXIS
400 Y = YO
410 FOR X = XO TO 319
420 GOSUB 1200 : REM ** PLOT A POINT
```

```
430 NEXT X
490 RETURN
```

Program 9-7b. Drawing a polar axis.

Now let's look at the actual plotting subroutine. We need to provide for the angle to sweep a full rotation. This is done with a FOR...NEXT loop ranging from 0 to 6.29. The number of points we want plotted may well depend on the size of the graph. We may want more points for larger graphs. That is why we let the calling routine establish the step size SP. A large step size will not give enough points of the graph, while too small a step size will take too long to plot. We can then experiment with each new equation until we obtain a satisfactory graph. See Program 9-7c.

```
     196 :
     198 REM ** PLOT POLAR GRAPH
     200 FOR G = 0 TO 6.29 STEP ST
-->210 R1 = 1 - 2 * COS(G)
-->220 R9 = RS * R1
     230 X1 = R9 * COS(G) : Y1 = R9 * SIN(G)
-->240 X=X0 + X1 : Y=Y0 - Y1 : GOSUB 1200
     250 NEXT G
     290 RETURN
```

Program 9-7c. Polar graph plotting subroutine.

In Program 9-7c, the polar equation is defined in line 210, the scaling factor is implemented in line 220, and the Cartesian X and Y values are calculated in line 240. It will be a simple matter to change the polar equation by changing line 210. We must be aware that other polar equations may contain points that are off the screen. We can test for out-of-range values and skip the plotting for those points. Further, we must be alert for equations that may cause BASIC to attempt to divide by zero.

Program 9-8 consists of five subroutines and one control routine.

```
     100 C = 6 : GOSUB 1000     : REM ** PREPARE HI-RES SCREEN
     110 Y0 = 100 : X0 = 160    : REM ** PLACE THE POINT (0,0)
     120 GOSUB 300              : REM ** PLOT A POLAR AXIS
     130 RS = 25 : ST = .1      : REM ** SET SCALE AND STEP
     140 GOSUB 200              : REM ** PLOT THE GRAPH
     150 GET A$ : IF LEN(A$) = 0 THEN 150
     160 GOSUB 1100             : REM ** RESTORE CHARACTER SCREEN
     190 END
     196 :
     198 REM ** PLOT POLAR GRAPH
     200 FOR G = 0 TO 6.29 STEP ST
-->210 R1 = 1 - 2 * COS(G)
-->220 R9 = RS * R1
     230 X1 = R9 * COS(G) : Y1 = R9 * SIN(G)
-->240 X=X0 + X1 : Y=Y0 - Y1 : GOSUB 1200
     250 NEXT G
     290 RETURN
     396 :
     398 REM  * PLOT POLAR AXIS
     400 Y = Y0
     410 FOR X = X0 TO 319
     420 GOSUB 1200 : REM ** PLOT A POINT
     430 NEXT X
```

```
    490 RETURN
    996 :
    998 REM ** BIT-MAP SCREEN SETUP
   1000 POKE 53265, PEEK(53265) OR 2^5 : REM ** BIT-MAP MODE ON
   1010 POKE 53272, PEEK(53272) OR 2^3 : REM ** SET MEMORY
   1020 FOR I9 = 8192 TO 16191          : REM ** CLEAR MEMORY
   1030 POKE I9, 0
   1040 NEXT I9
   1050 FOR I9 = 1024 TO 2023           : REM ** SET BIT-MAP COLOR
-->1060 POKE I9, C
   1070 NEXT I9
   1090 RETURN
   1096 :
   1098 REM ** RESTORE NORMAL CHARACTER SCREEN
   1100 POKE 53265, PEEK(53265) AND (255-2^5)
   1110 POKE 53272, PEEK(53272) AND (255-2^3)
   1120 PRINT CHR$(147);
   1190 RETURN
   1196 :
   1198 REM ** BIT MAP PLOTTING
   1200 TL = INT(Y/8)        : REM ** FIND TEXT LINE
   1210 BL = Y AND 7         : REM ** FIND BYTE WITHIN TEXT LINE
   1220 CP = INT(X/8)        : REM ** CHARACTER POSITION
   1230 MA = 8192 + TL*320 + CP*8 + BL
   1240 BP = 7 - (X AND 7) : REM ** FIND THE BIT POSITION
   1250 POKE MA, PEEK(MA) OR 2^BP
   1290 RETURN
```

Program 9-8. Complete polar graphing program.

See Figure 9-6 for a trial run.

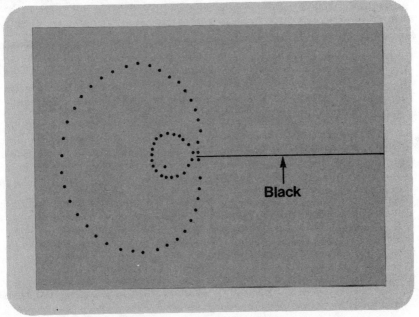

Figure 9-6. Execution of Program 9-8.

Problems for Section 9-3 . . . .

1. Write a program to plot a circle with our polar equation plotting program, using the polar equation

$$R = 1$$

2. There are lots of interesting polar graphs. Graph any of the following:

a. $R = 1 + 2 \cos (G) - 3 \sin (G)^2$
b. $R = 3 + \sin (3G)$
c. $R = 2 + \sin (2G)$
d. $R = \sin (G) + \cos (G)$

3. Many polar equations produce nice-looking graphs but will cause our polar plotting program to fail. Some points will lie off the graphics screen. Some values of G will cause division by zero. We can easily test whether a point is on the screen between lines 230 and 240 of Program 9-7c. If a point is off the screen, don't plot it. If the formula we enter at line 210 has an indicated division then we can put in a test between lines 200 and 210. If the current value of G would cause such a zero division, don't even execute line 210. Adding these features will enable you to draw graphs for any of the following:

a. $R \cos (G) = 1$
b. $R = 1 + R \cos (G)$
c. $R = \tan (G)$
d. $R = 2G$ (make the scale 1 and make G range from -50 to 50)
e. $R = 2/G$ (scale 25 and G from -10 to 10)

PROGRAMMER'S CORNER 9

Memory Use for Graphics . . . .

. . .Memory Allocation

As programs grow in size it may become important to be aware of where more things are in memory. Normally, BASIC programs begin at address 2049. This value is stored in two bytes at addresses 43 and 44. To confirm this information, we can type in the following line:

```
PRINT PEEK(43) + 256*PEEK(44)
```

If we are using the Hi-Res screen, our program must not expand past 8191. This leaves 6143, or just under 6K for our programs. It is a simple matter to move our BASIC program area by changing memory locations 43 and 44. (In practice, we will usually leave memory location 43 set to 1.)

In programs that use the Hi-Res screen it makes sense to set the beginning of program memory to 16385. That is the 16K boundary. Then we can use the Hi-Res screen at will. The magic number we want to POKE at 44 comes from 16384/256. We get 64. So we enter

```
POKE 44, 64
```

But that is not enough to make the move. We must also enter two more lines:

```
POKE 16384, 0
NEW
```

It turns out that BASIC requires a 0 byte just before program space. Look at memory location 2048 any time. When you have nothing important in memory sometime, try loading that location with a nonzero value. Then type NEW or RUN. It won't. POKE 2048, 0 brings it back. We must also type NEW to convey the change in memory pointers to BASIC itself. Now we have almost 24K for our program.

...**Program Size**

Sometimes it is desirable to compress our programs to occupy a minimum amount of memory. We can do this by combining statements on a single line and removing all unnecessary spaces. A program such as

```
100 FOR I = 832 TO 894
120 PRINT PEEK(I);
130 NEXT I
```

can be compressed into the following line:

```
100 FORI=832TO894:PRINTPEEK(I);:NEXT
```

Almost everything we might do to compress programs also makes them very hard to read. If space is the overriding concern, then we can do this. We can save space by eliminating all REM statements, too. If you decide to compress a program, be sure to keep a copy in a form that is easy to read and edit.

Chapter 10

Sprite Graphics

A Sprite is a marvelous graphics character. We can define many Sprites and place up to eight of them on a screen at one time. Normal Sprites are 24 dots wide and 21 dots high, measured in standard bit-map screen terms. Thus, a Sprite is three bytes wide and 21 lines high. We can command the Commodore 64 to double the width and/or height of any Sprite. (This can only be done once.) We can double a dimension and restore it to normal. Any Sprite can be displayed in any of the 16 Commodore 64 colors anywhere on the screen. We can use them on the character screen and on the Hi-Res screen. Sprites are very fast—fast enough to produce good animation in BASIC. The eight Sprites are identified by numbers from 0 to 7. Thus, some of the things we do to control them are accomplished by setting and unsetting a single bit in a byte designated for this purpose. Other features are controlled by setting a whole byte to a desired value. Sprites are priority ordered from 0 to 7, so that Sprite 0 will pass in front of Sprite 3. The Commodore 64 can tell our program when two Sprites are in collision.

There is a lot to control here. So we will have to learn a lot of detail to get the first Sprite on the screen. We will select a simple Sprite and get it on the screen with as little hassle as possible.

10-1...Our First Sprite: A Simple Figure

To simplify the making of our first Sprite, let's do a solid block. We will design more interesting figures in the next section. A Sprite is 24-by-21 dots—that is 63 bytes. If we set every bit on in a byte, the numeric value of the byte becomes 255. So, this

160

Sprite is defined by 63 bytes set to 255. Right now we need to give the computer the 63 bytes for this Sprite.

In order to store our Sprite data in memory, we need to decide where to put it. In order to do that, we need to understand more about the structure of the Sprite system. Once the data are stored our program must "point" to them. This is done in another memory location. Let's begin with this.

...Sprite Pointers

The eight memory locations from 2040 to 2047 are set aside to point at data for Sprites 0 to 7. (Our BASIC program begins at 2049 and BASIC uses 2048.) We need a scheme so that the values X and X + 1 point to adjacent Sprites. This means that a change of 1 in a Sprite pointer represents as close to 63 as possible. The number 64 is much better suited to reckoning in binary than 63. Since the largest value we can store in a single byte is 255, the largest address we can specify is 255°64 or 16320. This enables us to specify any 64-byte boundary in the first 16K of memory (16K is 16384 bytes.) A more advanced technique can be used to access memory above this address. We need to find an area of memory that is not used for something else that we are doing. We can use memory from 16192 to 16254 for our first Sprite. Remember that the Hi-Res screen ends at 16191. If our program does not use Hi-Res, then we can use memory below 16192. All of the examples in this chapter will be on the character screen. Later, you will be able to combine figures on the Hi-Res screen with Sprites. We have room for three Sprites from 16192 to 16383. 16383 is the end of the first 16K of memory. Address 16192 is 64°253. Therefore, we POKE 253 into memory location 2040 to point at 16192 for the first Sprite. That is Sprite 0.

Everything else about Sprites is controlled by bits in memory from 53248 to 53294. These 47 bytes are referred to as *registers*. Where possible, Sprite N is controlled by bit N. So, for example, to turn on Sprite 0, we set bit 0 in 53269 to 1 without disturbing the other bits. The other bits control the other 7 Sprites. We can make some of this a little easier if we set some base value to 53248 at the beginning of our programs and add a smaller number to arrive at the actual address. For example, for 53269 we can add 21 to the base value. So, register 21 is located at 53269 in memory.

In any case, in order to set the desired bit we must first obtain the current value using PEEK. We then set the bit we want and POKE the result. It looks like this:

```
100 B = 53248
110 POKE B + 21, PEEK(B + 21) OR 2^0
```

which is equivalent to

```
110 POKE 53269, PEEK(53269) OR 2^0
```

It seems easier to figure all of the Sprite registers from a variable set to 53248 rather than entering the five-digit memory address in every case.

...Sprite Colors

Sprite colors are set by the values of the registers from 39 to 46, or memory 53287 to 53294. Colors here are the same as for bit-map graphics. So, to set the color to Light Green for Sprite 5, we use a statement such as

```
235 POKE B + 39 + N, 13
```

...Sprite Position

Each Sprite has its own X and Y position registers. They are at 0 and 1 for Sprite 0, 2 and 3 for Sprite 1, and 14 and 15 for Sprite 7. So, for Sprite 0, we set the X and Y positions with

```
310 POKE B, X     : REM ** X POSITION FOR SPRITE 0
320 POKE B + 1, Y : REM ** Y POSITION FOR SPRITE 0
```

Let's put this all together for our first Sprite program. Program 10-1 creates a Sprite at 16192 and places it on the screen at (100, 50).

```
100 PRINT CHR$(147);
200 FOR I = 16192 TO 16192 + 62  : REM ** STORE SPRITE DATA
210 POKE I, 255
220 NEXT I
230 POKE 2040, 253               : REM ** POINT TO SPRITE 0
250 B = 53248
260 POKE B+21, PEEK(B+21) OR 2^0 : REM ** TURN ON SPRITE 0 ONLY
300 POKE B+39, 7                 : REM ** SPRITE 0 COLOR
310 POKE B, 100                  : REM ** X POSITION SPRITE 0
320 POKE B+1, 50                 : REM ** Y POSITION SPRITE 0
```

Program 10-1. Our first Sprite program.

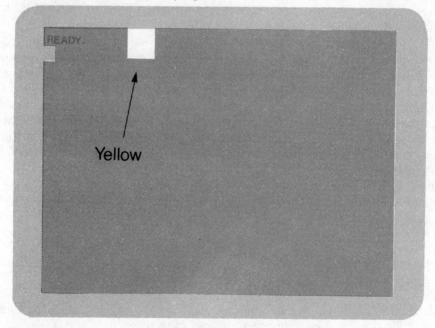

Figure 10-1. Execution of Program 10-1.

It is a good idea to type this program in and run it. This way, you will have a feel for what is happening. Once this program is typed in, you can easily create a second Sprite by making Sprite 1 point to the same place as Sprite 0. The way to distinguish between them is to assign a different color. Of course, eventually we will have differently shaped Sprites. That is the whole idea, after all. But we are trying to work up to that. With Program 10-1 in the computer, add the lines of Program 10-2.

```
240 POKE 2041, 253            : REM ** POINT TO SPRITE 1
270 POKE B+21, PEEK(B+21) OR 2^1 : REM ** TURN ON SPRITE 1 ONLY
400 POKE B + 40, 5            : REM ** SPRITE 1 COLOR
410 POKE B + 2, 200           : REM ** X POSITION SPRITE 1
420 POKE B + 3, 100           : REM ** Y POSITION SPRITE 1
```

Program 10-2. Adding a second Sprite to Program 10-1.

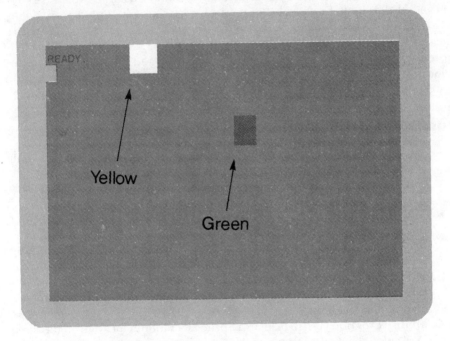

Figure 10-2. Execution of Program 10-2.

Now begin to experiment. Try moving things around by typing commands in immediate mode. Type

```
POKE B+3, 50
```

What happens? The Green block moved vertically, because you changed the value of Y. Now type

```
POKE B+3, 0
```

The Green block disappeared. It has simply been plotted off the screen. We'll look into this more a little later, but let's bring it back with

```
POKE B+3, 150
```

All these changes are pretty easy if you use the screen editing features of BASIC. Now, enter

```
POKE B, 255
```

This one takes the yellow block as far to the right as we can get it with a single memory POKE. We'll soon see that we have to coordinate this with yet another register to yield X values greater than 255.

...SUMMARY

A Sprite is a graphics figure that we control by using POKE to place information into registers provided for this purpose in the Commodore 64. Each Sprite is 24 dots wide and 21 dots high. For our first example, we have simply turned every dot on. Up to eight Sprites can be on the screen at the same time. Memory from 2040 to 2047 is set aside for Sprite pointers. Sprite registers begin at 53248 as the base. The bits of register 21 are used to turn the corresponding Sprite on and off. The color registers are located in the range 39 to 46. Each byte sets the color for a Sprite. The X and Y registers are paired by Sprite, 0 and 1 for Sprite 0, 2 and 3 for Sprite 1, etc.

Problems for Section 10-1 . . . .

1. Modify Program 10-1 to create eight Sprites by setting all of the Sprite pointers to point to the same Sprite data. Place all eight Sprites on the screen in a row across the screen with each Sprite in a different color in the range of 0 to 7. Use a PRINT statement to label the colors.

2. Modify Program 10-1 to create eight Sprites by setting all of the Sprite pointers to point to the same Sprite data. Place all eight Sprites on the screen in a row across the screen with each Sprite in a different color in the range 8 to 15. Use a PRINT statement to label the colors.

3. Modify Program 10-1 to create eight Sprites by setting all of the Sprite pointers to point to the same Sprite data. Place all eight Sprites on the screen along a diagonal.

4. Modify Program 10-1 to display a Sprite at a random location on the screen in a color selected at random. Use a delay loop to leave it on for a few seconds before moving it.

5. Set up the simple Sprite of this section. Move it across the screen in small steps with a delay loop between changing positions. Experiment with steps and the length of the delay to create smooth motion.

10-2...Spritemaking

Now that we know a little about controlling a Sprite, it is time to make one. Once we have thought of a figure, we need to lay it out on the 24-by-21 grid. Then we have to convert what is on the grid to numeric data that we POKE into memory. Let's draw a circle with a vertical line through the center. See Figure 10-3.

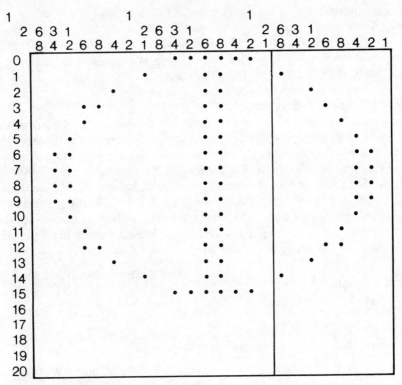

Figure 10-3. Sprite chart for a circle with a vertical line.

Each block in a Sprite chart represents a bit in a data value that we are going to POKE into memory. Remember in the example of Section 10-1 that we turned every bit on by using 255 for every data value. We are going to turn on only those bits that represent a point to be displayed in the bit map of our figure. The bytes are laid out in 21 rows of three bytes each. Clearly, the first byte in the upper left corner is 0, because there is no display in the first eight bits. The middle byte in the first row does have a value. It can be represented in binary as 01111110 or

$$2^6 + 2^5 + 2^4 + 2^3 + 2^2 + 2^1 \text{ which equals } 126$$

in base ten. The next byte in the top row is just like the first byte—nothing is displayed. So, the first three data values are 0, 126, and 0. Now to the second row. The first byte is 00000001. That is easy; the base ten value is 1. The second byte is 00011000 or

$$2^4 + 2^3 \text{ which equals } 24$$

in base ten. The third byte is 10000000, which comes out to 128. So, the data we have so far might be entered in data statements as follows:

```
1000 DATA 0,126,0
1001 DATA 1,24,128
```

165

We need to carry out the same operation on the rest of the figure. The final result is the 63 values we need for our Sprite.

This process is definitely tedious. The computer is very good at tedious things. We certainly ought to be able to get it to help us here. We can get it to do all of the work for us. Well, we will have to create the figures.

...A Simple Sprite Editor

Since Commodore 64 BASIC has such a versatile screen editor, let's take advantage of it here. We can easily draw our Sprite right on the screen and instruct the computer to convert the character data into numeric data. In order to do this we need to have the figure on the screen in a form that is easy for the computer to read. We could just put the figure there and read it with PEEK commands. That is one way. Here is another: create the figure in such a way that it is actually string data in the DATA statements of a program. This way, we can save the program on disk and easily make changes in it as we are perfecting a figure. We can even avoid typing the DATA statements in the first place. Look at Program 10-3a.

```
     100 D$ = "                        " : REM ** 24 SPACES
     105 FOR I = 100 TO 120
-->110 PRINT I; "DATA "; CHR$(34); D$; CHR$(34)
     115 NEXT I
     120 END
```

Program 10-3a. Displaying a Sprite grid on the screen.

In line 110 we create DATA statements by placing 24 spaces in quotes. We produce the quotes with CHR$(34). Now, we can use the cursor movers to draw our figure. We select a convenient character on the keyboard and place it wherever we want a point in the Sprite displayed. Of course, we will be careful not to scroll the figure off the screen. When we have a figure we are satisfied with, we simply place the cursor on DATA line 100 and press RETURN 21 times. The program that generated the chart is gone and in its place we have 21 DATA statements containing our figure in string form. Now we need a program that will analyze the string data and convert them to numeric data appropriate for placing into memory with POKE statements.

We can convert an eight-character string into a single data byte by turning on the bit corresponding to any character position that is occupied by the character we selected to draw the figure on the screen and leaving the other bits off. Program 10-3b converts such a Sprite string into a data byte.

```
     898 REM ** DATA BYTE FROM SPRITE STRING
     900 MB = 0            : REM ** ZERO THE DATA BYTE
     910 FOR I9 = 1 TO 8   : REM ** LOOK AT EACH CHARACTER
-->920 IF MID$(SP$,I9,1) <> "+" THEN 940
     930 MB = MB OR 2^(8-I9) : REM ** TURN ON THIS BIT
     940 NEXT I9
     990 RETURN
```

Program 10-3b. Calculating Sprite data from a Sprite drawing.

Line 920 looks for a plus sign in the Sprite drawing.

We also need a routine to read the 24-character string data in our Sprite drawing, break it up into three eight-character pieces, and display the numeric data for actual use. If we merely display the data then we will have to write them down somewhere and later type up DATA statements. Let's make the computer even POKE the data into the correct memory locations. Later, we can write a program to generate DATA statements. While we are at it, our program should POKE the correct Sprite pointer. Program 10-3c will POKE Sprite data into memory from a Sprite drawing in DATA statements on the screen.

```
498 REM ** SPRITE POKER
500 INPUT "SPRITE NUMBER"; SN
505 IF SN < 0 OR SN > 7 THEN 500
510 INPUT " BLOCK NUMBER"; BN
515 IF BN < 0 OR BN > 255 THEN 510
520 MA = 64*BN : POKE(2040+SN), BN : REM ** POKE THE POINTER
525 FOR I = 0 TO 20 : READ A$
530 FOR X = 0 TO 2
535 SP$ = MID$(A$,X*8+1,8) : GOSUB 900
540 POKE MA, MB : MA = MA + 1        : REM ** POKE SPRITE DATA
545 NEXT X
550 NEXT I
590 END
```

Program 10-3c. POKEing Sprite data from a Sprite drawing.

Putting this all together into one program, we can create our Sprite and POKE the corresponding data into memory. The first time we run the program it creates the DATA statements for us to use as a Sprite drawing palette. After we actually incorporate the DATA statements into the program by pressing RETURN 21 times, our program will POKE the data in the right place. If this is a Sprite we will be working on a lot, we may save the whole thing as a program on disk and retrieve it at any time.

```
100 D$ = "                        " : REM ** 24 SPACES
105 FOR I = 100 TO 120
110 PRINT I; "DATA "; CHR$(34); D$; CHR$(34)
115 NEXT I
120 END
498 REM ** SPRITE POKER
500 INPUT "SPRITE NUMBER"; SN
505 IF SN < 0 OR SN > 7 THEN 500
510 INPUT " BLOCK NUMBER"; BN
515 IF BN < 0 OR BN > 255 THEN 510
520 MA = 64*BN : POKE(2040+SN), BN : REM ** POKE THE POINTER
525 FOR I = 0 TO 20 : READ A$
530 FOR X = 0 TO 2
535 SP$ = MID$(A$,X*8+1,8) : GOSUB 900
540 POKE MA, MB : MA = MA + 1        : REM ** POKE SPRITE DATA
545 NEXT X
550 NEXT I
590 END
898 REM ** DATA BYTE FROM SPRITE STRING
900 MB = 0                   : REM ** ZERO THE DATA BYTE
910 FOR I9 = 1 TO 8     : REM ** LOOK AT EACH CHARACTER
920 IF MID$(SP$,I9,1) <> "+" THEN 940
```

167
. . .

```
930 MB = MB OR 2^(8-I9) : REM ** TURN ON THIS BIT
940 NEXT I9
990 RETURN
```

Program 10-4. Drawing Sprites and POKEing Sprite data.

We can use the Sprite data that our program POKEs into memory with any Sprite program we may write. Sprite data stays in memory until changed, rewritten, or replaced. If we have a very long program to write, this idea becomes important. We can write one program to load Sprites and another to use them for drawing graphics figures.

Now we can get back to drawing our circle with a line through it. Notice that we could create some of the international pictographs for no right turn, no smoking, no trucks, etc., by setting the line at an angle and then creating other Sprites for each of the different symbols. Placing the circle Sprite in the same position as a figure Sprite would create the whole sign. But we are getting ahead of ourselves. Running Program 10-4 and using the cursor movers, we can draw Figure 10-4a.

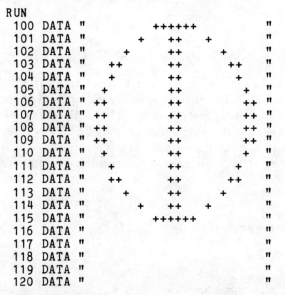

```
RUN
100 DATA "           ++++++          "
101 DATA "       +    ++    +        "
102 DATA "     +      ++      +      "
103 DATA "   ++       ++       ++    "
104 DATA "   +        ++        +    "
105 DATA "  +         ++         +   "
106 DATA " ++         ++         ++  "
107 DATA " ++         ++         ++  "
108 DATA " ++         ++         ++  "
109 DATA " ++         ++         ++  "
110 DATA "  +         ++         +   "
111 DATA "   +        ++        +    "
112 DATA "   ++       ++       ++    "
113 DATA "     +      ++      +      "
114 DATA "       +    ++    +        "
115 DATA "           ++++++          "
116 DATA "                          "
117 DATA "                          "
118 DATA "                          "
119 DATA "                          "
120 DATA "                          "
```

Figure 10-4a. Sprite screen drawing: circle with a vertical line.

Now we place the cursor on line 100 and press return 21 times. Run the program again. It will ask for the Sprite number and the block number. Remember blocks 253, 254, and 255 are beyond the end of the Hi-Res screen.

...Creating the Illusion of Motion

There isn't a whole lot that we can do with a circle having a line through it. But if we create a few more circles with the line in different positions, we can place different Sprites in slightly different locations on the screen in succession and produce the illusion that we have a wheel rolling across the screen. The Sprite data are in memory ready to use. Let's do the others.

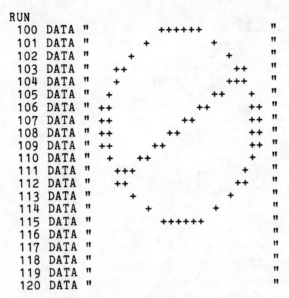

Figure 10-4b. Sprite screen drawing: circle with a diagonal line.

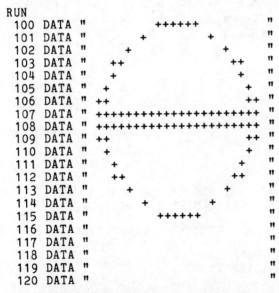

Figure 10-4c. Sprite screen drawing: circle with a horizontal line.

```
RUN
100 DATA "            ++++++           "
101 DATA "          +        +         "
102 DATA "        +            +       "
103 DATA "      ++                ++   "
104 DATA "      +++                +   "
105 DATA "    +    ++                +  "
106 DATA " ++      ++              ++ "
107 DATA " ++         ++          ++ "
108 DATA " ++           ++        ++ "
109 DATA " ++             ++      ++ "
110 DATA "   +              ++    +  "
111 DATA "    +              +++     "
112 DATA "    ++              ++     "
113 DATA "      +            +       "
114 DATA "       +          +        "
115 DATA "        ++++++            "
116 DATA "                          "
117 DATA "                          "
118 DATA "                          "
119 DATA "                          "
120 DATA "                          "
```

Figure 10-4d. Sprite screen drawing: circle with another diagonal line.

We discussed the use of 253, 254, and 255 as Sprite pointers beginning at 2040 to point to 16192, 16256, and 16320. That provides for three Sprites. There is a segment of memory used for the Datassette that we might use for additional Sprites. There is room for three Sprites beginning at 832. We may use pointers 13, 14, and 15 to take advantage of this area. Alternatively, since we are only using the character screen, we could just begin with pointer 252 and take up some of the Hi-Res screen. Once the Sprite data and Sprite pointer are in place, the Sprite drawing program is completely independent. Let's get on with our wheel-drawing program.

We need to do at least four things to display a Sprite:

1. Select a color.
2. Select a Y position.
3. Select an X position.
4. Turn it on.

Program 10-5 is a simple program to roll the wheel horizontally across the screen.

```
 98 REM ** ROLLING A WHEEL
100 B = 53248
110 FOR SP = 0 TO 3
-->120 POKE B + 39 + SP, 0      : REM ** ALL BLACK
130 POKE B + 2*SP + 1, 100 : REM ** Y POSITION
140 NEXT SP
150 PRINT CHR$(147);          : REM ** CLEAR THE SCREEN
196 :
198 REM ** CONTROL THE DISPLAY
200 FOR X = 100 TO 255 STEP 4
210 FOR SP = 0 TO 3
220 POKE B + 2*SP, X+SP                 : REM ** X POSITION
```

```
     230 POKE B + 21, PEEK(B+21) OR 2^SP : REM ** TURN THIS SPRITE ON
 -->240 FOR J = 1 TO 50 : NEXT J          : REM ** DELAY
     250 POKE B + 21, 2^SP                : REM ** TURN OTHER SPRITES OFF
     260 NEXT SP
     270 NEXT X
```

Program 10-5. Moving four Sprites across the screen.

We can experiment with various components of this short program until we have created an effect we really like. We can change the color in line 120. Line 240 controls the delay. We might want to change the Y position value and make the wheel go uphill or downhill.

...X Positions Greater Than 255

Note that the value for the X position of a Sprite must be entered into a Sprite register by using POKE. That means that the largest value can be 255. But, the screen is 320 dots wide. A second register is used to specify that the X value indicates the distance from 255. For example, if we want to place a Sprite at 300 for X, we must set the X value at $300 - 256$, or 44, and then turn on the corresponding bit in the register that keeps track of which Sprites are past 255 in the horizontal position. This is done in register 16. Thus we need a statement such as

```
     POKE B+16, PEEK(B+16) OR 2^SP
```

In order to access the left side of the screen with that Sprite later on, we must turn that bit off with something like

```
     POKE B+16, PEEK(B+16) AND (255-2^SP)
```

Or we could move all Sprites to the left side of the screen with POKE B + 16, 0.

...SUMMARY

We have developed a system to generate Sprite data from a Sprite figure drawn as strings in DATA statements. With Sprites loaded into memory, it is a simple matter to write programs to control Sprites on the screen. By drawing several slightly different Sprites in sequence in different positions, we have created the illusion of motion.

Problems for Section 10-2 ....

Using the techniques of this section, you are limited only by your imagination. You can draw any figures on the screen that you have the patience to create and control. Experiment; be adventuresome. Try your own figures. We offer here problems to create additional programs that will serve as tools to further facilitate your Sprite program writing.

1. Write a program to read Sprite data and POKE it into the designated memory. Include the Sprite number and the memory block number for the Sprite pointer. Use the following data:

```
999   DATA 0, 13 : REM ** SPRITE 0, DATA BLOCK 13
1000  DATA 0,126,0,1,24,128,4,24,32
1001  DATA 24,24,24,16,24,8,32,24,4
1002  DATA 96,24,6,96,24,6,96,24,6
1003  DATA 96,24,6,32,24,4,16,24,8
1004  DATA 24,24,24,4,24,32,1,24,128
1005  DATA 0,126,0,0,0,0,0,0,0
1006  DATA 0,0,0,0,0,0,0,0,0
```

These are the data for the circle of this section with a vertical line. (The next step in this program would be to work with data for several Sprites.)

2. Write a program to display DATA statements given a Sprite number. Suggestion: produce seven lines of data and number them in such a way that the Sprite number is part of the line number. For example, code Sprite 0 in lines 1000 through 1006, Sprite 7 in lines 1070 through 1076. After each Sprite DATA statement is done, move the cursor to the first new DATA statement and press RETURN seven times. When you have all the DATA statements you need, then you must remove the lines of the program that generated all this in the first place. Save the resulting DATA block on disk if possible; otherwise use tape. The resulting DATA statements will resemble those in Problem 1 above without line 999.

3. Design Sprites for the six faces of a die. Write a program to roll a die at random and display the corresponding face.

10-3...An Animation Example

No treatment of animation is complete without a little person moving about the screen. Let's have our little person climbing a set of stairs. We can create the stairs with the SHIFT-O graphics character. That can be displayed by printing CHR$(111).

We need at least two slightly different figures of our little person to help create the illusion of smooth motion. Using the technique for creating figures developed in the last section, we can produce the Sprites of Figures 10-5a and b.

```
RUN
100 DATA "                          "
101 DATA "                          "
102 DATA "           +              "
103 DATA "         ++ ++            "
104 DATA "                          "
105 DATA "          + +             "
106 DATA "          +     +         "
107 DATA "          +    +          "
108 DATA "          ++ +            "
109 DATA "          ++ +            "
110 DATA "          ++   + +        "
111 DATA "                          "
112 DATA "         +   +            "
113 DATA "        +    +            "
114 DATA "       +                  "
115 DATA "       +       +          "
116 DATA "               +          "
```

172

```
117 DATA "                          "
118 DATA "                          "
119 DATA "                          "
120 DATA "                          "
```

Figure 10-5a. Sprite screen drawing of a little person.

```
RUN
 100 DATA "                          "
 101 DATA "                          "
 102 DATA "            +             "
 103 DATA "          ++ +            "
 104 DATA "                          "
 105 DATA "          + +             "
 106 DATA "          +               "
 107 DATA "          +    +          "
 108 DATA "          ++  +           "
 109 DATA "          +++     +       "
 110 DATA "          ++ + +          "
 111 DATA "                          "
 112 DATA "         +    +           "
 113 DATA "        +    +            "
 114 DATA "        +      +          "
 115 DATA "               +          "
 116 DATA "       +                  "
 117 DATA "                          "
 118 DATA "                          "
 119 DATA "                          "
 120 DATA "                          "
```

Figure 10-5b. Modified Sprite screen drawing of a little person.

Even these crude figures will fool the viewer into seeing a little person on the screen. Sprites do not need to be completely realistic. Often they merely suggest the figure we have in mind. Once we have entered the data for these figures into memory, we need a program to move things around. Program 10-6 manages that for us.

```
1 REM ** 147 => CLEAR SCREEN
2 REM ** 144 => BLACK COLOR
3 REM ** 183 => THICK LINE FOR FLOOR
4 REM **  19 => HOME
5 REM ** 111 => STEP CHARACTER
6 REM ** 154 => LT BLUE COLOR
10 PRINT CHR$(147); CHR$(144);
15 PRINT : PRINT : PRINT
20 PRINT "        ";
25 FOR I9 = 1 TO 8 : PRINT CHR$(183); : NEXT I9
30 PRINT "        ";
35 FOR I9 = 1 TO 8 : PRINT CHR$(183); : NEXT I9
40 PRINT CHR$(19) : PRINT : PRINT
45 FOR I = 1 TO 13
50 PRINT TAB(24-I); CHR$(111)
55 NEXT I
98 REM ** SET SPRITES UP
100 B=53248
120 POKE B+39, 0 : POKE B+40,0
130 POKE B,100   : POKE B+1,100
```

```
140 POKE B+2,100 : POKE B+3,100
196 :
198 REM ** WALK UP STAIRS
200 FOR I = 100 TO 200 STEP 8
207 POKE B+1,254-I : POKE B+3,254-I
210 FOR J = 1 TO 140 : NEXT J
220 POKE B,I : POKE B+21,1
230 FOR J = 1 TO 140 : NEXT J
240 POKE B+2,I+4 : POKE B+21,2
290 NEXT I
296 :
298 REM ** WALK ON SECOND FLOOR
300 FOR I = 200 TO 255 STEP 3
310 FOR J = 1 TO 90
320 POKE B,I : POKE B+21,1
330 FOR J = 1 TO 90 : NEXT J
340 POKE B+2,I : POKE B+21,2
390 NEXT I
400 PRINT CHR$(154);
```

Program 10-6. Person climbing stairs.

We have produced all of the graphics characters by printing the CHR$ of their numeric value for easy reading with a character printer. The values are easily obtained by using GET A$ in a program to determine the ASC of each character we want. Or we can find the characters we like from Appendix C. When we write a program like this we should experiment with delay loops and step increments until we achieve a smooth motion that conveys the image we have in mind. This program can be fine-tuned still more. We include a figure showing stages on the screen, but you will have to type it all in to get the true feel of the display.

Figure 10-6. Execution of Program 10-6.

We have included a Spritemaking chart to summarize all of the features of Sprite graphics in Programmer's Corner 10. You may want to refer to it often.

PROGRAMMER'S CORNER 10

Additional Sprite Features and Techniques . . . .

. . .The Sprite Screen
The visible Sprite screen has the same dimensions as the Hi-Res screen—320-by-200 bits. It is laid out in such a way that any Sprite can be "displayed" completely off the visible screen. This makes it possible to have a figure appear to be emerging from the edge.

A Sprite will be fully visible if the Y value is in the range 50 to 249 and the X value is in the range 24 to 343. If either value falls outside its range, then part or all of the figure will be off the visible screen. The value of Y may range from 0 to 255. The value of X may range from 0 to 255 with the corresponding Sprite bit in register 16 set to 0. With the Sprite bit in register 16 turned on, the value of X may range from 0 to 88.

. . .Sprite Expansion
Sprites can easily be displayed at double the X dimension by turning on the corresponding Sprite bit in register 29. Register 23 controls the Y direction. Note that we can display only normal or double. We cannot double a second time. The Sprite is restored to normal size by turning the corresponding bit off.

```
450 POKE B + 29, PEEK(B+29) OR 2^SN
```

doubles the width of Sprite SN. The upper left corner of the Sprite does not move. All positioning is from this point on the Sprite. We restore Sprite SN to normal width with

```
550 POKE B + 29, PEEK(B+29) AND (255-2^SN)
```

We can POKE B + 29, 255 to double all Sprites, and POKE B + 29, 0 to make them all normal.

. . .Collision Detection
Two registers are used for collision detection. Register 30 reflects collisions of Sprites with other Sprites. Register 31 reflects collisions of Sprites with figures in the background. Each bit that is turned on in the register means that the corresponding Sprite is involved in a collision. So, if register 30 reads 3, then Sprites 0 and 1 are in collision, because 3 is the combination of 1 and 2, or bit 0 and bit 1. Similarly, 9 implies that Sprites 0 and 3 are in collision. Suppose the value of register 30 is 15. Then Sprites 0 through 3 are all involved in collisions. It is up to the programmer to monitor the collision registers and find the collisions in pairs before the pattern becomes too complex to sort out.

When using PEEK to read the collision registers, you should know that you have to enter PEEK once to clear the register and a second time to read the current condition.

...Memory Allocation

One technique for working with more than eight Sprites is to have more Sprite data in memory and then simply change the Sprite pointers in memory locations 2040 to 2047 as needed.

In Programmer's Corner 9 we saw how to move the beginning of BASIC program memory. In programs that use the Hi-Res screen it makes sense to set the beginning of program memory to 16385, the 16K boundary. Then we can use the Hi-Res screen at will and load all the Sprites we might ever need in the area from 2148 to 8190. Each Sprite uses 64 bytes. So, we could put data for 96 Sprites in there.

We found in Chapter 10 that we could enter Sprite data in one program and use them in another. This technique saves a lot of program memory. Another method is to use disk files to store Sprite data and read them with our Sprite programs.

...Spritemaker's Table of Sprite Registers

	POKE FOR SPRITE N (base address = 53248)
Turn on the Sprite	B + 21, PEEK(B+21) OR 2^N turn off with AND $(255-2^N)$
Sprite pointer	2040 + N, pointer to 64-byte boundary requires bank info above 255 (16320)
Sprite color	B + 39 + N, color
Low order of X position	B + 2*N, X
High order of X position	B + 16, PEEK(B+16) OR 2^N : B + 2*N, X−256 turn off with: PEEK(B+16) AND $(255-2^N)$
Y position	B + 2*N + 1, Y
Double Sprite width	B + 29, PEEK(B+29) OR 2^N restore with AND $(255-2^N)$
Double Sprite height	B + 23, PEEK(B+23) OR 2^N restore with AND $(255-2^N)$
Sprite collision	IF PEEK(B+30) AND $2^N = 2^N$ this Sprite is involved in a collision PEEK clears this register
Background collision	IF PEEK(B+31) AND $2^N = 2^N$ this Sprite collides with the background PEEK clears this register

Table 10-1. Sprite register specifications

Chapter 11

Programming Sound and Music

by Scott Banks

The Commodore 64 offers a fully programmable electronic music synthesizer. By writing relatively simple BASIC programs, we will be able to produce songs with three-part harmony. With equal ease we will discover how to create exciting sound effects. This powerful capability is provided by a device known as SID, short for Sound Interface Device.

SID appears as 29 memory locations in the range 54272 through 54300. We give instructions to SID by using the POKE statement to place values in the first 25 of these special locations. (The remaining four locations may be accessed with a PEEK command to obtain the status of the SID operation and are not important for our purposes here.) To use SID, you must be familiar with the POKE statement (see Chapter 3), logical bit values, and the use of AND and OR (see Chapter 7).

In an effort to make programming easier and clearer, all of the examples and exercises in this chapter will begin with the following statements:

```
10 S=54272
20 FOR I=0 TO 24 : POKE S+I,0 : NEXT I
```

Line 10 frees us from having to remember and use numbers like 54272 and 54276. By setting S equal to 54272, the start of SID's memory range, we can refer to any SID location by simply adding to S a value from 0 to 24. Later, we will be careful never to change the value of S.

Line 20 is included to initialize the SID for the beginning of each program run. We POKE a zero into each of the 25 SID locations to put the synthesizer into a known condition before proceeding. Perhaps most important, the system is guaranteed to be quiet at this time!

177

Each of the SID locations controls a specific aspect of the sound or sounds currently being generated. We must POKE values into particular locations to begin to produce sound. Thereafter, we may POKE other values to modify or enhance the sound.

11-1...Frequency and Volume

In the simplest case, a musical note is composed of two essential ingredients, frequency and volume. The frequency of a note is nothing more than its pitch. A low-pitched note has a low frequency and a high-pitched note has a high frequency. As far as SID is concerned, we must tell it just what frequency we desire. A number in the range from 1 to 65535 can describe all of the frequencies that SID is able to produce. The higher the number, the higher the frequency and of course, the higher the pitch. To SID, a frequency number of 4291 corresponds to the piano note middle C. Specifying a frequency of zero is allowed and produces no sound. (By the way, the frequency numbers used by SID are not the actual hertz or cycles per second values, but are proportional by a factor of 16.4). Table 11-1 lists musical notes and their corresponding SID frequency values.

NOTE	FREQ	NOTE	FREQ
C—0	268	C—4	4291
C#—0	284	C#—4	4547
D—0	301	D—4	4817
D#—0	318	D#—4	5103
E—0	337	E—4	5407
F—0	358	F—4	5728
F#—0	379	F#—4	6069
G—0	401	G—4	6430
G#—0	425	G#—4	6812
A—0	451	A—4	7217
A#—0	477	A#—4	7647
B—0	506	B—4	8101
C—1	536	C—5	8583
C#—1	568	C#—5	9094
D—1	602	D—5	9634
D#—1	637	D#—5	10207
E—1	675	E—5	10814
F—1	716	F—5	11457
F#—1	758	F#—5	12139
G—1	803	G—5	12860
G#—1	851	G#—5	13625
A—1	902	A—5	14435
A#—1	955	A#—5	15294
B—1	1012	B—5	16203
C—2	1072	C—6	17167

NOTE	FREQ	NOTE	FREQ
C#—2	1136	C#—6	18188
D—2	1204	D—6	19269
D#—2	1275	D#—6	20415
E—2	1351	E—6	21629
F—2	1432	F—6	22915
F#—2	1517	F#—6	24278
G—2	1607	G—6	25721
G#—2	1703	G#—6	27251
A—2	1804	A—6	28871
A#—2	1911	A#—6	30588
B—2	2025	B—6	32407
C—3	2145	C—7	34334
C#—3	2273	C#—7	36376
D—3	2408	D—7	38539
D#—3	2551	D#—7	40830
E—3	2703	E—7	43258
F—3	2864	F—7	45830
F#—3	3034	F#—7	48556
G—3	3215	G—7	51443
G#—3	3406	G#—7	54502
A—3	3608	A—7	57743
A#—3	3823	A#—7	61176
B—3	4050	B—7	64814

Table 11-1. Musical Notes and SID Frequencies. (Courtesy of Commodore Electronics Limited.)

SID is able to produce three different notes simultaneously. To do this, SID has three independent tone sources called Voice 1, Voice 2, and Voice 3. To begin, we need only concern ourselves with Voice 1. We choose a frequency for Voice 1 by executing POKE statements to locations S and S+1. Assuming F to be a value in the range 0 to 65535, the following statements will instruct SID to use frequency F for Voice 1:

```
POKE S,(F-32768) AND 255
POKE S+1,F/256
```

The first POKE assigns the low-order byte of F to location S. By subtracting 32768, we obtain a proper integer value. The low byte is isolated by using AND 255. The second POKE isolates the high byte of F with a simple division. The POKE will automatically trim the quotient to an integer. We must use such a technique to split frequency values into two bytes for SID.

The volume is controlled by a number in the range 0 to 15. A volume setting of 0 means no sound at all, while a volume of 15 tells SID to produce maximum sound output. A POKE to location S+24 is used to set the volume.

```
10 S=54272
20 FOR I=0 TO 24 : POKE S+I,0 : NEXT I
100 POKE S+24,15
120 POKE S+6,15*16
140 POKE S+4,16+1
200 INPUT "FREQ"; F
220 IF F<0 OR F>65535 THEN 900
240 POKE S,(F-32768) AND 255
250 POKE S+1,F/256
290 GOTO 200
900 END
```

Program 11-1. Frequency test.

Program 11-1 is a short example designed to demonstrate how easy it really is to choose a frequency for SID. Lines 10 and 20 are standard initialization for our sound programs. Line 100 sets the volume to 15, the maximum. Use the manual volume control on your TV set to adjust the sound to a comfortable level. It isn't necessary to understand why just yet, but lines 120 and 140 are required to make Voice 1 available for our use. Later, we'll see just what they do. At line 200, a value is accepted for F. The purpose of line 220 is to ensure that F is in the range 0 to 65535, causing the program to terminate if it is not. Line 240 and 250 POKE the high and low bytes of F, as described earlier. The program loops via line 290.

When you run this program, you are prompted for a frequency value. Enter a legal value, such as 4291. Assuming your TV is properly adjusted, a note will sound immediately. And if you don't do anything else, that note will play forever! In the meantime, the computer will prompt again for a new frequency value. As soon as you enter another value, the new note will play instead.

Try entering the values 4291, 4817, and 5407. This will sound like do re me (C, D, and E on the piano). By entering the full range of allowed values, you can hear the eight-octave span of your computer's voice. Enter 0 to obtain silence. Enter −1 (or any value out of range) to exit the program.

...SUMMARY

In this section we have met SID, the Sound Interface Device contained within your Commodore 64 computer. SID appears as 29 memory locations, starting with 54272. We use the POKE statement to place values into the first 25 of these locations. To make life easier, we always assign the value 54272 to the variable S, adding an offset in the range of 0 to 24 to S for each POKE.

SID is easily able to sound a musical tone, but must be told the desired volume and frequency of the note. The volume may range from 0 to 15. We have learned how to specify the frequency using a value ranging from 0 to 65535.

Problems for Section 11-1 . . . .

1. Modify line 100 of Program 11-1, trying other values from 0 to 15 for the volume. Further modify the program to prompt for a volume as well as frequency. Add the appropriate POKE to have SID change the volume along with the frequency.

2. Write a program that employs a FOR loop to change the value of F. Make F span the range 0 to 65535 by using various STEP increments. Each value of F should be transmitted to SID with a POKE so you can hear the result. Try having F go from 65535 to 0 (use a negative STEP value). A further enhancement would be to insert a delay loop, so the tone remains steady for each value of F.

3. Now try changing the volume by using a FOR loop. Choose a frequency and let it sound continuously. Change the volume automatically by using a POKE to location S+24.

11-2...Waveforms

In Program 11-1, the following line was included:

```
140 POKE S+4,16+1
```

The SID location S+4 is known as the *control register* for Voice 1. Each of the eight bits of this register controls some aspect of Voice 1 operation. The four high-order bits allow us to select a waveform. The four low-order bits of this register have a purpose too. We really don't want to concern ourselves very much with the low-order bits at this time. It is worth noting, however, that the lowest order bit (with a value of 1) is the *gate* bit and is required to initiate sound output. In the example line 140 above, the value 16+1 is entered into the control register location with a POKE. The number 16 represents one of the high-order bits and selects a waveform. We add one to this to set the gate bit as well.

The names of the waveforms are based on their appearance on an electronic instrument called an oscilloscope. The four waveforms available are triangle, sawtooth, pulse, and noise. Each is selected by setting the proper bit in the register, using values of 16, 32, 64, and 128, respectively. In the previous example, the triangle waveform was selected by using the value 16. That's a good place to start.

...The Triangle Waveform
The triangle waveform is an approximation of a sine wave. In musical terms, however, it does contain odd harmonics (although it is not particularly rich in them). It is pleasant and somewhat hollow sounding, rather like a flute.

...The Sawtooth Waveform
For a brighter, more brassy sound than the triangle waveform, you would select the sawtooth wave. The sawtooth contains odd and even harmonics, both in reasonably high proportion.

...The Pulse Waveform
The pulse waveform is really an adjustable rectangular wave. The pulse width of a rectangular wave determines its harmonic content. For SID, the pulse width can range from 0 to 4095. The value 2048, right in the middle of the range, will cause a

square wave to be emitted. We must use a set of two POKE statements to assign the desired pulse width to locations S+2 and S+3, similar to the way we assigned the frequency. For our sample programs, we will use these statements to assign the pulse width P to SID's Voice 1:

```
POKE S+2,P AND 255
POKE S+3,P/256
```

In contrast to a frequency value, a pulse width value cannot exceed 32768. Therefore we are able to use a simpler expression for the first POKE.

You will be able to generate a tone that varies from bright and hollow (a square wave, PW = 2048) to nasal and reedy (a narrow pulse, PW = 50). Pulse width values in the range from 0 to 2047 will sound just like those in the range 4095 to 2049. Values less than about 50 or greater than about 4045 are generally too quiet to be useful. Note that locations S+2 and S+3 will only affect the sound output when the pulse waveform is selected.

...The Noise Waveform

The noise waveform is of a random nature. Although the noise waveform is essentially unpitched, the frequency value selected does have a significant effect. The output can be varied from a scratchy rumble to a rushing or hissy sound. Noise waves make it possible to simulate drums that are highly percussive and have no definite pitch. They are also useful for special effects such as explosions, missiles, gunshots, wind, etc.

...SUMMARY

We have learned that SID is capable of a variety of waveforms. Each waveform, because of its harmonic content, produces a unique sound. The triangle and sawtooth waves are the basis of conventional music. The pulse waveform, in addition to frequency control, has a variable pulse width. The noise waveform is most useful for special effects.

To produce any sound output at all from any of the voices, a waveform must be selected for that voice. It is strongly suggested that you select only one waveform per voice, however. As it happens, the waveforms do not add together, as you might expect. Furthermore, there is a possibility that the noise output will "lock up" if it is selected along with any other waveform.

Problems for Section 11-2 . . . .

1. Modify line 140 of Program 11-1, replacing the value 16 with 32 and 128. This will allow you to sample the sawtooth and noise waveforms, respectively. Be sure to include +1 after the waveform selection value. A further program modification would be to prompt for a waveform value in addition to the frequency. In this way you could readily compare the different waveforms at various frequencies.

2. Create a program that selects the pulse waveform for Voice 1. For simplicity, select one frequency and use it for the duration of the program. For

this experiment, frequencies in the range from 500 to 4000 will probably be most effective. Prompt for a pulse width in the same way we accepted a frequency in Program 11-1. Remember to use two POKE statements to place the pulse width into locations S+2 and S+3.

11-3...The Envelope Generator

In addition to a tone source, each of SID's voices has an envelope generator. (Once again, although we will limit ourselves to Voice 1, what we learn will apply to all of the voices.) The job of an envelope generator is to control the volume of a musical tone as it is played. There are a few instruments (an organ, for example), that simply switch their tones on and off. More often, when a note is first played, it takes a little time for the note to reach full volume. Even more significant is that most instruments don't end their notes immediately, but rather take a while to fade away. We may program the envelope generator to produce realistic imitations of common instruments as well as creating new instruments of our own.

...Gating

In the previous section we discovered the control register for Voice 1. The low-order bit (value 1) was termed the *gate* bit. It is helpful to think of the gate bit as a piano key. We learned that the gate bit must be set to 1 to cause sound to be produced by the tone source. This bit tells SID to begin to sound the note. It's much like pressing a piano key. Then, should you reset this bit, the note will cease to sound. This action, of course, is just like releasing the piano key.

We will gate the tone source for Voice 1 by controlling only the gate bit within the Control Register. After all, we don't want to change the waveform that we have selected. Assuming that we have the waveform selection stored in the variable W (having the value 16, 32, 64, or 128), the following will gate Voice 1:

```
POKE S+4, W+1
```

To release Voice 1, we would execute:

```
POKE S+4, W
```

At the time we choose to gate the tone source, we will have already set the proper parameters (for example, frequency) for the note we wish to play. Then we would release the note, change the frequency, and gate the next note.

It is plain to see that the gate bit is used to turn the tone source on and off. But gating really controls the envelope generator, and it is the envelope generator that actually controls the voice.

...Attack/Decay/Sustain/Release

The envelope generator controls four parameters: *attack time*, *decay time*, *sustain level*, and *release time*. Each of these is fully programmable by specifying a value ranging from 0 to 15.

Attack time is defined as the time it takes for a note to reach its maximum volume after it has been gated. Specifying an attack time of 0 tells SID to use the minimum time of 0.002 seconds. The maximum attack is eight seconds and is obtained with the value 15. The attack period begins when the gate bit is set to 1. During the attack period, the volume of the tone source will gradually increase until it reaches maximum.

The decay period begins as soon as the attack period ends. Using the values 0 to 15, the decay may range from a minimum of 0.006 seconds to a maximum of 24 seconds. The volume of the tone source will decrease evenly until, at the end of the decay phase, it reaches the sustain level.

The sustain level, ranging from 0 to 15, determines the volume of the tone source during the remainder of the gating. After the decay period ends, the volume will remain indefinitely at the sustain level—as long as the gate bit stays set.

When the gate bit is finally cleared, the release period starts. The release values 0 to 15 have the same absolute time durations as the decay values. During the release phase, the volume of the tone source will gradually decrease until it finally reaches zero. The voice will then remain quiet until it is once again gated.

The acronym ADSR is commonly used to represent the attack/decay/sustain/ release cycle. Each of the conventional musical instruments has its own natural envelope. Although natural envelopes are often complicated and even change dynamically, we can approximate many instruments by choosing the proper ADSR.

An organ, for example, has ADSR values of 0/0/15/0. This means that, once gated, the sound takes a minimum amount of time to build up to a full sustain level. The sound remains at full volume until the gate bit is cleared, and then stops almost immediately. On the other hand, the ADSR of a piano is more like 0/10/0/0. Like the organ, the piano sound begins immediately. But, unlike an organ, the volume of a piano note begins to decrease just after the key is pressed. The sustain is zero because, no matter how long you hold the key, the sound will decay to nothing. The release value is also zero, ensuring that the sound ends as soon as the key is released, even if this is before the decay period has finished.

Figure 11-1 is a graphic representation of the ADSR cycle. You can see that, before gating, the volume is zero. The attack period begins immediately when the gate bit is set, and is then followed by the decay. The volume remains at the intermediate level until the gate bit is reset. Then the release interval begins, with the volume returning to zero. The actual time values for the attack, decay, and release periods are given in Table 11-2.

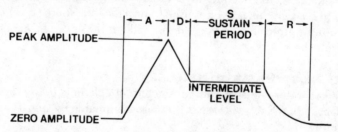

Figure 11-1. The ADSR cycle. (Courtesy of Commodore Electronics Limited.)

VALUE	ATTACK RATE (Time/Cycle)	DECAY/RELEASE RATE (Time/Cycle)
0	2 ms	6 ms
1	8 ms	24 ms
2	16 ms	48 ms
3	24 ms	72 ms
4	38 ms	114 ms
5	56 ms	168 ms
6	68 ms	204 ms
7	80 ms	240 ms
8	100 ms	300 ms
9	250 ms	750 ms
10	500 ms	1.5 s
11	800 ms	2.4 s
12	17 s	3 s
13	3 s	9 s
14	5 s	15 s
15	8 s	24 s

Table 11-2. ADSR Timing Values. (Courtesy of Commodore Electronics Limited.)

...Playing a Song with SID

It's time to see how the various things we've learned about SID fit together. Program 11-2 does just that. Before we go into the analysis of how this program works, you might want to enter and run it.

```
10 S=54272
20 FOR I=0 TO 24 : POKE S+I,0 : NEXT I
100 POKE S+5, 0*16 +10
110 POKE S+6, 0*16 + 0
120 W=16
180 POKE S+24,15
200 READ F,D : IF F=0 THEN 900
210 POKE S,(F-32768) AND 255
220 POKE S+1,F/256
300 POKE S+4,W+1
320 FOR I=1 TO D*50 : NEXT I
360 POKE S+4,W
390 GOTO 200
900 END
9000 DATA 4291,4
9010 DATA 4817,2
9020 DATA 5407,4
9030 DATA 4817,4
9040 DATA 5407,2
9050 DATA 5728,4
9060 DATA 5407,2
9070 DATA 4817,4
9080 DATA 4291,4
```

```
9090 DATA 4817,2
9100 DATA 5407,4
9110 DATA 4817,2
9120 DATA 4291,6
9130 DATA 5407,4
9140 DATA 4817,8
9999 DATA 0,0
```

Program 11-2. Playing a melody.

Program 11-2 plays the melody of a simple song. The melody and rhythm are stored in DATA statements. The data are read and transmitted by POKE statements to the SID locations that control Voice 1. Although the program was originally intended to sound like a piano, you can easily change the waveform and ADSR parameters. The DATA statements, of course, may be replaced to play any song you wish. Let's see how it works . . .

The first two lines of the program, 10 and 20, are our standard SID initialization. The attack and decay periods are determined by line 100. To sound like a piano, we have chosen an attack of 0 and a decay of 10. Rather than simply POKE the value 10 into location S+5, we chose to clearly demonstrate that the high nibble is 0 and the low nibble is 10. Also, should you decide to alter line 100 to provide other values, it will be very easy to edit. Line 110 sets the sustain level and decay interval in a similar way. Both values are set to 0 for the piano sound.

Line 120 assigns the desired waveform value to W. The triangle waveform, value 16, has been selected. The volume level is set to maximum at line 180 by putting the value 15 into location S+24. This concludes the one-time setup of Voice 1.

Line 200 begins the main loop. The READ statement picks up two values from the next DATA statement. The variables F and D are assigned to the frequency and the duration of the note about to be played, respectively. The frequency value F is entered into the proper locations by the POKE statements in lines 210 and 220. This technique, detailed previously, allows the DATA statements to contain F values in the range of 1 to 65535. The last DATA statement should contain an F value of 0, to terminate the program. Line 200 detects this condition and transfers control to the END at 900.

With the frequency now properly set, it is time to gate Voice 1. Line 300 enters the value W+1 into the control register. This selects the waveform W and sets the gate bit. Now the ADSR cycle begins and the voice plays. However, we only want it to play for a specified duration, D. So, the FOR loop at line 320 delays for the duration of the note. It is a do-nothing loop, designed just to wait a while. It waits for a time period that is proportional to the value of D. The timing parameters are chosen so that D may represent the number of sixteenth-note counts required. For example, a whole note would have a D value of 16, a half note would be eight, a quarter note would be four, an eighth note would be two, and a sixteenth note would be one.

When the wait loop is done, the note must be released. This is accomplished by resetting the gate bit. However, we don't want to change the selected waveform. So we POKE the value W into the control register, but without adding one. Now the decay phase begins, with the volume falling off at a rate determined by the decay setting. Line 390 returns control to line 200, which will read the F and D values for the next note to be played. This loop will continue on and on, playing one note after another, until the last DATA statement is reached.

Let's also take a look at the DATA statements, which begin at line 9000. Each DATA line represents one note to be played. The frequency values are selected from Table 11-1. This particular song only requires four notes, C, D, E, and F. The values 4291, 4817, 5407, and 5728 were chosen from the table. The first value corresponds to middle C on a piano. As explained above, the duration values supply the information necessary to reproduce the rhythm of the song. The last DATA statement, line 9999, contains two 0 values, allowing the program to end in an orderly way.

...SUMMARY

In this section we have learned about SID's mechanism for gating and envelope generation. Gating is the process by which the volume of a tone source is controlled. The envelope generator is supplied with four parameters; attack, decay, sustain, and release. Also known as ADSR, these values control the rise and fall of a musical note as it is played.

We have introduced a program capable of playing a melody. The program is flexible enough to be easily modified to play any desired tune. The waveform and ADSR parameters may be changed quickly also.

Problems for Section 11-3 . . . .

1. Supply Program 11-2 with new DATA statements. You can convert the melody of your favorite song, especially if you have the sheet music. Or, if you have access to a piano or other instrument, perhaps you can do it by ear. Another idea is to try random values, not necessarily from Table 11-1, to create a computer music effect.

2. Modify lines 100 and 110 of Program 11-2, experimenting with different ADSR cycles. Use 0/0/15/0 to simulate an organ. Try some of your own. Then modify line 120 to assign other waveforms to W. (If you try the pulse waveform, don't forget to set a pulse width with two POKE statements.)

11-4...The Three Voices

As we know, SID has three independent voices (tone sources). Voices 2 and 3 function in an identical manner to Voice 1. For each voice you must choose a waveform, frequency, ADSR, and (if the pulse waveform is selected) a pulse width. The voices sound simultaneously, allowing you to create three-part harmony or complex melodies.

Voice 1 uses seven SID locations, S through S+6. Voice 2 uses the next seven, S+7 through S+13. The following seven locations, S+14 through S+20, are dedicated to Voice 3. The registers for Voices 2 and 3 are mapped in the same order as for Voice 1. You can add seven to any Voice 1 location to find the equivalent Voice 2 location. Add 14, and you convert from Voice 1 to Voice 3. For example, the control register for Voice 1 is S+4. Therefore, the control register for Voice 2 is S+11, while for Voice 3 it is S+18.

...SID Locations

Table 11-3 is a chart of all 29 SID locations. It shows each of the locations along with its offset. The offset is the value you add to S; it can range from 0 to 28. This table allows you to visualize the bit functions of the registers. The first 21 locations are divided into three groups of seven, corresponding to the three voices. We have learned how to use these SID registers.

BIT VALUES

REG #	128 D_7	64 D_6	32 D_5	16 D_4	8 D_3	4 D_2	2 D_1	1 D_0	REG NAME	REG TYPE
									Voice 1	
0	F_7	F_6	F_5	F_4	F_3	F_2	F_1	F_0	FREQ LO	WRITE-ONLY
1	F_{15}	F_{14}	F_{13}	F_{12}	F_{11}	F_{10}	F_9	F_8	FREQ HI	WRITE-ONLY
2	PW_7	PW_6	PW_5	PW_4	PW_3	PW_2	PW_1	PW_0	PW LO	WRITE-ONLY
3	—	—	—	—	PW_{11}	PW_{10}	PW_9	PW_8	PW HI	WRITE-ONLY
4	NOISE	⊓⊔	∿	∧	TEST	RING MOD	SYNC	GATE	CONTROL REG	WRITE-ONLY
5	ATK_3	ATK_2	ATK_1	ATK_0	DCY_3	DCY_2	DCY_1	DCY_0	ATTACK/DECAY	WRITE-ONLY
6	STN_3	STN_2	STN_1	STN_0	RLS_3	RLS_2	RLS_1	RLS_0	SUSTAIN/RELEASE	WRITE-ONLY
									Voice 2	
7	F_7	F_6	F_5	F_4	F_3	F_2	F_1	F_0	FREQ LO	WRITE-ONLY
8	F_{15}	F_{14}	F_{13}	F_{12}	F_{11}	F_{10}	F_9	F_8	FREQ HI	WRITE-ONLY
9	PW_7	PW_6	PW_5	PW_4	PW_3	PW_2	PW_1	PW_0	PW LO	WRITE-ONLY
10	—	—	—	—	PW_{11}	PW_{10}	PW_9	PW_8	PW HI	WRITE-ONLY
11	NOISE	⊓⊔	∿	∧	TEST	RING MOD	SYNC	GATE	CONTROL REG	WRITE-ONLY
12	ATK_3	ATK_2	ATK_1	ATK_0	DCY_3	DCY_2	DCY_1	DCY_0	ATTACK/DECAY	WRITE-ONLY
13	STN_3	STN_2	STN_1	STN_0	RLS_3	RLS_2	RLS_1	RLS_0	SUSTAIN/RELEASE	WRITE-ONLY
									Voice 3	
14	F_7	F_6	F_5	F_4	F_3	F_2	F_1	F_0	FREQ LO	WRITE-ONLY
15	F_{15}	F_{14}	F_{13}	F_{12}	F_{11}	F_{10}	F_9	F_8	FREQ HI	WRITE-ONLY
16	PW_7	PW_6	PW_5	PW_4	PW_3	PW_2	PW_1	PW_0	PW LO	WRITE-ONLY
17	—	—	—	—	PW_{11}	PW_{10}	PW_9	PW_8	PW HI	WRITE-ONLY
18	NOISE	⊓⊔	∿	∧	TEST	RING MOD	SYNC	GATE	CONTROL REG	WRITE-ONLY
19	ATK_3	ATK_2	ATK_1	ATK_0	DCY_3	DCY_2	DCY_1	DCY_0	ATTACK/DECAY	WRITE-ONLY
20	STN_3	STN_2	STN_1	STN_0	RLS_3	RLS_2	RLS_1	RLS_0	SUSTAIN/RELEASE	WRITE-ONLY
									Filter	
21	—	—	—	—	—	FC_2	FC_1	FC_0	FC LO	WRITE-ONLY
22	FC_{10}	FC_9	FC_8	FC_7	FC_6	FC_5	FC_4	FC_3	FC HI	WRITE-ONLY
23	RES_3	RES_2	RES_1	RES_0	FILTEX	FILT 3	FILT 2	FILT 1	RES/FILT	WRITE-ONLY
24	3 OFF	HP	BP	LP	VOL_3	VOL_2	VOL_1	VOL_0	MODE/VOL	WRITE-ONLY
									Misc	
25	PX_7	PX_6	PX_5	PX_4	PX_3	PX_2	PX_1	PX_0	POT X	READ-ONLY
26	PY_7	PY_6	PY_5	PY_4	PY_3	PY_2	PY_1	PY_0	POT Y	READ-ONLY
27	O_7	O_6	O_5	O_4	O_3	O_2	O_1	O_0	OSC_3/RANDOM	READ-ONLY
28	E_7	E_6	E_5	E_4	E_3	E_2	E_1	E_0	ENV_3	READ-ONLY

Table 11-3. SID Locations. (Courtesy of Commodore Electronics Limited.)

Locations S+21 through S+24 control the filter circuit. These four registers allow further modification of all three tone sources. We already know that location S+24 controls the volume, but our map reveals that this register has additional functions in the bits of the high nibble. We will examine the filter in the next section.

Finally, SID locations S+25 through S+28 are read-only registers, and are accessed with the PEEK( ) function. These locations, as well as certain bits of locations we have already covered, allow experienced programmers access to even more SID features.

...Playing the Voices Together

Our next goal is to coordinate the three voices, allowing us to achieve three-part harmony. The design of a multiple-voice program is more complicated because of the need to maintain the same timing (rhythm) for each voice. For example, Voice 1 may sound a half note (eight counts) while Voice 2 may be required to simultaneously sound two quarter notes (four counts each). And who knows what Voice 3 may be called upon to do!

Previously, Program 11-2 played a melody directly from notes that were encoded into DATA statements. But for three voices, this approach is extremely difficult. It becomes a confusion of which voice or voices must be gated on, which voice(s) must be gated off, and which voice(s) must change pitch. One way to ease this dilemma is to build a separate set of DATA statements for each voice. Then the computer can construct an array containing all of the SID instructions in their proper timing relationship.

Program 11-3 may be used to play any song in three-part harmony. The DATA statements at the end appear in three groups, one for each voice. In addition, an improved encoding scheme is used that allows you to read a song directly from sheet music. Enter and run this program and then we'll see how it works.

```
10 S=54272
20 FOR I=S TO S+24 : POKE I,0 : NEXT I
40 DIM HF%(2,200), LF%(2,200)
50 DIM WC%(2,200), MF(13)
100 PRINT "STANDBY..."
200 GOSUB 4000
220 GOSUB 2000
400 GOSUB 1000
420 Z$="" : INPUT "PLAY IT AGAIN"; Z$
440 IF LEFT$(Z$,1) = "Y" THEN 400
900 END

1000 REM ** PLAY TUNE
1020 FOR I=1 TO S+14 STEP 7
1030 POKE I+5,0*16+0
1040 POKE I+6,15*16+0
1090 NEXT I
1100 POKE S+24,15
1200 FOR I=1 TO CT
1220 POKE S,   LF%(0,I)
1230 POKE S+ 1,HF%(0,I)
1240 POKE S+ 7,LF%(1,I)
```

```
1250 POKE S+ 8,HF%(1,I)
1260 POKE S+14,LF%(2,I)
1270 POKE S+15,HF%(2,I)
1280 POKE S; 4,WC%(0,I)
1282 POKE S;11,WC%(1,I)
1284 POKE S;18,WC%(2,I)
1400 FOR J=1 TO 50 : NEXT
1490 NEXT I
1800 POKE S+24,0
1990 RETURN
2000 REM ** LOAD ARRAYS FROM DATA
2020 FOR V=0 TO 2 : CT = 0
2040 PRINT "LOADING VOICE"; V+1
2100 READ D$ : IF D$ = "*" THEN 2900
2110 B = 7-VAL(LEFT$(D$,1))
2200 F = ASC(MID$(D$,2,1))
2400 Z$ = MID$(D$,3,3) : H=0
2410 IF ASC(Z$) >= 48 THEN 2500
2420 H=1
2430 IF LEFT$(Z$,1) = "-" THEN H=-1
2440 Z$ = MID$(Z$,2,2)
2500 IF F > 71 THEN F=0 : GOTO 2600
2510 F=F-67 : IF F < 0 THEN F=F+7
2520 F = 2*F + 1 : IF F > 5 THEN F=F-1
2530 F = MF(F+H) / 2^B
2600 D = VAL(Z$)

2800 FOR I=1 TO D : CT = CT+1
2810 WC%(V,CT)=17-(1 AND I=D AND D<>1)
2820 LF%(V,CT) = (F-32768) AND 255
2830 HF%(V,CT) = F/256
2840 NEXT I
2890 GOTO 2100
2900 NEXT V
2980 PRINT "LOADING COMPLETE" : PRINT
2990 RETURN

4000 REM ** SETUP MASTER FREQ ARRAY
4020 FOR I=0 TO 13 : READ MF(I) : NEXT I
4100 DATA 32407
4110 DATA 34334, 36376, 38539, 40830
4120 DATA 43258, 45830, 48556, 51443
4130 DATA 54502, 57743, 61176, 64814
4140 DATA 68668
4190 RETURN

6000 REM ** DATA FOR VOICE 1
6010 DATA OR8, 4B4, 4E4
6020 DATA OR2, 4G+2, 4F+2, 4E2
6022 DATA 4F+2, 4D+2, 4E2, 4F+2
6030 DATA OR2, 4F+2, 4E2, 4D+2
6032 DATA 4E2, 4C+2, 4D+2, 4E2
6040 DATA OR2, 4E2, 4D+6, 4D+2, 4C+6
6052 DATA OR2, 3B6, 4C+2, 4D4
6060 DATA 4C+2, 3B2, 4C+2, 4D2
6062 DATA 4E2, 4D2, 4C+2, 3B2
```

```
6070 DATA 4C+8,4C+8
6990 DATA *
7000 REM ** DATA FOR VOICE 2
7010 DATA 0R8,4G+4,4A2,4B2
7020 DATA 5C+8,4B4,3B2,3B2
7030 DATA 4B8,4A4,3A2,3A2
7040 DATA 4A6,4B2,4G+6,4A2
7050 DATA 4F+2,4E2,4F+4
7052 DATA 4F+2,4A2,4G+2,4F+2
7060 DATA 4E+2,4D+2,4E+2,4F+2
7062 DATA 4G+2,4F+2,4E+2,4D+2
7070 DATA 4E+16
7990 DATA *

8000 REM ** DATA FOR VOICE 3
8010 DATA 0R8,3E2,3E2,3F+2,3G+2
8020 DATA 3A16
8030 DATA 3G+16
8040 DATA 3F+8,3E8
8050 DATA 3D4,3D2,3C+2,3D4,2B4
8060 DATA 3C+12,2G+4
8070 DATA 3C+8,3C+8
8990 DATA *
```

Program 11-3. Three-part harmony.

Lines 10 through 900 of Program 11-3 are the control section. Our standard SID initialization takes place in lines 10 and 20. The DIM statements at lines 40 and 50 define the data storage arrays we will use. The arrays HF%( ), LF%( ), and WC%( ) are each two-dimensional, with the first subscript representing the voice (the values 0, 1, and 2 stand for Voices 1, 2, and 3), and the second subscript representing the beat count. The arrays HF%( ) and LF%( ) contain the low-order and high-order bytes of the current frequency of the voice. The array WC%( ) contains the waveform control byte. The MF( ) array holds the master frequency values from which the frequencies of all the possible notes are obtained.

The 4000 routine is called to initialize the master frequency array. Then, a GOSUB 2000 loads the data values into the working arrays. It is the subroutine at 1000 that actually plays the song. Lines 420 and 440 allow the song to be replayed immediately, as the data remain in the arrays. Line 900 terminates the program when no more play is requested.

The 1000 subroutine plays the song from the HF%( ), LF%( ), and WC%( ) arrays. Lines 1020 through 1090 set up the ADSR envelopes. All three voices are set to imitate an electronic organ. The volume is turned to full at line 1100. The main play loop appears from lines 1200 to 1490. The variable CT contains the number of beat counts in the entire song. Each value of I represents one beat. The variable I is used to index the arrays to assign the high and low frequency bytes from LF%( ) and HF%( ), and the control register bytes from WC%( ). After the parameters for all three voices are entered with POKE statements, line 1400 delays to allow the tones to sound for one beat time. Line 1800 turns off the volume at the end of play, and line 1990 returns to the caller.

The DATA statements are loaded into the working arrays by the subroutine at line 2000. Voice 1 is loaded from its own set of DATA statements. Then Voices 2 and 3 are loaded, in order, from theirs. It takes a significant amount of time for all three voices to be loaded, but this approach allows the play subroutine (line 1000) to produce three properly synchronized voices.

The precise internal workings of the 2000 subroutine are left as an exercise for the reader. Only conventional programming techniques are employed, without relation to the SID. However, some discussion of the note encoding scheme is required, as well as the data array formats.

Look at the data for Voice 1, beginning at line 6000. Each note is expressed by a sequence of letters and numbers. These are all of the same format: a number, a letter, and a number, for example, 3C8. Here, the first number represents the octave band, 0 to 7 (SID is capable of an eight-octave musical range). The letter in the middle represents the musical note: C, D, E, F, G, A, or B. The letter R may also be used to denote a rest, causing that voice to be silent. The final number, called the *duration*, is the number of beats to hold the note. Values in the range of 1 to 16 allow us to specify sixteenth notes through whole notes, as in Program 11-2. Duration values greater than 16 may be used to produce even longer notes.

As a matter of convention, the zero octave band is used for rest notes, such as 0R8. Also, we may make any note sharp ($\#$) or flat ($\flat$) by appending either + or −, respectively, to the letter. For instance, an F-sharp quarter note in the third octave band would be described as 3F + 4. Even notation such as E$\#$ and C$\flat$ (really the E-sharp and C-flat) can be processed. The lowest possible note is 0C− and the highest is 7B. The DATA statements for Voice 1 end with a single asterisk*. Voices 2 and 3 use the same format for their data at lines 7000 and 8000. It is important that the voices match up with one another and that the total number of beats be equal for each voice.

The number of array elements required for a note depends on its duration. A half note, for example, has a duration value of eight. Therefore, it would require eight elements each of LF%( ), HF%( ), and WC%( ). For these eight elements, the frequency values would all be the same (it is the same note). But, the WC%( ) values would cause the voice to be gated on for the first WC%( ) element, remain gated for elements 2 to 7, and release the gate bit for the final element. The DIM statements allow for a maximum of 200 beat counts, which provides room for 12 measures of 4/4 time music. The DIM statements may be increased for longer songs.

Problems for Section 11-4 . . . .

1. Write a program that plays a simple melody, using Program 11-2 as a starting point. Have the melody play through Voice 1. But have Voices 2 and 3 also play. To create a choir effect, don't use the same frequency values for the second two voices. Assuming that F is the frequency of Voice 1, play Voice 2 at 1.01*F and play Voice 3 at 1.02*F. Try other multipliers as well.
2. Modify Program 11-3 to vary the waveforms selected for the voices. Try changing the delay loop at line 1400 to alter the tempo.

3. Create your own set of DATA statements for Program 11-3. Producing three-part harmony will require you (or a helper) to have some musical knowledge. This is easiest if you can read sheet music prepared for a piano. Generally, it makes sense to assign Voice 1 to the melody or vocal part. Use Voice 2 to build harmony. Voice 3 can be used to help complete chord structures or to provide a bass line. Don't be afraid to spread the voices over the various octave bands.

11-5...The Filter Section

SID has a programmable filter that allows frequencies in a certain range to be excluded from the sound output. All of the tone source waveforms produce harmonic frequencies in addition to the fundamental frequency that determines their pitch. The filter makes it possible to further shape the waveform by tailoring the harmonic content. Therefore, a wider variety of sounds are possible and natural instrument sounds can become more realistic.

The four locations S+21 through S+24 control the filter. Although the filter has a 12-bit cutoff register, it will be entirely sufficient for us to deal only with the high-order byte. We will ignore location S+21. The location S+22 will be used to set the filter's cutoff frequency. This byte may range from 0 (the lowest cutoff frequency) to 255 (the highest). Let's see how the cutoff frequency changes the sound.

The low-order nibble of location S+24 controls the volume. As we have seen, a value in the range 0 to 15 will dictate the overall sound level of all the voices. To activate the filter, we must also set one of the high-order bits of S+24. Referring to Table 11-3, we see that the bit values 16, 32, and 64 correspond to LP, BP, and HP. These are the three basic modes of the filter, and stand for low-pass, band-pass, and high-pass. When the filter is in low-pass mode, frequencies below the cutoff are passed, but higher frequencies are reduced. The higher the frequency, the more it is reduced. The high-pass mode does just the opposite. The high frequencies are undisturbed, but low frequency components are reduced in level. The band-pass mode allows frequencies near the cutoff to pass, while attenuating those above and below the cutoff. We select the filter's mode by setting the appropriate bit in S+24. Normally only one of the three mode bits is set. However, LP and BP may both be set, creating a notch effect. This reduces only those frequencies near the cutoff.

Location S+23 provides further control of the filter. The lowest three bits of this register determine which voices are affected by the filter section. Setting the value of bit 1 causes the output of Voice 1 to be routed through the filter, rather than going directly to the sound output. The bit values 2 and 4 apply to Voices 2 and 3, respectively. If all three bits are zero, the filter has no effect.

The upper nibble of location S+23 controls the resonance of the filter. This parameter may vary from 0 to 15. Higher values of resonance cause a peaking effect near the cutoff frequency. You may use the resonance feature to create a sharper sound by emphasizing the filter's effect.

...Using the Filter

Program 11-4 demonstrates the action of the filter. Enter this program to hear how it uses the filter to modify the tone of Voice 1.

Lines 10 and 20 should be quite familiar by now. At line 100 we assign a constant value to the high-order frequency register for Voice 1. For the duration of the program, the frequency of the tone source will not change. Line 110 sets the sustain level of the ADSR envelope to maximum, allowing us to produce a continuous tone. The sawtooth waveform for Voice 1 is selected at line 120; the tone source is gated. We chose the sawtooth because it is rich in harmonics. Line 130 instructs the filter to process the output of Voice 1. The volume is set to maximum and the low-pass filter mode is selected at line 140.

At this point, Voice 1 is producing a constant tone. The filter's cutoff frequency is zero (S+22 was cleared by line 20), so there is practically no output. Remember that a low-pass filter removes frequencies above the cutoff, and right now the cutoff is zero. Line 200 executes and begins a FOR loop, causing C to go from 0 to 255. The variable C represents the filter's cutoff frequency. Sure enough, we POKE the value of C into the cutoff register at line 210. Line 220 is a delay loop, allowing us time to hear each step as the cutoff frequency changes. The effect is that, as the loop progresses, more and more of the high-frequency components of the tone source can be heard. Line 300 turns off the volume at the end of the program.

```
10 S=54272
20 FOR I=0 TO 24 : POKE S+I,0 : NEXT I
100 POKE S+1,25
110 POKE S+6,15*16
120 POKE S+4,32+1
130 POKE S+23,1
140 POKE S+24,16+15
200 FOR C = 0 TO 255
210 POKE S+22,C
220 FOR J=1 TO 10 : NEXT J
240 NEXT C
300 POKE S+24,0
```

Program 11-4. Filter demonstration.

The filter can be used to help produce sound effects, as Program 11-5 illustrates. Try running this example. You will hear a jet plane approach take-off velocity and leave the runway. This program uses the noise waveform to generate the rushing sound of the jet engines. The filter cutoff frequency is swept from low to high, causing the initial low-pitched rumble to build to a mighty roar.

```
10 S=54272
20 FOR I=0 TO 24 : POKE S+I,0 : NEXT I
100 POKE S+1,100
110 POKE S+6,15*16 + 13
120 POKE S+4,128+1
130 POKE S+23,1
140 POKE S+24,16+15
200 FOR C = 0 TO 255
210 POKE S+22,C
```

```
220 FOR J=1 TO 10 : NEXT J
240 NEXT C
300 POKE S+4,128
```

Program 11-5. Jet aircraft departure.

Program 11-5 was derived from Program 11-4 above. Only four lines are different—100, 110, 120, and 300. A higher frequency is selected at line 100. Line 110 provides the ADSR with a release period of nine seconds. This gives the jet the appearance of fading into the sky at the end. The noise waveform is activated and gated at line 120. Rather than abruptly turn off the volume at line 300 as above, this program simply turns off the gate bit at the end. This way, the ADSR envelope does the work of letting the volume fade off gradually.

...SUMMARY

The SID programmable filter allows you to easily remove unwanted harmonics from the tone sources. The filter mode—low-pass, high-pass, band-pass, or notch—is selected according to the effect desired. The filter's cutoff frequency and resonance are determined by simple POKE statements. Any or all of the three voices may optionally be processed by the filter, as required. One of the main uses of the filter is in achieving realistic sound effects.

PROGRAMMER'S CORNER 11

Synchronization and Ring Modulation . . . .

There are two additional bits in the control register of each voice that allow further modification of the harmonic content of the tone source. The principal use of both features is in the creation of special sound effects. Bit value 2, when added to the control register data value, enables the synchronization feature. Ring modulation is effected by adding bit value 4.

If either of these options is activated for Voice 1, then Voice 3 will have an effect upon the first voice. Only the frequency value of Voice 3 is important; it need not be gated or have any waveform selected. The frequency of Voice 3 must be nonzero, however. Should these special bit values be selected for Voices 2 or 3, then they will be affected by Voice 1 or 2, respectively. Synchronizing one voice with another has the effect of drastically altering the harmonic structure of the waveform.

Ring modulation creates nonharmonic overtones and is useful for bell and gong sounds. Only the triangle waveform may be selected, along with the ring modulation bit. Program 11-6 simulates a gong by using this technique.

```
10 S=54272
20 FOR I=0 TO 24 : POKE S+I,0 : NEXT I
30 POKE S+1,50
40 POKE S+6,15*16 + 13
60 POKE S+14,2
70 POKE S+15,20
80 POKE S+24,15
90 POKE S+4,16+4+1
100 FOR J=1 TO 500 : NEXT J
110 POKE S+4,16+4
```

Program 11-6. Gong sound.

Line 30 assigns a frequency value to Voice 1. The ADSR envelope is set to 0/0/15/13 by line 40. Lines 60 and 70 set up the frequency for Voice 3. At line 80, the volume is turned on. Line 90 selects the triangle waveform, ring modulation, and gate bit for Voice 1. After the delay loop at line 100, the Voice 1 gate is released by line 110.

...The Output Registers

Locations S+27 and S+28 change dynamically as SID produces your music and sound effects. Location S+27 is known as the oscillator 3 output. Location S+28 is the output of the Voice 3 envelope generator.

As Voice 3 oscillates, location S+27 tracks the waveform. The following statement will read this location:

```
X = PEEK(S+27)
```

If the triangle waveform is selected for Voice 3, the value read will have smooth transitions from 0 to 255. The noise waveform will have random values. These values will change at a rate determined by the frequency of Voice 3. Typically, the oscillator three output value is used to modify the frequency of the other tone sources for a vibrato effect. You may also use this value to affect the volume for a tremolo effect.

Location S+28 tracks the ADSR envelope for Voice 3 and may be accessed by a PEEK statement at any time. Again, the value from this location may be used to affect other SID registers that control frequency, volume, etc.

In the register at location S+24, the bit value 128 may be set. This completely cuts off the sound output from Voice 3. Generally, when the Voice 3 output registers are used for modulation purposes, the output is not desired.

Special Print Characters

(How They Appear in Quote Mode)

Upper-case Mode

CHR$	KEYS TO PRESS	HOW IT APPEARS IN PROGRAM	ACTION
144	CTRL !/1	■	BLACK
5	CTRL "/2	▄	WHITE
28	CTRL #/3	£	RED
159	CTRL $/4	◤	CYAN
156	CTRL %/5	▚	PURPLE
30	CTRL &/6	↑	GREEN
31	CTRL '/7	←	BLUE
158	CTRL (/8	π	YELLOW
129	C= !/1	♠	ORANGE
149	C= "/2	◝	BROWN
150	C= #/3	⊠	LIGHT RED
151	C= $/4	⊙	GRAY 1

CHR$	KEYS TO PRESS		HOW IT APPEARS IN PROGRAM	ACTION
152	⬤	% 5	♣	GRAY 2
153	⬤	& 6	▌▌	LIGHT GREEN
154	⬤	' 7	◆	LIGHT BLUE
155	⬤	(8	✚	GRAY 3
18	CTRL	) 9	R	REVERSE ON
147	SHIFT	CLR HOME	♥	CLEAR THE SCREEN AND HOME
19	CLR HOME		S	HOME
145	SHIFT	CRSR	▢	CURSOR UP
17	CRSR		Q	CURSOR DOWN
157	SHIFT	CRSR	▌▌	CURSOR LEFT
29	CRSR		▟	CURSOR RIGHT
148	SHIFT	INST/DEL	▌▌	INSERT

Lowercase Mode

186	SHIFT	@	✓	CHECK MARK
169	SHIFT	£	◩	DIAGONAL HASHING
127	⬤	*	◨	DIAGONAL HASHING
126	⬤	↑	▦	CHECKERBOARD

Appendix B

Commodore 64 Screen Codes

The Commodore 64 has an upper-case character set and a lower-case character set. We move from one to the other by pressing the Ⓔ and SHIFT keys. Characters from only one set at a time can be displayed on the screen. Screen codes are distinguished from ASCII codes in that screen codes are used for PEEK and POKE with memory locations in the range 1024 to 2023 (the character screen), and ASCII codes are used for PRINT statements and the CHR$( ) function.

In order for a character to be displayed on the character screen, a corresponding location in color memory must be accessed by POKE with a color code. Character screen memory from 1024 to 2023 is mapped onto color memory from 55296 to 56295.

We present here a chart of code values and characters in the range 0 to 127. Values in the range 128 to 255 are correlated with the reverse display of the codes 0 to 127.

Upper-case Screen Codes

CHARACTER	VALUE TO POKE	CHARACTER	VALUE TO POKE	CHARACTER	VALUE TO POKE	CHARACTER	VALUE TO POKE
@	0	D	4	H	8	L	12
A	1	E	5	I	9	M	13
B	2	F	6	J	10	N	14
C	3	G	7	K	11	O	15

CHARACTER	VALUE TO POKE	CHARACTER	VALUE TO POKE	CHARACTER	VALUE TO POKE	CHARACTER	VALUE TO POKE
P	16	&	38	<	60	(graphic)	82
Q	17	'	39	=	61	(heart)	83
R	18	(	40	>	62	(graphic)	84
S	19	)	41	?	63	(graphic)	85
T	20	*	42	(graphic)	64	(graphic)	86
U	21	+	43	(spade)	65	(circle)	87
V	22	,	44	(graphic)	66	(club)	88
W	23	-	45	(graphic)	67	(graphic)	89
X	24	.	46	(graphic)	68	(diamond)	90
Y	25	/	47	(graphic)	69	(cross)	91
Z	26	0	48	(graphic)	70	(graphic)	92
[	27	1	49	(graphic)	71	(graphic)	93
£	28	2	50	(graphic)	72	π	94
]	29	3	51	(graphic)	73	(graphic)	95
↑	30	4	52	(graphic)	74	SPACE	96
←	31	5	53	(graphic)	75	(graphic)	97
SPACE	32	6	54	(graphic)	76	(graphic)	98
!	33	7	55	(graphic)	77	(graphic)	99
"	34	8	56	(graphic)	78	(graphic)	100
#	35	9	57	(graphic)	79	(graphic)	101
$	36	:	58	(graphic)	80	(checker)	102
%	37	;	59	(circle)	81	(graphic)	103

CHARACTER	VALUE TO POKE	CHARACTER	VALUE TO POKE	CHARACTER	VALUE TO POKE	CHARACTER	VALUE TO POKE
	104		110		116		122
	105		111		117		123
	106		112		118		124
	107		113		119		125
	108		114		120		126
	109		115		121		127

Lower-case Screen Codes

CHARACTER	VALUE TO POKE	CHARACTER	VALUE TO POKE	CHARACTER	VALUE TO POKE	CHARACTER	VALUE TO POKE
@	0	n	14	£	28	*	42
a	1	o	15	]	29	+	43
b	2	p	16	↑	30	,	44
c	3	q	17	←	31	-	45
d	4	r	18	SPACE	32	.	46
e	5	s	19	!	33	/	47
f	6	t	20	"	34	0	48
g	7	u	21	#	35	1	49
h	8	v	22	$	36	2	50
i	9	w	23	%	37	3	51
j	10	x	24	&	38	4	52
k	11	y	25	'	39	5	53
l	12	z	26	(	40	6	54
m	13	[	27	)	41	7	55

CHARACTER	VALUE TO POKE	CHARACTER	VALUE TO POKE	CHARACTER	VALUE TO POKE	CHARACTER	VALUE TO POKE
8	56	J	74		92		110
9	57	K	75		93		111
:	58	L	76		94		112
;	59	M	77		95		113
<	60	N	78	SPACE	96		114
=	61	O	79		97		115
>	62	P	80		98		116
?	63	Q	81		99		117
	64	R	82		100		118
A	65	S	83		101		119
B	66	T	84		102		120
C	67	U	85		103		121
D	68	V	86		104		122
E	69	W	87		105		123
F	70	X	88		106		124
G	71	Y	89		107		125
H	72	Z	90		108		126
I	73		91		109		127

Appendix C

PRINT Codes on the Commodore 64

The character sets and certain control functions are produced by using PRINT CHR$(C), where C is a value from this appendix. Sometimes it is useful to determine the code value from an entry from the keyboard. This is easily accomplished with GET A$ and PRINT ASC (A$). ASC will return the numeric value associated with the character in A$. This is particularly useful for the function keys (f1 to f8) at the right on the keyboard.

The Commodore 64 has an upper-case and a lower-case character set. Characters from only one at a time can be displayed. We switch from one to the other by pressing the **C=** and SHIFT keys. We may also specify lower-case display by using CHR$(14) in a PRINT statement. To switch to upper-case, use CHR$(142) in a PRINT statement.

Upper-case PRINT Codes

DISPLAY OR ACTION	CHR$( )	DISPLAY OR ACTION	CHR$( )	DISPLAY OR ACTION	CHR$( )	DISPLAY OR ACTION	CHR$( )
	0	White	5		10		15
	1		6		11		16
	2		7		12	CRSR ↑	17
	3	Disable SHIFT C=8		RETURN	13	RVS ON	18
	4	Enable SHIFT C=9		Switch to Lower Case	14	HOME	19

DISPLAY OR ACTION	CHR$( )	DISPLAY OR ACTION	CHR$( )	DISPLAY OR ACTION	CHR$( )	DISPLAY OR ACTION	CHR$( )
DEL	20	*	42	@	64	V	86
	21	+	43	A	65	W	87
	22	,	44	B	66	X	88
	23	-	45	C	67	Y	89
	24	.	46	D	68	Z	90
	25	/	47	E	69	[	91
	26	0	48	F	70	£	92
	27	1	49	G	71	]	93
Red	28	2	50	H	72	↑	94
CRSR→	29	3	51	I	73	←	95
Green	30	4	52	J	74		96
Blue	31	5	53	K	75	♠	97
SPACE	32	6	54	L	76		98
!	33	7	55	M	77		99
"	34	8	56	N	78		100
#	35	9	57	O	79		101
$	36	:	58	P	80		102
%	37	;	59	Q	81		103
&	38	<	60	R	82		104
•	39	=	61	S	83		105
(	40	>	62	T	84		106
)	41	?	63	U	85		107

DISPLAY OR ACTION	CHR$( )	DISPLAY OR ACTION	CHR$( )	DISPLAY OR ACTION	CHR$( )	DISPLAY OR ACTION	CHR$( )
	108		130	Gray 2	152		174
	109		131	Light green	153		175
	110		132	Light blue	154		176
	111	f1	133	Gray 3	155		177
	112	f3	134	Purple	156		178
	113	f5	135	CRSR	157		179
	114	f7	136	Yellow	158		180
	115	f2	137	Cyan	159		181
	116	f4	138	SPACE	160		182
	117	f6	139		161		183
	118	f8	140		162		184
	119	SHIFT RETURN	141		163		185
	120	Switch to Upper Case	142		164		186
	121		143		165		187
	122	Black	144		166		188
	123	CRSR	145		167		189
	124	RVS OFF	146		168		190
	125	CLR	147		169		191
π	126	INST	148		170		
	127	Brown	149		171		
	128	Light red	150		172		
	129	Gray 1	151		173		

Lower-case PRINT Codes

DISPLAY OR ACTION	CHR$( )	DISPLAY OR ACTION	CHR$( )	DISPLAY OR ACTION	CHR$( )	DISPLAY OR ACTION	CHR$( )
	0		21	*	42	?	63
	1		22	+	43	@	64
	2		23	,	44	a	65
	3		24	-	45	b	66
	4		25	.	46	c	67
White	5		26	/	47	d	68
	6		27	0	48	e	69
	7	Red	28	1	49	f	70
Disable [SHIFT] [C=]	8	CRSR→	29	2	50	g	71
Enable [SHIFT] [C=]	9	Green	30	3	51	h	72
	10	Blue	31	4	52	i	73
	11	SPACE	32	5	53	j	74
	12	!	33	6	54	k	75
RETURN	13	"	34	7	55	l	76
Switch to Lower Case	14	#	35	8	56	m	77
	15	$	36	9	57	n	78
	16	%	37	:	58	o	79
CRSR↑	17	&	38	;	59	p	80
RVS ON	18	•	39	<	60	q	81
HOME	19	(	40	=	61	r	82
DEL	20	)	41	>	62	s	83

DISPLAY OR ACTION	CHR$( )	DISPLAY OR ACTION	CHR$( )	DISPLAY OR ACTION	CHR$( )	DISPLAY OR ACTION	CHR$( )
t	84	J	106		128	Light red	150
u	85	K	107	Orange	129	Gray 1	151
v	86	L	108		130	Gray 2	152
w	87	M	109		131	Light green	153
x	88	N	110		132	Light blue	154
y	89	O	111	f1	133	Gray 3	155
z	90	P	112	f3	134	Purple	156
[	91	Q	113	f5	135	←CRSR	157
£	92	R	114	f7	136	Yellow	158
]	93	S	115	f2	137	Cyan	159
↑	94	T	116	f4	138	SPACE	160
←	95	U	117	f6	139		161
	96	V	118	f8	140		162
A	97	W	119	SHIFT RETURN	141		163
B	98	X	120	Switch to Upper Case	142		164
C	99	Y	121		143		165
D	100	Z	122	Black	144		166
E	101		123	↓CRSR	145		167
F	102		124	RVS OFF	146		168
G	103		125	CLR	147		169
H	104	↑	126	INST	148		170
I	105		127	Brown	149		171

DISPLAY OR ACTION	CHR$( )	DISPLAY OR ACTION	CHR$( )	DISPLAY OR ACTION	CHR$( )	DISPLAY OR ACTION	CHR$( )
	172		177		182		187
	173		178		183		188
	174		179		184		189
	175		180		185		190
	176		181		186		191

CODES 192–223 ARE THE SAME AS 96–127
CODES 224–254 ARE THE SAME AS 160–190
CODE 255 IS THE SAME AS 126

Appendix D

The Disk

Adding a 1541 Commodore disk drive to the Commodore 64 computer creates a powerful computer system. Now we can purchase a wide variety of applications programs for education, business, and entertainment. We can write programs of our own and save them to use later. These programs are easily used with simple commands in BASIC. The disk is much faster and more versatile than tape. This appendix contains information for maintaining programs on a disk. For information on sequential files, see Chapter 8.

The disk drive is connected to the computer with a single cable that fits only in the correct socket at the rear of the keyboard unit. A standard power cord is also supplied. All connections of any computer components should be made only with power switches turned off. Once the connections are made, turning the disk drive power switch on should cause the red light on the front to come on momentarily; the green light should come on and stay on until the power switch is turned off. Only after the power is on should you insert a disk. The disk should always be removed before power is turned off. Failure to observe these rules could result in damage to the data stored on the disk.

To insert a disk, first remove it from the protective paper envelope. Then, with the label facing up and the little notch toward the side the lights are on, gently slide it all the way in. To do this you must slide a finger part way into the one-inch by two-inch opening in the center. Then gently press down on the door cover. It should slide easily past a little spring and stay down. This process very quickly becomes automatic.

To remove a disk, press the door cover into the disk drive (toward the rear) with a firm motion. The door will spring up and the disk will be propelled part way out of the slot.

Always be careful when you are handling disks. Never touch the exposed parts of the Mylar disk enclosed within the square jacket. Fingerprints, dust, and dirt are enemies of the recording surface. Always use a soft tip marker to write on the label. Never use a ball point pen, as this could dent the disk, causing permanent damage.

...The Directory

One way to look at a directory of files stored on a disk is to type the following:

```
LOAD "$",8
```

(We'll get to the LOAD command shortly.) Then type LIST. If your disk has a large number of files on it you may want to press the CTRL key to hold the display on the screen long enough to read it all. Each file name will contain a PRG, SEQ, USR, or REL to distinguish the four types of files available on the Commodore 64. The two file types discussed in this book are PRG and SEQ. All BASIC programs are labelled PRG. All sequential files (see Chapter 8) are labelled SEQ.

At the left in each entry of the directory is a number. That is the number of 256-byte blocks required to store the file on the disk. A disk will hold 664 blocks for a total of about 170K.

Be careful. Reading the directory in this way destroys any BASIC program in memory at the time. Yes, the directory is read into main memory by the procedure described above. Once you have read the directory, it is necessary to clear it out by typing NEW or by loading a program from disk. Turning the machine off will do it, too.

We can also examine the directory without displacing any BASIC program in memory. This is done by using a program supplied on the test/demo disk included with the 1541 disk drive.

...LOAD

In order to use any program on disk, we must first load it into the computer. This command causes a copy of a program to be transferred to memory in the Commodore 64. It is a good idea to begin with the test/demo disk supplied with the 1514 drive. It should contain a program called C-64 WEDGE. On some disks it may be called DOS SUPPORT or a similar name. If one of these names isn't present, check the directory by entering LOAD "$", 8 and LIST as described above. The wedge provides some convenient commands not available in BASIC, and it doesn't use any of the memory normally available to a BASIC program. To use it type

```
LOAD "C-64 WEDGE", 8
```

We need to tell the Commodore 64 that we want to access the disk. The disk is number 8 to this computer. Other values are used for other devices. 0 is the screen, 1 is the Datassette. Additional values represent other peripherals like a printer. So, we use the number 8 in our command. That is called the *device number*. The first disk is always taken to be device number 8. The Commodore 64 should reply

```
SEARCHING FOR C-64 WEDGE
LOADING
READY.
```

Next, we type RUN and the new commands are in place. All programs are used in this way, by first loading the program and then running it. We may use an asterisk to request the first program on the directory.

With the C-64 WEDGE in place we can easily examine the directory by entering the command

```
@$
```

We don't even have to give the device number. The biggest benefit is that we can examine the directory and maintain a program in memory at the same time.

...SAVE

Every disk must be properly formatted once to prepare it for storing programs (see "Formatting a New Disk" below).

To save a program with the name FIRST on disk we simply type

```
SAVE "FIRST",8
```

The computer will display

```
SAVING FIRST
```

on the screen. The disk will whir for a few seconds. When it shuts off and the red light goes out, typing @$ will reveal that indeed our program named FIRST is on the list.

If it happens that we already have a program named FIRST, there will be no discernable difference on the screen. However, (and this is a *however*), the red light on the drive will flash. Whenever the red light on the drive flashes, there's trouble. Press @ and RETURN. (With the WEDGE in place, @ reads disk errors.) The red light will go out and the following message will appear on the screen:

```
63, FILE EXISTS,00,00
```

This means just what it says. Disk errors are numbered for the Commodore 1541 drive. The error number 63 is the FILE EXISTS error. The other two numbers are the track and sector. With track and sector, the advanced programmer can diagnose the exact location on the disk where the difficulty lies. Track 18 has to do with the directory. (Errors are discussed under the section entitled "DOS Commands.")

We need a special instruction to tell the computer to replace the existing program. It is

```
SAVE "@:FIRST",8
```

The at-sign-colon (@:) causes the replacement.

...DOS Commands

Certain things that we do on disk are controlled by the disk drive itself. In order to do those things, we must create a communications link between BASIC and a program in the disk drive called DOS (*Disk Operating System*). The communications link is called the *command channel* and is always numbered 15. In addition, we must specify a file number in the range 1 to 127 in an OPEN statement.

```
OPEN 3,8,15
```

This OPEN statement connects file 3 to the command channel. The 8 refers to the disk drive as before. The OPEN statement can be issued in immediate or deferred mode. Now we can send commands to the disk drive through PRINT# statements. We will get to the commands soon.

Following any command and at the end of a task, we must be sure to close the file. In the case above

```
CLOSE 3
```

does it for us.

...Formatting a New Disk (NEW)

Before we can save programs on a disk it must be formatted. That is, a pattern must be written on the disk so that the computer can organize data stored on it.

We can write a program to format a disk. See Program D-1.

```
100 OPEN 3,8,15
110 PRINT# 3, "NEW:FIRST DISK,00"
130 CLOSE 3
```

Program D-1. Formatting a disk.

The formatting command appears in quotes in line 110. The NEW command may be abbreviated to "N." The colon separates the command from the disk name. We are allowed up to 16 characters for a name. The comma separates the name from a two-character identification (ID). This ID is checked by DOS. If we improperly change disks during an operation DOS will produce an error. (We'll also get to errors.)

Alternatively, the command can be included right in the OPEN statement, as in Program D-2.

```
100 OPEN 3,8,15,"N:FIRST DISK,00"
130 CLOSE 3
```

Program D-2. Formatting with the OPEN statement.

Following the NEW command the red light will come on and the disk will whir for about a minute and a half. The red light will go out and the disk is ready for use.

We can format a disk by typing the lines of either Program D-1 or D-2 in immediate mode as well.

Omitting the two-character ID at the end will cause DOS to simply erase all directory entries. This is a way to reformat a disk with unwanted programs on it. This operation will erase all programs.

...Disk Errors

If the red light ever blinks continuously, something is wrong. We have to look at the light—BASIC does not necessarily display an error message. Even when BASIC does display a message, it may not reflect the real problem. The easy way to determine what the error might be is to have the C-64 WEDGE program in place at all times. Then we can simply press the @ symbol and the error will be displayed for us.

Without the WEDGE program we must write a program to read the ERROR channel. See Program D-3.

```
     100  OPEN 3,8,15
-->110  INPUT# 3, E,E$,T,S
     120  PRINT E;E$;T;S
     130  CLOSE 3
```

Program D-3. Reading the error channel.

Errors are read through the command channel, 15. Line 110 of Program D-3 uses a variation of the INPUT statement—it simply takes its INPUT from file 3. The value of E is the error number. These numbers are keyed to a table of errors in the VIC 1541 user's manual. The second value is a string with a readable error message. The symbols T and S stand for the disk track and sector where the error was detected. In rare instances where a valuable disk has been damaged, advanced programmers can use this information to bypass the error and recover lost data. Usually the error is something simple that beginners tend to do. After a few days, we gain experience and most errors cease to occur.

Some of the silly things that cause errors are not putting a disk in the drive, not closing the door, putting the disk in upside down, and not turning the disk drive on. It takes a little experience to interpret the meaning of the error messages.

DRIVE NOT READY can mean several things. An unformatted disk will produce this message. Inserting a disk part way will, too. So will putting a disk in upside down. They all amount to the same thing: the drive is not ready.

The best way to deal with errors is to acknowledge that there is an error and search for the cause. It is a great temptation to be certain that *we* couldn't possibly have made a mistake. Well, we can and we do.

...SCRATCH

Any program that we have no further use for should be erased from the disk with the SCRATCH command. This can be done right in an OPEN statement or with PRINT#, as with NEW. Here is a two-line program to do it:

```
     100  OPEN 1,8,15,"S:OLD FILE"
     110  CLOSE 1
```

The same two lines may be used in immediate mode. If we choose to do this with a PRINT# statement, we must remember to open a file for this purpose and then close it.

Be sure to check the little red light or the error channel.

...RENAME

Occasionally we want to rename a program. This can be done without LOAD and SAVE, by using RENAME.

```
100 OPEN 3,8,15,"R:NEW=OLD"
110 CLOSE 3
```

...INITIALIZE

It may happen that an error condition will keep us from proceeding further with some disk operation. We can initialize the disk drive to the condition it has when turned on with

```
100 OPEN 3,8,15,"I"
110 CLOSE 3
```

This should be a rarely used command.

...VALIDATE

After SAVE and SCRATCH have been used on a disk many times it is possible for small areas to become inaccessible to DOS.

```
100 OPEN 3,8,15,"V"
110 CLOSE 3
```

will reorganize things on the disk to maximize the space that can be used.

If you are using the advanced technique of random files, this command must not be issued. It will destroy data in random files.

... C-64 WEDGE Commands

We have discussed the benefits of using @$ to examine the disk directory of files. We have also mentioned the use of @ by itself to read errors on the command channel. Many of the commands discussed above are available in abbreviated form with C-64 WEDGE. OPEN and CLOSE are not required for any of these commands.

...NEW

We can format a disk easily with

```
@N:NAME,OO
```

To reformat an old disk, just omit the two-character ID.

...SCRATCH

We can erase an unwanted program with

```
@S:FILENAME
```

...RENAME

```
@R:NEWNAME=OLDNAME
```

renames a program for us on disk.

...INITIALIZE
The drive can be restored to its initial state at power-up with

```
@I
```

...VALIDATE
If a disk has accumulated little unusable blocks of space because of repeated use of the SAVE and SCRATCH commands, we can recover by validating the disk with

```
@V
```

...LOAD
Even LOAD can be shortened.

```
/PROGRAM NAME
```

is equivalent to

```
LOAD "PROGRAM NAME", 8
```

...LOAD and RUN
We can load and run a BASIC program with

```
█PROGRAM NAME
```

That is an up arrow, found next to the RESTORE key.

...SAVE
We have a shortened command for SAVE.

```
←PROGRAM NAME
```

That is the left arrow key, found to the left of the digit 1 on the keyboard.

If you use the Commodore 64 day in and day out, then it is definitely worth learning these shortened forms. It isn't too much of a chore to learn the @ commands. And certainly it is well worthwhile to use @ to read errors and @$ to see the directory. These two commands alone justify installing C-64 WEDGE routinely every time you turn the disk drive on.

Appendix E

Index of Programs

Appendix F

Solution Programs for Even-Numbered Problems

Each two-page spread should be read from top to bottom as one individual page.

Chapter 1

Problem No. 2

```
100 PRINT "ENTER FIVE NUMBERS";
110 INPUT A1, A2, A3, A4, A5
120 PRINT A1+A2+A3+A4+A5

RUN
ENTER FIVE NUMBERS? 3,98,2.1,21,109
 233.1

READY.
```

Problem No. 4

```
100 X = 1/3
110 PRINT X, 3*X, X + X + X

RUN
```

Chapter 2

Section 1

Problem No. 2

```
10 REM ** ENTER THE FOLLOWING LINES:
232 IF WT = 0 THEN GOTO 999
295 PRINT
297 PRINT
300 GOTO 200
999 END

RUN
WT 1? 179
WT 2? 182
WT 3? 181
WT 4? 180
WT 5? 179
ACCEPT THIS LOT
```

WT 120

READY.

Problem No. 4

```
100  READ A,B,C,D
110  PRINT " SCORES:"; A; B; C; D
120  PRINT "AVERAGE:"; (A + B + C + D) / 4
900  DATA 100, 86, 71, 92
```

RUN
```
  SCORES: 100   86   71   92
AVERAGE: 87.25
```

Problem No. 6

```
100 REM ** COUNT AND SUM INTEGERS FROM
1001 TO 2213 DIVISIBLE BY ELEVEN
150  C1 = 0
160  J1 = 1001
170  SM = 0
210  C1 = C1 + 1
220  SM = SM + J1
280  J1 = J1 + 11
290  IF J1 <= 2213 THEN GOTO 210
310  PRINT C1; "NUMBERS"
320  PRINT SM; "SUM"
```

RUN
```
  111 NUMBERS
  178266 SUM
```

Problem No. 8

```
100 REM ** DOUBLE WAGES EACH DAY FOR 30
DAYS
150  DA = 1
```

.333333333   1   1

READY.

Problem No. 6

```
100  N = 1/2 + 1/3
110  D = 1/3 - 1/4
120  PRINT N/D
```

RUN
```
  10
```

READY.

Problem No. 8

```
100 PRINT 1*2*3*4*5*6*7*8*9*10
```

RUN
```
  3628800
```

READY.

Problem No. 10

```
100  PRINT " ENTER FIRST FRACTION N,D";
110  INPUT N1, D1
130  PRINT "ENTER SECOND FRACTION N,D";
140  INPUT N2, D2
160  PRINT N1*D2 + N2*D1; "/"; D1*D2
```

RUN
```
  ENTER FIRST FRACTION N, D? 1, 4
  ENTER SECOND FRACTION N, D? 2, 3
  11 / 12
```

READY.

Section 1 *Problem No. 8 (continued)*

```
160 WA = .01
170 T1 = 0
198 REM
200 T1 = T1 + WA
210 W1 = WA
220 WA = WA * 2
230 DA = DA + 1
290 IF DA <= 30 THEN GOTO 200
300 PRINT "30TH DAY WAGES = $"; W1
310 PRINT "    TOTAL WAGES = $"; T1

RUN
30TH DAY WAGES = $ 5368709.12
     TOTAL WAGES = $ 10737418.2
```

Problem No. 10

```
100 REM **    CALCULATE THE AMOUNT OF AN
    ORDER
200 BK = 4 * 10.95 * (1 - .25)
220 RC = 3 * 7.98 * (1 - .15)
240 RP = 59.95
290 T1 = BK + RC + RP
300 T = T1 * (1 - .02)
400 PRINT "AMOUNT $"; T

RUN
AMOUNT $ 110.88602
```

Problem No. 12

```
100 REM ** G FOR GIFTS
102 REM ** D FOR DAY NUMBER
104 REM ** G1 FOR GIFTS THIS DAY
150 G = 0
160 D = 1
```

RUN
HTTTTHHTTHHHTHHHTHHTHHHTTHTTTHHHHHHHHTH
16 TAILS

Problem No. 4

```
100 REM ** ROLLING TWO DICE TEN TIMES
150 C1 = 1
200 D1 = INT(RND(1) * 6 + 1)
210 D2 = INT(RND(1) * 6 + 1)
220 PRINT D1, D2
250 C1 = C1 + 1
290 IF C1 <= 10 THEN 200

RUN
6    2
5    3
5    1
6    5
5    1
5    4
6    4
1    6
2    4
1    3
```

Section 3
Problem No. 2

```
100 REM **  COUNT ODD INTEGERS FROM 5 TO
    1191
190 C1 = 0
200 FOR IN = 5 TO 1191 STEP 2
210 C1 = C1 + 1
290 NEXT IN
300 PRINT "ODD INTEGERS FROM 5 TO 1191 ="; C1
```

```
RUN
ODD INTEGERS FROM 5 TO 1191 = 594
```

Problem No. 4

```
100 REM ** CALCULATE WAGES FOR DOUBLING
    EACH DAY FOR 30 DAYS
180 WA = .01
190 T1 = .01
200 FOR DA = 2 TO 30
230 WA = WA * 2
230 T1 = T1 + WA
290 NEXT DA
300 PRINT "30TH DAY WAGES = $"; WA
310 PRINT " TOTAL WAGES = $"; T1
```

```
RUN
30TH DAY WAGES = $ 5368709.12
   TOTAL WAGES = $ 10737418.2
```

Problem No. 6

```
100 REM ** G FOR GIFTS
102 REM ** D FOR DAY NUMBER
104 REM ** G1 IS GIFTS TODAY
150 G = 0
160 FOR D = 1 TO 12
190 G1 = 0
200 FOR T = 1 TO D
220 G1 = G1 + T
230 NEXT T
240 G = G + G1
300 NEXT D
400 PRINT "TOTAL NUMBER OF GIFTS IS:"; G
```

```
RUN
TOTAL NUMBER OF GIFTS IS: 364
```

```
200 G1 = 0
210 G1 = G1 + 1
220 G = G + G1
230 IF G1 = D THEN GOTO 300
240 GOTO 210
300 PRINT G1, G
305 D = D + 1
310 IF D <= 12 THEN GOTO 200
390 PRINT
400 PRINT "TOTAL NUMBER OF GIFTS IS:"; G
```

```
RUN
1    1
2    4
3    10
4    20
5    35
6    56
7    84
8    120
9    165
10   220
11   286
12   364
```

```
TOTAL NUMBER OF GIFTS IS: 364
```

Section 2

Problem No. 2

```
10 REM ** TYPE IN PROGRAM 2-9 AND ENTER
   THE FOLLOWING LINES:
150 TA = 0
255 TA = TA + 1
295 PRINT
300 PRINT TA; "TAILS"
```

RUN
LET'S DO SOME ADDITION DRILL

HOW MANY PROBLEMS DO YOU WANT? 5

ENTER RANGE OF NUMBERS DESIRED? 10,41

28 + 11 =? 38
NO, THAT WOULD BE 39

10 + 19 =? 29
RIGHT

18 + 22 =? 40
RIGHT

30 + 29 =? 39
NO, THAT WOULD BE 59

14 + 33 =? 47
RIGHT

YOU GOT 3 CORRECT OUT OF 5

Chapter 3

Section 1

Problem No. 2

```
98 REM ** DISPLAY A ONE AND A THREE
100 PRINT "☐";
1098 REM ** DISPLAY "1"
1100 PRINT "R"
1110 PRINT "R"
1120 PRINT "R"
1130 PRINT "R"
1140 PRINT "R"
```

Section 3 *(continued)*

Problem No. 8

```
100 REM ** USING FOR...NEXT
150 FOR DO = 1 TO 5
198 REM ** 39 FLIPS 5 TIMES
200 FOR FL = 1 TO 39
230 IF RND(1) < .5 THEN 270
250 PRINT "T";
260 GOTO 280
270 PRINT "H";
280 NEXT FL
295 PRINT
296 PRINT
300 NEXT DO
999 END
```

RUN
TTTTTTHTTHHHTHHHHTHTHTTHHHTHHHTHHT

HHHTHHHHTHHHTTHTTHTTHTHTTTHHHHHHHT

HTTTTTHHTTHTHTHTTTTTTHHHTHHTHTHTTTTHT

TTTHTTTHHTTTTTTTTTTTTHHTTHHTTTTTTHHTHTHT

HTTHTHTHTTTTTTHTTHTHHTTHTHHTTHTTHTTTT

Problem No. 10

```
100 REM ** USING FOR...NEXT
150 TA = 0
198 REM ** FLIP A COIN 1000 TIMES
200 FOR FL = 1 TO 1000
230 IF RND(1) < .5 THEN 270
250 REM
255 TA = TA + 1
```

```
1298 REM ** DISPLAY "3"
1300 PRINT "▨"
1310 PRINT "▨"
1320 PRINT "▨"
1330 PRINT "▨"
1340 PRINT "▨"
```

Problem No. 4

```
100  PRINT "□"
1098 REM ** DISPLAY "1"
1100 PRINT " ▨ "
1110 PRINT " ▨ "
1120 PRINT " ▨ "
1130 PRINT " ▨ "
1140 PRINT " ▨ "
```

Problem No. 6

```
98   REM ** THREE OF HEARTS
100  PRINT "□"
110  PRINT
120  PRINT
130  PRINT
140  PRINT
150  PRINT
160  PRINT
170  PRINT
180  PRINT
190  PRINT
200  PRINT
210  PRINT
220  PRINT
230  PRINT
```

```
260 GOTO 280
270 REM
280 NEXT FL
295 PRINT
300 PRINT TA; "TAILS"
999 END

RUN

534 TAILS
```

Problem No. 12

```
200 PRINT "LET'S DO SOME ADDITION DRILL"
205 PRINT
210 PRINT "HOW MANY PROBLEMS DO YOU WANT";
220 INPUT NØ
250 PRINT
260 PRINT "ENTER RANGE OF NUMBERS DESIRED";
270 INPUT LO,HI
290 RT = Ø
298 REM ** BEGIN DRILL HERE
300 FOR PR = 1 TO NØ
310 N1 = INT(RND(1) * (HI - LO + 1) + LO)
320 N2 = INT(RND(1) * (HI - LO + 1) + LO)
330 SM = N1 + N2
340 PRINT
350 PRINT N1; "+"; N2; "=";
360 INPUT AN
400 IF AN = SM THEN 450
410 PRINT "NO, THAT WOULD BE"; SM
420 GOTO 480
450 PRINT "RIGHT"
460 RT = RT + 1
480 NEXT PR
500 PRINT
510 PRINT "YOU GOT"; RT; "CORRECT OUT OF"; NØ
```

Section 2

Problem No. 2

```
200 R = INT(RND(1)*6) + 1
210 PRINT "□";
910 IF R = 1 THEN GOSUB 1100
920 IF R = 2 THEN GOSUB 1200
930 IF R = 3 THEN GOSUB 1300
940 IF R = 4 THEN GOSUB 1400
950 IF R = 5 THEN GOSUB 1500
960 IF R = 6 THEN GOSUB 1600
990 END
1098 REM ** DISPLAY "1"
1100 PRINT "R    ="
1110 PRINT "R    ="
1120 PRINT "R  ● ="
1130 PRINT "R    ="
1140 PRINT "R    ="
1190 RETURN
1198 REM ** DISPLAY "2"
1200 PRINT "R    ="
1210 PRINT "R  ● ="
1220 PRINT "R    ="
1230 PRINT "R ●  ="
1240 PRINT "R    ="
1290 RETURN
1298 REM ** DISPLAY "3"
1300 PRINT "R    ="
1310 PRINT "R  ● ="
1320 PRINT "R ●  ="
1330 PRINT "R  ● ="
1340 PRINT "R    ="
1390 RETURN
1398 REM ** DISPLAY "4"
1400 PRINT "R ●  ="
1410 PRINT "R    ="
1420 PRINT "R ●  ="
1430 PRINT "R ●  ="
```

```
940 IF R = 4 THEN GOSUB 1400
950 IF R = 5 THEN GOSUB 1500
960 IF R = 6 THEN GOSUB 1600
990 RETURN
998 REM ** PLACE CURSOR
1000 IF L = 0 THEN 1090
1010 FOR I9 = 1 TO L
1020 PRINT
1030 NEXT I9
1090 RETURN
1098 REM ** DISPLAY "1"
1100 PRINT TAB(X); "R    ="
1110 PRINT TAB(X); "R    ="
1120 PRINT TAB(X); "R  ● ="
1130 PRINT TAB(X); "R    ="
1140 PRINT TAB(X); "R    ="
1190 RETURN
1198 REM ** DISPLAY "2"
1200 PRINT TAB(X); "R    ="
1210 PRINT TAB(X); "R ●  ="
1220 PRINT TAB(X); "R    ="
1230 PRINT TAB(X); "R  ● ="
1240 PRINT TAB(X); "R    ="
1290 RETURN
1298 REM ** DISPLAY "3"
1300 PRINT TAB(X); "R ●  ="
1310 PRINT TAB(X); "R    ="
1320 PRINT TAB(X); "R ●  ="
1330 PRINT TAB(X); "R  ● ="
1340 PRINT TAB(X); "R    ="
1390 RETURN
1398 REM ** DISPLAY "4"
1400 PRINT TAB(X); "R ●  ="
1410 PRINT TAB(X); "R    ="
1420 PRINT TAB(X); "R ●  ="
1430 PRINT TAB(X); "R ●  ="
1440 PRINT TAB(X); "R    ="
1490 RETURN
1498 REM ** DISPLAY "5"
```

```
1440 PRINT "R       "
1490 RETURN
1498 REM ** DISPLAY "5"
1500 PRINT "R  •   • R"
1510 PRINT "R        R"
1520 PRINT "R    •   R"
1530 PRINT "R        R"
1540 PRINT "R  •   • R"
1590 RETURN
1598 REM ** DISPLAY "6"
1600 PRINT "R  •   • R"
1610 PRINT "R        R"
1620 PRINT "R  •   • R"
1630 PRINT "R        R"
1640 PRINT "R  •   • R"
1690 RETURN
```

Problem No. 4

```
98  REM ** FIRST DIE
100 R = INT(RND(1)*6) + 1
110 PRINT "☐";
120 X = 1
130 L = 19
140 GOSUB 1000
150 GOSUB 910
198 REM ** SECOND DIE
200 R = INT(RND(1)*6) + 1
210 PRINT "S";
220 X = 9
230 L = 19
240 GOSUB 1000
250 GOSUB 910
260 PRINT "S";
290 END
898 REM ** SELECT DIE TO DISPLAY
910 IF R = 1 THEN GOSUB 1100
920 IF R = 2 THEN GOSUB 1200
930 IF R = 3 THEN GOSUB 1300
```

```
1500 PRINT TAB(X); "R  •   • R"
1510 PRINT TAB(X); "R        R"
1520 PRINT TAB(X); "R    •   R"
1530 PRINT TAB(X); "R        R"
1540 PRINT TAB(X); "R  •   • R"
1590 RETURN
1598 REM ** DISPLAY "6"
1600 PRINT TAB(X); "R  •   • R"
1610 PRINT TAB(X); "R        R"
1620 PRINT TAB(X); "R  •   • R"
1630 PRINT TAB(X); "R        R"
1640 PRINT TAB(X); "R  •   • R"
1690 RETURN
```

Problem No. 6

```
1  REM ** TYPE IN THE SOLUTION TO PROBLEM
   NO. 4 ABOVE AND THE FOLLOWING LINES:
8  REM ** ROLL THE DICE
10 FOR J9 = 1 TO 25
20 R = INT(RND(1)*6) + 1
30 PRINT "H";
40 X = INT(RND(1)*32) + 1
50 L = INT(RND(1)*19) + 1
60 GOSUB 1000
70 GOSUB 910
80 NEXT J9
120 X = INT(RND(1)*32) + 1
130 L = INT(RND(1)*19) + 1
220 X = INT(RND(1)*32) + 1
230 L = INT(RND(1)*19) + 1
```

Chapter 4

Section 1

Problem No. 2

```
100 PRINT "COMPARE COMPOUND INTEREST"
110 PRINT "ON $100000 FOR A YEAR"
```

Section 1 Problem No. 2 (continued)

```
120 PRINT
130 PRINT ,360; TAB(27); 365
200 P = 100000
210 A = P*(1+.055/360)^360 - P
220 A1 = P*(1+.055/365)^365 - P
230 PRINT " 5.5%", A; TAB(25); A1
240 A = P*(1+.125/360)^360 - P
250 A1 = P*(1+.125/365)^365 - P
260 PRINT "12.5%", A; TAB(25); A1
300 PRINT
310 PRINT "WE WOULD LOSE 4 CENTS AT 12.5%"
```

```
RUN
COMPARE COMPOUND INTEREST
ON $100000 FOR A YEAR

             360           365
5.5%     5653.6304    5653.64285
12.5%   13312.3911    13312.4347

WE WOULD LOSE 4 CENTS AT 12.5%
```

Problem No. 4

```
100 PRINT "COMPARE COMPOUND INTEREST"
110 PRINT "ON $100000 FOR A YEAR"
120 PRINT
130 PRINT ,360; TAB(27); 365
200 P = 100000
210 R = 5.5
220 DA = 360
230 GOSUB 900
240 A = A9 - P
250 DA = 365
260 GOSUB 900
270 A1 = A9 - P
```

```
160 GOTO 120
200 PRINT
210 PRINT "THE EARLIEST IS: "; E$
890 END
900 DATA GEORGE, ASTER, CAMERA
910 DATA TELEVISION, ALPHABET
999 DATA THE END
```

```
RUN
THE WORDS:
GEORGE
ASTER
CAMERA
TELEVISION
ALPHABET

THE EARLIEST IS: ALPHABET
```

Problem No. 4

```
998 REM ** YES-NO PROCESSOR
1000 AN = -5
1010 INPUT A$
1020 IF A$ = "YES"  THEN AN = 1
1030 IF A$ = "Y"    THEN AN = 1
1040 IF A$ = "NO"   THEN AN = 0
1050 IF A$ = "N"    THEN AN = 0
1060 IF AN > -5 THEN 1090
1070 PRINT "'Y' OR 'N', PLEASE"
1080 GOTO 1010
1090 RETURN
```

Section 2

Problem No. 2

```
100 W$ = "SUNDAY  MONDAY  TUESDAY  WED
NESDAYTHURSDAY FRIDAY "
```

```
290 PRINT "  5.5%", A; TAB(25); A1
300 P = 100000
310 R = 12.5
320 DA = 365
330 GOSUB 900
340 A = A9 - P
350 DA = 365
360 GOSUB 900
370 A1 = A9 - P
390 PRINT "12.5%", A; TAB(25); A1
989 REM ** CALCULATE INTEREST
900 P9 = P
910 FOR X = 1 TO DA
920 A9 = P9 + P9*(R/100/DA)
930 P9 = A9
940 NEXT X
990 RETURN

RUN
COMPARE COMPOUND INTEREST
ON $100000 FOR A YEAR

                        365
5.5%      5653.61746    5653.62402
12.5%     13312.3867    13312.4206
```

Chapter 5

Section 1

Problem No. 2

```
100 PRINT "THE WORDS:"
110 E$ = "ZZZZ"
120 READ A$
130 IF A$ = "THE END" THEN 200
140 PRINT A$
150 IF A$ < E$ THEN E$ = A$
```

```
200 FOR L = 0 TO 8
210 FOR D = 0 TO 6
220 P = D*9 + 1 + L
230 PRINT " "; MID$(W$,P,1); " ";
240 NEXT D
250 PRINT
260 NEXT L
```

Problem No. 4

```
8 REM ** INSERT THE FOLLOWING LINES:
1040 IF LEFT$(D$,1) = " " THEN D$ = MID$
(D$,2)
1050 D$ = "$" + D$

RUN
TEST VALUE? 19
19 = $19.00

TEST VALUE? -9999
```

Problem No. 6

```
8 REM ** INSERT THE FOLLOWING LINE:
1040 IF M1 = 0 THEN D$ = "0.00"

RUN
TEST VALUE? 0
0 = 0.00
```

Problem No. 8

```
100 PRINT "CONVERT STRING TO NUMERIC VALUE"
110 PRINT "<$1234.56> BECOMES -1234.56"
120 PRINT
200 INPUT "ENTER TEST STRING"; M$
210 PRINT
220 IF M$ = "STOP" THEN END
```

Section 2 *Problem No. 8 (continued)*

```
230 GOSUB 1200
235 IF E = 1 THEN 200
240 PRINT M$; " BECOMES "; M9
250 PRINT
260 GOTO 200
1198 REM ** FIND SPECIAL CHARACTERS
1200 S$ = "$<>" : S1$ = "0123456789."
1205 M9$ = "" : E = 0
1210 FOR I9 = 1 TO LEN (M$)
1215 FOR J9 = 1 TO LEN (S$)
1220 IF MID$(M$,I9,1) = MID$(S$,J9,1) THEN 1260
1225 NEXT J9
1230 FOR J9 = 1 TO LEN(S1$)
1235 IF MID$(M$,I9,1) = MID$(S1$,J9,1) THEN 1255
1240 NEXT J9
1245 PRINT "ILLEGAL CHARACTER" : E = 1
1250 GOTO 1290
1255 M9$ = M9$ + MID$(M$,I9,1)
1260 NEXT I9
1265 IF RIGHT$(M$,1) = ">" THEN M9$ = "_" + M9$
1270 M9 = VAL(M9$)
1290 RETURN

RUN
CONVERT STRING TO NUMERIC VALUE
<$1234.56> BECOMES -1234.56

ENTER TEST STRING? TEST STRING

ILLEGAL CHARACTER
ENTER TEST STRING? <$56.98>

<$56.98> BECOMES -56.98

ENTER TEST STRING? STOP
```

```
240 PRINT "□"; B$;
250 FOR X9 = 1 TO 80 : NEXT X9
260 NEXT I9
290 GOTO 210
900 DATA "                                      "
902 DATA "THIS IS A SAMPLE SCROLLING MESSAGE. "
904 DATA "WE CAN EASILY CHANGE THE MESSAGE "
906 DATA "BY CHANGING THE DATA STATEMENTS. "
989 DATA "                                      "
990 DATA DONE
```

Section 3

Problem No. 2

```
100 READ L$
110 IF L$ = "DONE" THEN END
120 PRINT TAB(12-LEN(L$)); L$;
130 GET A$ : IF LEN(A$) = 0 THEN 130
140 PRINT ASC(A$)
150 GOTO 100
1000 DATA CURSOR UP, CURSOR DOWN
1010 DATA CURSOR LEFT, CURSOR RIGHT
1020 DATA CLR, HOME, INST, DEL
1090 DATA DONE

RUN
   CURSOR UP 145
 CURSOR DOWN 17
 CURSOR LEFT 157
CURSOR RIGHT 29
         CLR 147
        HOME 19
        INST 148
         DEL 20
```

Chapter 6

Section 1

Problem No. 2

```
10 REM ** MAKE THE FOLLOWING CHANGES:
170 DH = 1 : DL = 1
230 IF W(J) > H THEN H = W(J) : DH = J
240 IF W(J) < L THEN L = W(J) : DL = J
320 PRINT "HIGHEST TEMP:"; H; "ON DAY"; DH
330 PRINT " LOWEST TEMP:"; L; "ON DAY"; DL
```

Problem No. 4

```
10 REM ** MAKE THE FOLLOWING CHANGES TO PROGRAM 6-2:
180 UN = 0
200 FOR J = 1 TO 10
250 IF A(R) = 0 THEN UN = UN + 1 : GOTO 210
295 PRINT UN; "UNUSED DRAWS"
```

Problem No. 6

```
100 HV = -1E38
110 READ A$ : IF A$ = "STOP" THEN 200
120 X = VAL(A$)
130 IF X > HV THEN HV = X
140 GOTO 110
200 PRINT "HIGHEST VALUE IS"; HV
900 DATA 3, 9, 10, -192, 31
910 DATA -54.9, 89, 100
920 DATA 63121, 0, 96
999 DATA STOP

RUN
HIGHEST VALUE IS 63121
```

Problem No. 10

```
95 PL = 3
97 REM ** PL IS THE NUMBER OF PLACES
100 INPUT "TEST VALUE"; M1
110 IF M1 = 0 THEN END
120 GOSUB 1000
130 PRINT M1; "= "; D$
140 PRINT
150 GOTO 100
996 :
998 REM ** FORMAT TO ANY NUMBER OF PLACES
1000 M9 = INT(M1 * 10^PL + .5)
1010 X$ = STR$(M9)
1020 IF LEFT$(X$,1) <> " " THEN 1040
1030 X$ = MID$(X$,2) : GOTO 1020
1040 IF LEN(X$) > PL THEN 1070
1050 T$ = "00000000000000"
1060 X$ = RIGHT$(T$,PL + 1 - LEN(X$)) + X$
1070 D9 = LEN(X$) - PL
1080 D$ = LEFT$(X$,D9) + "." + RIGHT$(X$,PL)
1090 RETURN

RUN
TEST VALUE? 102.01
  102.01 = 102.010

TEST VALUE? .09
  .09 = 0.090

TEST VALUE? 0
```

Problem No. 12

```
200 READ B$
210 READ A$ : IF A$ = "DONE" THEN END
220 FOR I9 = 1 TO LEN (A$)
230 B$ = RIGHT$(B$,39) + MID$(A$,I9,1)
```

Section 1 *(continued)*

Problem No. 8

```
100 PRINT CHR$(147);
110 DIM A(20)
120 FOR J = 1 TO 20
130 A(J) = 2*J,
140 NEXT J
196 :
200 PRINT "DISPLAY IN ORDER"
210 FOR J = 1 TO 20
220 PRINT A(J);
230 NEXT J
240 PRINT : PRINT
296 :
300 PRINT "DISPLAY IN REVERSE ORDER"
310 FOR J = 20 TO 1 STEP -1
320 PRINT A(J);
330 NEXT J
990 END
```

```
RUN
DISPLAY IN ORDER
 2  4  6  8  10  12  14  16  18  20  22
24  26  28  30  32  34  36  38  40

DISPLAY IN REVERSE ORDER
40  38  36  34  32  30  28  26  24  22
20  18  16  14  12  10   8   6   4   2
```

Problem No. 10

```
10 PRINT CHR$(147);
90 REM ** DISPLAY COMPOSITE OF TWO ARRAYS
95 DIM A1(15),A2(15),A3(30)
100 READ N1
110 FOR J = 1 TO N1
```

```
110 FOR RE = 1 TO 3
120 READ TE(DA,RE)
130 NEXT RE
140 NEXT DA
150 GOSUB 2000
165 :
170 PRINT " MAXIMUM"
180 PRINT "DAY TEMP"
200 FOR DA = 1 TO 7
210 PRINT DA; " "; TE(DA,4)
220 NEXT DA
230 PRINT
900 END
980 :
1000 DATA 76,79,75, 72,77,76
1020 DATA 74,79,81, 75,80,83
1040 DATA 80,77,70, 68,65,65
1060 DATA 65,67,76
1996 :
1998 REM ** FIND MAXIMUM TEMPERATURES HERE
2000 FOR DA = 1 TO 7
2010 TE(DA,4) = TE(DA,1)
2020 NEXT DA
2050 FOR DA = 1 TO 7
2060 FOR RE = 1 TO 3
2070 IF TE(DA,RE) > TE(DA,4) THEN TE(DA,4) = TE(DA,RE)
2080 NEXT RE
2090 NEXT DA
2095 RETURN
```

```
RUN
  MAXIMUM
DAY TEMP
 1   79
 2   77
 3   81
 4   83
```

232

```
5   80
6   68
7   76
```

Problem No. 4

```
90 REM ** FILLING ARRAYS WITH RANDOM NUMBERS
95 DIM R1(4,5),R2(4,5),S(4,5)
100 FOR R = 1 TO 4 : FOR C = 1 TO 5
120 R1(R,C) = INT(RND(1) * 398 + 101)
130 NEXT C : NEXT R
200 FOR R = 1 TO 4 : FOR C = 1 TO 5
220 R2(R,C) = INT(RND(1) * 398 + 101)
230 NEXT C : NEXT R
296 :
300 PRINT "       FIRST ARRAY"
310 FOR R = 1 TO 4
320 FOR C = 1 TO 5
330 PRINT R1(R,C);
340 NEXT C
350 PRINT
360 NEXT R
370 PRINT
396 :
400 PRINT "       SECOND ARRAY"
410 FOR R = 1 TO 4
420 FOR C = 1 TO 5
430 PRINT R2(R,C);
440 NEXT C
450 PRINT
460 NEXT R
470 PRINT
496 :
498 REM ** ENTER SUMS HERE
500 FOR R = 1 TO 4 : FOR C = 1 TO 5
520 S(R,C) = R1(R,C) + R2(R,C)
530 NEXT C : NEXT R
596 :
```

```
120 READ A1(J)
130 NEXT J
200 READ N2
210 FOR J = 1 TO N2
220 READ A2(J)
230 NEXT J
300 FOR J = 1 TO N1
305 J3 = J
310 A3(J) = A1(J)
315 NEXT J
325 FOR J = 1 TO N2
330 FOR K = 1 TO J3
335 IF A3(K) = A2(J) THEN 365
340 NEXT K
345 J3 = J3 + 1
350 A3(J3) = A2(J)
355 GOTO 365
360 NEXT K
365 NEXT J
400 PRINT "THE COMPOSITE ARRAY:"
410 FOR J = 1 TO J3
420 PRINT A3(J);
430 NEXT J
800 END
900 DATA 3,  6,  3,  9
910 DATA 4,  2,  8,  6,  5

RUN
THE COMPOSITE ARRAY:
 6  3  9  2  8  5
```

Section 2

Problem No. 2

```
90 REM ** FIND MAXIMUM TEMP FOR EACH DAY
95 DIM TE(7,4)
100 FOR DA = 1 TO 7
```

Chapter 7

Section 1

Problem No. 2

```
10 REM ** REPLACE 170 OF PROGRAM 7-1
   WITH THE FOLLOWING:
170 R = INT(N - I*T + .5)
```

Problem No. 4

```
90 REM ** REVERSE THE DIGITS OF A NUMBER
100 INPUT "ENTER AN INTEGER"; N
110 IF N < 1 THEN END
120 IF INT(N) <> N THEN 100
130 NU = N
140 GOSUB 1000
150 PRINT NU, RE
160 PRINT
170 GOTO 100
996 :
998 REM ** REVERSE HERE
1000 X$ = MID$(STR$(NU),2)
1010 RE = 0
1020 FOR I = 1 TO LEN(X$)
1030 D = VAL(MID$(X$,I,1))
1040 RE = RE + D*10^(I-1)
1050 NEXT I
1090 RETURN
```

```
RUN
ENTER AN INTEGER? 123456789
 123456789          987654321

ENTER AN INTEGER? 0
```

Section 2 Problem No. 4 (continued)

```
600 PRINT "                SUMS"
610 FOR R = 1 TO 4
620 FOR C = 1 TO 5
630 PRINT S(R,C);
640 NEXT C
650 PRINT
660 NEXT R
```

```
RUN
        FIRST ARRAY
216  380  273  368  221
196  373  118  298  212
398  402  345  134  377
379  203  154  259  274

        SECOND ARRAY
122  167  130  240  497
418  291  131  490  392
263  329  190  349  369
271  110  291  334  416

           SUMS
338  547  403  608  718
614  664  249  788  604
661  731  535  483  746
650  313  445  593  690
```

Section 3

Problem No. 2

```
1 REM ** CHANGES IN COMPUTER RESPONSE SUBROUTINE
  FOR MORE RANDOM SELECTION
2 :
4 REM ** FIRST REMOVE LINES 5000, 5010, AND 5015
6 REM ** THEN ENTER THE FOLLOWING LINES:
```

```
5000 BG = INT(RND(1) * N0 + 1)
5002 FOR I9 = BG TO N0
5004 IF LEFT$(NA$(I9),1) = RIGHT$(PE$(I9),1)
AND AV(I9) = 1 THEN 5050
5006 NEXT I9
5010 FOR I9 = 1 TO BG
5012 IF LEFT$(NA$(I9),1) = RIGHT$(PE$(I9),1)
AND AV(I9) = 1 THEN 5050
5014 NEXT I9
```

Problem No. 4

```
90 REM ** FIND THE ALPHABETICALLY FIRST NAME
95 DIM WE$(7)
100 GOSUB 900
196 :
200 SM$ = WE$(1) : PO = 1
210 FOR I9 = 2 TO 7
220 IF WE$(I9) < SM$ THEN SM$ = WE$(I9) : PO = I9
230 NEXT I9
240 PRINT "ALPHABETICALLY FIRST = "; SM$
250 PRINT "    IN POSITION NUMBER:"; PO
800 END
896 :
898 REM ** READ NAMES - DAYS OF THE WEEK
900 FOR I9 = 1 TO 7
910 READ WE$(I9)
960 NEXT I9
990 RETURN
996 :
1000 DATA SUNDAY, MONDAY, TUESDAY
1010 DATA WEDNESDAY, THURSDAY, FRIDAY
1020 DATA SATURDAY

RUN
ALPHABETICALLY FIRST = FRIDAY
    IN POSITION NUMBER: 6
```

Problem No. 6

```
90 REM ** REVERSE THE DIGITS OF A PRIME
91 REM ** NUMBER.  ELIMINATE DUPLICATES
95 DIM SA(43)
97 SS = 0
100 FOR X = 100 TO 900 STEP 200
110 FOR Y = 1 TO 99 STEP 2
120 N = X + Y
130 FOR Z = 3 TO N STEP 2
140 IF Z*Z > N THEN 170
150 IF INT(N/Z) = N/Z THEN 370
160 NEXT Z
170 GOSUB 1000
196 :
198 REM ** IS REVERSE PRIME??
200 FOR Z = 3 TO RE STEP 2
210 IF Z*Z > RE THEN 270
220 IF INT(RE/Z) = RE/Z THEN 370
230 NEXT Z
270 IF SS = 0 THEN 320
280 FOR I9 = 1 TO SS
290 IF RE = SA(I9) THEN 370
300 NEXT I9
320 SS = SS + 1
330 SA(SS) = N
370 NEXT Y
380 NEXT X
396 :
398 REM ** DONE - DISPLAY THE RESULTS
400 FOR I9 = 1 TO SS
410 PRINT SA(I9),
420 NEXT I9
990 END
996 :
998 REM ** REVERSE HERE
1000 X$ = MID$(STR$(N),2)
```

Section 1 Problem No. 6 (continued)

```
1010 RE = 0
1020 FOR I = 1 TO LEN(X$)
1030 D = VAL(MID$(X$,I,1))
1040 RE = RE + D*10^(I-1)
1050 NEXT I
1090 RETURN
```

```
RUN
101  107  113  131
149  151  157  167
179  181  191  199
313  337  347  353
359  373  383  389
709  727  739  757
769  787  797  919
929
```

Section 2

Problem No. 2

```
10 REM ** ENTER PROGRAM 7-3 AND ENTER
11 REM    THE FOLLOWING LINES:
400 T1 = 0
402 FOR J = 1 TO 16
406 T1 = T1 + A(J) : IF T1 = 0 THEN 420
410 PRINT MID$(STR$(A(J)),2);
```

Problem No. 4

```
100 REM ** TWO'S COMPLEMENT
100 DIM A(16)
200 INPUT "ENTER A NEGATIVE INTEGER"; I
210 IF I >= 0 THEN 999
220 IF I < 0 AND I > -32769 THEN 290
230 PRINT "OUT OF RANGE" : PRINT : GOTO 200
```

```
1000000110000000000

ENTER A NEGATIVE INTEGER? -127
1111111110000001

ENTER A NEGATIVE INTEGER? 0
```

Section 4

Problems of General Interest

Problem No. 2

```
90 PRINT CHR$(147);
100 PRINT " I WILL THINK OF A NUMBER BETWEEN 1 AND N.  ";
110 PRINT "HOW LARGE WOULD YOU LIKE"
120 PRINT "N TO BE";
130 INPUT N
140 IF N < 1 THEN : PRINT "TOO SMALL": GOTO 110
150 N1 = INT(RND(1) * N + 1)
200 PRINT
205 INPUT "YOUR GUESS"; G
210 IF G < 1 THEN 450
220 IF G > N THEN 400
230 IF G = N1 THEN 500
240 IF G < N1 THEN 300
250 PRINT "LOWER"
260 GOTO 200
300 PRINT "HIGHER"
310 GOTO 200
400 PRINT "THAT'S BIGGER THAN YOUR LIMIT"
410 GOTO 200
450 PRINT "TOO SMALL"
460 GOTO 200
500 PRINT "YOU GOT IT ***"
510 END
```

290 N = ABS(I)
296 :
298 REM ** LOAD THE ARRAY
300 FOR J = 16 TO 1 STEP -1
310 IF N / 2 = INT(N / 2) THEN A(J) = 0
320 IF N / 2 <> INT(N / 2) THEN A(J) = 1
340 N = INT(N / 2)
360 NEXT J
396 :
398 REM ** REVERSE THE DIGITS
400 FOR J = 1 TO 16
410 IF A(J) = 0 THEN A(J) = 1 : GOTO 430
420 IF A(J) = 1 THEN A(J) = 0
430 NEXT J
496 :
498 REM ** NOW ADD ONE
500 FOR J = 16 TO 1 STEP -1
510 IF A(J) = 0 THEN A(J) = 1 : GOTO 800
520 A(J) = 0
530 NEXT J
538 REM ** THE ADD IS DONE WHEN EXECUTION
    EXITS AT LINE 510
796 :
798 REM ** DISPLAY RESULTS
800 T1 = 0
804 FOR J = 1 TO 16
806 T1 = T1 + A(J) : IF T1 = 0 THEN 820
810 PRINT MID$(STR$(A(J)),2);
820 NEXT J
855 PRINT : PRINT
860 GOTO 200
999 END

RUN
ENTER A NEGATIVE INTEGER? -1
1111111111111111

ENTER A NEGATIVE INTEGER? -32000

RUN
I WILL THINK OF A NUMBER BETWEEN 1 AND
N. HOW LARGE WOULD YOU LIKE
N TO BE?91

YOUR GUESS? 45
HIGHER

YOUR GUESS? 66
LOWER

YOUR GUESS? 55
LOWER

YOUR GUESS? 50
HIGHER

YOUR GUESS? 52
YOU GOT IT ***

Problem No. 4

10 PRINT CHR$(147);
110 GOSUB 1100
120 GOSUB 1200
130 GOSUB 1300
140 GOSUB 1400
150 GOSUB 1500
200 PRINT : PRINT "MONTHLY PAYMENT = $"; P$
210 PA = VAL(P$) * N1
220 GOSUB 1500
230 PRINT " TOTAL PAYMENTS = $"; P$
240 PA = VAL(P$) - P
250 GOSUB 1500
260 PRINT " TOTAL INTEREST = $"; P$
900 END
1096 :
1098 REM ** GET INTEREST RATE

Section 4 Problem No. 4 (continued)

```
1100 PRINT "ANNUAL INTEREST RATE (%)";
1110 INPUT I
1120 IF I > 1 THEN 1140
1125 PRINT "PERCENTAGE PLEASE"
1130 PRINT : GOTO 1100
1140 I1 = I / 100
1150 I1 = I1 / 12
1188 REM ** EXIT WITH MONTHLY RATE IN I1
1190 RETURN
1196 :
1198 REM ** GET PRINCIPAL
1200 PRINT "        ENTER PRINCIPAL ($)";
1210 INPUT P
1290 RETURN
1296 :
1298 REM ** GET NUMBER OF YEARS
1300 PRINT "          NUMBER OF YEARS";
1310 INPUT N
1320 N1 = N * 12
1388 REM ** EXIT WITH NUMBER OF PAYMENTS IN N1
1390 RETURN
1396 :
1398 REM ** COMPUTE MONTHLY PAYMENT
1400 X = (1 + I1) ^ N1
1410 PA = (P * I1 * X) / (X - 1)
1490 RETURN
1496 :
1498 REM ** FORMAT PAYMENT
1500 X = INT(PA * 100 + .5)
1510 P$ = STR$(X)
1520 Y = LEN(P$) - 2
1530 P$ = LEFT$(P$,Y) + "." + RIGHT$(P$,2)
1590 RETURN

RUN
ANNUAL INTEREST RATE (%)? 17
```

```
200 FOR NU = 2 TO 32767 STEP 2
210 SU = 1
220 F1 = 1
230 FA(F1) = 1
250 FOR IN = 2 TO SQR(NU)
260 X = NU / IN
270 IF X <> INT(X) THEN 330
280 FA(F1 + 1) = IN
290 FA(F1 + 2) = X
300 F1 = F1 + 2
310 SU = SU + IN + X
320 IF SU > NU THEN 420
330 NEXT IN
340 IF SU <> NU THEN 420
350 PRINT NU; "IS PERFECT"
360 FOR I9 = 1 TO F1
370 PRINT FA(I9);
380 NEXT I9
390 PRINT : PRINT
400 C1 = C1 + 1
410 IF C1 = 4 THEN END
420 NEXT NU
900 END

RUN
6 IS PERFECT
1  2  3

28 IS PERFECT
1  2  14  4  7

496 IS PERFECT
1  2  248  4  124  8  62  16  31

8128 IS PERFECT
1  2  4064  4  2032  8  1016  16  508  32  254  64  127
```

ENTER PRINCIPAL ($)? 50000
NUMBER OF YEARS? 30

MONTHLY PAYMENT = $ 712.84
TOTAL PAYMENTS = $ 256622.40
TOTAL INTEREST = $ 206622.40

Math Oriented Problems

Problem No. 2

```
50 REM ** EUCLID'S ALGORITHM
100 INPUT " FIRST NUMBER"; N1
105 IF N1 = 0 THEN END
110 INPUT "SECOND NUMBER"; N2
150 Q = INT(N1 / N2)
160 R = N1 - N2 * Q
170 IF R = 0 THEN 200
175 N1 = N2
180 N2 = R
190 GOTO 150
200 PRINT "GREATEST COMMON FACTOR:"; N2
210 PRINT
220 GOTO 100

RUN
  FIRST NUMBER? 1001
  SECOND NUMBER? 1300
GREATEST COMMON FACTOR: 13

  FIRST NUMBER? 0
```

Problem No. 4

```
10 PRINT CHR$(147);
50 REM ** FIND PERFECT NUMBERS
100 DIM FA(50)
110 C1 = 0
```

Problem No. 6

```
10 PRINT CHR$(147);
50 REM ** FIND PYTHAGOREAN TRIPLES
100 FOR L1 = 1 TO 25
120 FOR L2 = L1 + 1 TO 25
130 X = L1 * L1 + L2 * L2
140 FOR HY = L2 + 1 TO 50
150 X1 = HY * HY
155 IF X1 > X THEN 180
160 IF X1 < X THEN 170
165 PRINT L1, L2, HY
170 NEXT HY
180 NEXT L2
190 NEXT L1

RUN
3    4    5
5    12   13
6    8    10
7    24   25
8    15   17
9    12   15
10   24   26
12   16   20
15   20   25
18   24   30
20   21   29
```

Problem No. 8

```
10 PRINT CHR$(147);
50 REM ** FIND PI FROM A SEQUENCE
100 PI = 2
110 FOR I9 = 1 TO 1500 STEP 4
120 PI = PI + 16 / ((I9) * (I9 + 2) * (I9 + 4))
140 NEXT I9
150 PRINT "APPROXIMATE VALUE:"; PI
```

Section 4 Problem No. 8 (continued)

```
900 END

RUN
APPROXIMATE VALUE: 3.14159176
```

Chapter 8

Section 3

Problem No. 2

```
10 F$ = "PLACES"
15 OPEN 15,8,15
20 DIM NA$(500), AV(500)
30 GOSUB 8000 : REM ** READ NAMES ARRAY
90 PRINT CHR$(147);
100 GOSUB 12000 : REM ** EDIT PLACE NAMES
140 GOSUB 8500 : REM ** REWRITE THE NAMES FILE
150 CLOSE 15
190 END
796 :
798 REM ** READ ERROR CHANNEL,
800 INPUT# 15, E,E$,T,S
810 IF E < 20 THEN 890
820 PRINT E$
830 STOP
890 RETURN
7996 :
7998 REM ** READ NAMES FILE
8000 OPEN 2,8,2, F$ + ",S,R" : GOSUB 800
8010 INPUT# 2, N0
8030 FOR I9 = 1 TO N0
8040 INPUT# 2, NA$(I9)
8050 NEXT I9
8060 CLOSE 2
8090 RETURN
8496 :
```

```
5006 NEXT I9
5010 FOR I9 = 1 TO BG
5012 IF LEFT$(NA$(I9),1) = RIGHT$(PE$(I9),1)
     AND AV(I9) = 1 THEN 5050
5014 NEXT I9
```

Chapter 9

Section 1

Problem No. 2

```
5 REM ** ENTER PROGRAM 9-1 LESS LINES 200-290
6 REM    AND ENTER THE FOLLOWING LINES:
200 READ X1,Y1,X2,Y2,X3,Y3,X4,Y4
205 M$ = "BAD DATA"
210 IF Y1 <> Y2 THEN PRINT M$ : STOP
215 IF X2 <> X3 THEN PRINT M$ : STOP
220 IF Y3 <> Y4 THEN PRINT M$ : STOP
225 IF X4 <> X1 THEN PRINT M$ : STOP
230 FOR X = X1 TO X2
240 Y = Y1 : GOSUB 1200 : Y = Y3 : GOSUB 1200
250 NEXT X
260 FOR Y = Y1 TO Y3
270 X = X1 : GOSUB 1200 : X = X2 : GOSUB 1200
280 NEXT Y
290 RETURN
300 DATA 10,10, 309, 10
302 DATA 309,189, 10,189
```

Problem No. 4

```
1 REM ** EXAMPLE DATA
8996 :
8998 REM ** TIC-TAC-TOE BOARD
9000 DATA 20,30, 80,30
9005 DATA 40,10, 40,70
9010 DATA 60,10, 60,70
```

9015 DATA 20,50, 80, 50
9999 DATA -1,0,0,0

Section 2

Problem No. 2

```
1 REM ** ENTER PROGRAM 9-2 AND THE
2 REM    FOLLOWING DATA:
8996 :
8998 REM ** A SIMPLE SAILBOAT
9000 DATA 30,40, 40,50
9005 DATA 30,40, 30,52
9010 DATA 30,50, 40,50
9015 DATA 26,52, 46,52
9020 DATA 26,52, 28,56
9025 DATA 28,56, 44,56
9030 DATA 44,56, 46,52
9999 DATA -1,0,0,0
```

Section 3

Problem No. 2

```
1 REM ** SIMPLY REPLACE LINE 210 IN PROGRAM 9-5
2 REM    WITH ANY OF THE LISTED EQUATIONS
```

Chapter 10

Section 1

Problem No. 2

```
100 PRINT CHR$(147);
200 FOR I = 16192 TO 16192 + 62 : REM **
    STORE SPRITE DATA
210 POKE I, 255
220 NEXT I
230 FOR I = 2040 TO 2040 + 7 : REM **
```

```
8498 REM ** UPDATE NAMES FILE
8500 OPEN 2,8,2,"@:" + F$ + ",S,W" : GOSUB 800
8520 PRINT# 2, NØ
8530 FOR I9 = 1 TO NØ
8535 PRINT# 2, NA$(I9)
8540 NEXT I9
8580 CLOSE 2
8590 RETURN
11996 :
12000 PRINT "EDITING PLACE NAMES"
12005 PRINT
12010 INPUT "FIX NAME"; X$
12015 IF X$ = "DONE" THEN 12090
12020 FOR I9 = 1 TO NØ
12025 IF NA$(I9) = X$ THEN 12040
12030 NEXT I9
12035 PRINT "NOT FOUND" : GOTO 12005
12040 INPUT "NEW PLACE"; X$
12045 FOR J9 = 1 TO NØ
12050 IF X$ = NA$(J9) THEN 12070
12055 NEXT J9
12060 NA$(I9) = X$
12065 GOTO 12005
12070 PRINT "DUPLICATE NAME - REENTER"
12075 GOTO 12005
12090 RETURN
```

Problem No. 4

```
1 REM ** CHANGES IN COMPUTER RESPONSE SUBROUTINE
  FOR MORE RANDOM SELECTION
2 :
4 REM ** FIRST REMOVE LINES 5000, 5010, AND 5015
6 REM ** THEN ENTER THE FOLLOWING LINES:
5000 BG = INT(RND(1) * NØ + 1)
5002 FOR I9 = BG TO NØ
5004 IF LEFT$(NA$(I9),1) = RIGHT$(PE$(I9),1)
  AND AV(I9) = 1 THEN 5050
```

Section 1 *Problem No. 2 (continued)*

```
    STORE POINTERS
232 POKE I, 253
234 NEXT I
250 B = 53248
260 POKE B + 21, 255 : REM ** ALL SPRITES ON
300 FOR I = 39 TO 39 + 7
302 POKE B + I, I - 31 : REM ** SPRITE COLOR
304 NEXT I
310 FOR I = Ø TO 14 STEP 2
312 POKE B + I, 26 + 16*I : REM ** X POSITION
314 POKE B + I + 1, 55 : REM ** Y POSITION
316 NEXT I
400 PRINT : PRINT
410 PRINT "RNG BRN LRD GR1 GR2 LGN LBL GR3"
```

Problem No. 4

```
100 PRINT CHR$(147);
200 FOR I = 16192 TO 16192 + 62 : REM **
    STORE SPRITE DATA
210 POKE I, 255
220 NEXT I
230 POKE 2040, 253 : REM ** POINT TO SPRITE Ø
250 B = 53248
260 POKE B+21, PEEK(B+21) OR 2^Ø
300 C = INT(RND(1)*16)
310 X = INT(RND(1)*256)
320 Y = INT(RND(1)*256)
330 POKE B+39, C
340 POKE B, X
350 POKE B+1, Y
360 FOR I = 1 TO 300 : NEXT I
370 GOTO 300
```

Chapter 11

Section 1

Problem No. 2

```
10 S = 54272
20 FOR I = S TO S+24 : POKE I, Ø : NEXT I
100 POKE S+24, 15
120 POKE S+6, 15*16
140 POKE S+4, 16+1
200 FOR F = Ø TO 65535 STEP 200
240 POKE S, (F-32768) AND 255
250 POKE S+1, F/256
290 NEXT F
400 POKE S+24, Ø
9999 REM ** ALSO TRY :
    200 FOR F = 65535 TO Ø STEP -500
```

Section 2

Problem No. 2

```
10 S = 54272
20 FOR I = S TO S+24 : POKE I, Ø : NEXT I
100 POKE S+24, 15
120 POKE S+6, 15*16
140 POKE S+4, 16+1
200 F = 2000
240 POKE S, (F-32768) AND 255
250 POKE S+1, F/256
300 INPUT "PULSE WIDTH"; P
320 IF P < Ø OR P > 4095 THEN 400
340 POKE S+2, P AND 255
350 POKE S+3, P/256
390 GOTO 300
400 POKE S+24, Ø
900 END
```

Section 2

Problem No. 2

```
100 INPUT "SPRITE NUMBER"; SN
105 IF SN < 0 OR SN > 7 THEN 100
110 MA = 64 * PEEK(2040 + SN)
115 FOR D = 0 TO 6
120 PRINT 1000 + 10*SN + D; "DATA ";
125 FOR DP = 1 TO 9
130 X = PEEK(MA)
135 PRINT MID$(STR$(X),2);
140 IF DP < 9 THEN PRINT ",";
145 MA = MA + 1
150 NEXT DP
155 PRINT
160 NEXT D
190 END
```

Section 3

Problem No. 2

```
5 REM ** ADD THE FOLLOWING LINES TO PROGRAM 11-2
  FOR ORGAN SOUND
100 POKE S+5, 0*16+0
110 POKE S+6, 15*16+0
119 REM ** AFTER YOU TRY LINES 100 AND 110,
F TRY ADDING THIS LINE:
120 W = 32
```

Section 4

Problem No. 2

```
1 REM ** ADD EITHER ONE OR BOTH OF THE FOLLOWING
  LINES TO PROGRAM 11-3:
1400 FOR J = 1 TO 15 : NEXT J
2810 WC%(V,CT)=33-(1 AND I=D AND D<>1)
```

Index